THE ANALYST'S ANALYST

THE ANALYST'S ANALYST

Selected Papers of
Milton H. Horowitz, M.D.

Edited by Herbert M. Wyman, M.D.

Introduction by Philip Herschenfeld, M.D.

IPBOOKS.net
International Psychoanalytic Books

International Psychoanalytic Books (IPBooks)
New York • http://www.IPBooks.net

The Analyst's Analyst: Selected Papers of Milton H. Horowitz, M.D.

Published by IPBooks, Queens, NY
Online at: www.IPBooks.net

Edited by: Herbert M. Wyman, M.D.

ISBN: 978-1-956864-60-1

Contents

Editor's Preface ix

Milton H. Horowitz M.D.: A Personal Portrait xi

Introduction to Selected Papers xxiii

Chapter 1: Hatred in the Analytic Situation 3
    Introduction 3
    Case History 5
    Affective Resonance and The Analytic Situation......... 11
    The Analyst's Insight and the Understanding of
        Powerful Affects 13
    Miscarriages of the Analyst's Insight in the Face of
        Explosive Affect.. 16
    The Immediate Here and Now Affective Experience and
        Analytic Process 18
    The Analyst's Provocation of Hatred 19
    Summary.. 21
    References 21

Chapter 2: How Character Shapes Transference 23
    I   23
    References 31

Chapter 3: On the Difficulty of Analyzing Character 33
    References 40

Chapter 4: New York Psychoanalytic Association Symposium
            in Honor of Leo Stone, M.D., December 5, 1992............ 43
   Preface.. 43
   Transference 44
   Orientation 50
   Projections of Aspects of the Patient's Personality: The
      Special Contribution to Transference..................................... 53
   Projection of Defense and Projection of the Need for
      Punishment as Specific Aspects of Narcissistic
      Coloration of Transference 56
   Conclusion 58
   References 59

Chapter 5: The Durability of Unconscious Fantasy 61
   References 67

Chapter 6: The Fear of Knowledge... 71
   References 96

Chapter 7: Some Notes on Insight and its Failures 99
   Abstract.. 99
   The Structure of Insight 104
   The Response of Interpretation and the Process of Insight 112
   The Vulnerability of Insight to Regression.............................. 114
   Conclusions.. 116
   References 118

Chapter 8: On the Fate of Unconscious Fantasies: Experiences
            in Middle Life 121
   References 132

Chapter 9: IPTAR Lecture: Revenge and Masochism 133
   On the Role of Transference in Self-Directed Revenge 142
   Revenge and Suicidal Fantasy.. 143

Masturbation and Revenge Fantasies.................................... 144

The Self-Contained Unit–Subject and Object United Through 146

Self-hatred and Masochistic Revenge..................................... 148

Hatred of the Self and Masochistic Exhibitionism 151

Bondage and Masochism.. 152

The Beating Fantasy Turned on the Self—The Revenge of the
    Victim-Sibling upon the Patient's Own Self....................... 153

Conclusion 155

References 155

Chapter 10: For the Psychoanalytic Forum: The Fear of Intimacy...... 157

I. Clinical Realities of Treating Patients Afraid of Intimacy 167

II. The Initial Interviews.. 168

III. Special Problems of Transference 172

References 174

Chapter 11: On The Reaction of Men to the Menopause of Women . 175

The Post-Menopausal Woman and the Mythology of Witches. 181

Summary... 183

Discussion 183

Conclusion 187

References 187

Chapter 12: Object Loss, Fetishism, and Creativity 189

An Historical Review 202

References 220

Chapter 13: The 1994 Freud Lecture: Adolescent Daydream
    and Creative Impulse 223

Preface.. 223

The Place of Adolescence in Psychoanalytic Theory
    and Practice 243

After the Ball 246

References 247

Chapter 14: Self-Observation, Self-Analysis and Re-Analysis 251
Introduction 251
Self-Observation and Self-Analysis 254
Self-Observation and Self-Analysis in the Analytic Situation .. 257
Re-analysis 258
References 260

Chapter 15: On Beginning a Reanalysis 263
The Initial Consultation 264
Fantasies of Therapeutic Success or Failure 267
Transference Responses at the Onset of Reanalysis 268
Resistances in Reanalysis 270
Why Analyses Fail 270
The Importance of Fantasy Life in the Maintenance
of Resistance 273
Reanalysis of Transferences to the Previous Analyst 275
References 277

Chapter 16: Freud's Enduring Legacy: The Flexibility of
Psychoanalytic Technique 279
New Clinical Entities 283
References 285

Chapter 17: On The Evolution of Psychoanalytic Technique 287
References 319

Chapter 18: Discussions for the Panel: The Relevance of Frequency
of Sessions to the Creation of an Analytic Experience 323
On The Relevance of Frequency 323
References 326

Editor's Preface

"The second analyst should remember that if his reanalysis yields better results than the first, it is more likely because the patient is a more experienced and better patient than because the analyst is a better analyst." (2001)

With these modest words Milton Horowitz concluded his seminar on Reanalysis, held on January 30, 2001, for the benefit of the Faculty of the New York Psychoanalytic Institute. These words were remarkable because at that time no one was a more renowned second analyst than Dr. Horowitz. Remarkable but not surprising to those who were fortunate enough to know Dr. Horowitz. His primary concern was not for himself but for the well-being and progress of his patients. This priority was dramatically illustrated when the *Journal of Clinical Psychoanalysis (*of which I was co-editor) was about to publish an issue in his honor in 2003. Dr. Horowitz requested that an interview and profile of him, composed by his lifelong friend and colleague Dr Manuel Furer, be withheld from publication at that time, lest it complicate in any way the transferences of his patients.

Fortunately, this portrait has been preserved and is now included at the beginning of this collection of Dr. Horowitz' papers. It is a pleasure to present these wonderfully rich papers in an accessible one volume format, organized topically for ease of reference. This project was inspired by Dr. Philip Herschenfeld who has provided an excellent introduction to the papers.

Here is a contemporaneous succinct summary: "Milton Horowitz is not only a skilled and experienced analyst, he is an effective one." (Jacobs 2003) Readers of these papers will find that as a writer he was likewise effective.

Herbert M Wyman MD

Jacobs, T (2003) Reprise: On Blocks, Impasses, and Repeated Scenarios in Reanalysis. in Reanalysis: :Papers in Honor of Milton H Horowitz MD. *Journal of Clinical Psychoanalysis* 12:1, pp 73-84.

Milton H. Horowitz M.D.: A Personal Portrait

by Manuel Furer M.D. 2003

INTRODUCTION

In many large psychoanalytic centers in this country there can often be found an analyst who is consulted by other analysts when problems arise in their work, particularly in training analyses or in analyses of those in the psychoanalytic community. Some time ago in New York City this was Dr. Phyllis Greenacre, who was generally regarded as possessing special gifts in her understanding, intuition, and concern with the early period of development. When an impasse occurred in an analysis and an issue of early development or trauma was felt to be involved, Dr. Greenacre was called in as a consultant and/or referred the patient. She was likewise consulted when even more serious trouble occurred in an analysis requiring the delicate work for which she was known.

Dr. Milton Horowitz, for some time now, has been such a resource in the New York area. When there is trouble in an analysis, an impasse in an ongoing analysis, or persisting discomfort in a previously analyzed patient, Dr. Horowitz is called in to assess the problem and recommend a solution, whether continuation or change of analysts in an ongoing situation, or re-analysis in a post-analytic situation. His sensitivity and tact in regard to particular mismatches of patient and analyst is remarkable and much appreciated by the community.

As will appear below in the interview with Dr. Horowitz, referrals for re-analysis occur most frequently when the outcome of the prior analytic work, although seemingly satisfactory and successful in many regards, has not resulted in the patient feeling ultimately that he was living a better life. This is apparent in Dr. Horowitz's initial questions to patients, "How can I help you?"

INTERVIEW

What follows is derived from an interview with Dr. Horowitz on the evening of Tuesday, January 16th, 2002, as well as from forty-eight years of friendship with my classmate at the New York Psychoanalytic Institute, and also from thirty-five years of collegiate membership in Study Group Two of the Center for Advanced Psychoanalytic Studies at Princeton. It will be clear that Dr. Horowitz captured my mind as he does with all who have the privilege of listening to him.

Dr. Horowitz began life in an apartment on Ocean Parkway in Brooklyn at its furthest end near Brighton Beach, and very close to the house of his maternal grandfather, who first inspired Dr. Horowitz's intellectual interests. Grandfather had been trained as a Rabbi in Vilna, but was picked up on the street, as was the custom then, and impressed into the Czar's Army for the usual term of twenty-five years. He had had a previous exposure to a Cossack troop who had invaded his house during Passover when he was a child. Luckily he had escaped unharmed on that occasion. Like many rabbinical students, he had married at a very early age. His wife gave birth to Dr. Horowitz's mother just one year before he was conscripted. The Grandfather's family had a saddlery business and so he was assigned to a cavalry troop. One might call them Cossacks. Fortunately, he once more escaped and emigrated to Hamburg, Germany, where his brother lived, and from Hamburg to New York City. From the moment of landing he devoted his life to bringing his wife and young daughter to safety in the United States.

In this country the grandfather's interest in rabbinical matters diminished but he substituted with equal intensity, other interests, particularly opera. Dr. Horowitz remembers the wonderful times sitting on the porch listening to records of old favorites like Enrico Caruso. The grandfather's excitement was contagious for the little boy. The Grandfather was a born teacher and taught his grandson to read Yiddish before he read English. This allowed them to go further and learn about Yiddish culture.

Dr. Horowitz's father bought him his first "grown up" book, *Treasure Island*. Ever since then despite his encyclopedic reading he has always been excited by adventure stories, such as he originally shared with his father.

When the family moved to the Bronx, the young Dr. Horowitz quickly located the library where he borrowed as many books as he was allowed. At first children's books, which he read through very quickly, and then he wheedled permission from the librarian to read grown-up books, although in many cases he didn't understand them.

He was singled out by the teachers as a smart youngster. There was one teacher he loved above the others who was also the school librarian. In fourth grade she told him that he would grow up to be a professor, and as he recalls he believed this was his future. The librarian-teacher was very beautiful and in his mind was of a higher social status than the other teachers in the school. She recommended books to him, talked to him about his reading, and encouraged him to write brief reports on the books as a guide to the other children, indicating what they might like and what they probably wouldn't like.

This teacher's image stayed with Dr. Horowitz. He remembered an incident when he was stationed on Staten Island in the Public Health Service during the Korean War. He was coming back to Manhattan on the ferry when he noticed a small woman in front of him. Her hair was gray, although in his image it had been bright red; and she had had green eyes. She still looked very pretty to him. He recognized her and called her name! She turned around and said "Hello, Milton." She too had remembered.

As was the practice at the time in the New York City School System, bright students were skipped many grades and Dr. Horowitz was one of them. As a child he was tiny, both short and skinny. He did not grow to his adult height until college. That kept him from participating with other children in some of their favorite activities like sports, such as football, which was a great disappointment to Dr. Horowitz, since his father was a very good athlete. The children called him "professor" because he wore glasses and was always reading. In their eyes, but also in Dr. Horowitz's eyes, he was different from the others.

Each time he skipped to a new grade he was able to find a teacher who acted as a mentor. The one catastrophe of his schooling was being forced to use his right hand although he was naturally left-handed. This resulted in a stutter, an impediment, which made it difficult to get along with the other children. However, disastrous as that policy was in the school system in New York, the school also provided him with speech therapy. Only in his analysis did Dr. Horowitz discover how infuriated he was with this physical restraint. Prior to the analysis, he only remembered how inferior he felt he was. When the stutter finally cleared up during the analysis, his wife said, "Once you talk, you never stop."

Dr. Horowitz's teacher-mentors were those in English and History. They encouraged him to read the English poets and historians. He remembers reading McCauley, everything he wrote, despite having been told that many historians were dismissive of McCauley's approach and bias. However, what impressed Dr. Horowitz, and this is crucial in him, is that McCauley wrote so well. He wrote a narrative, and it was the narrative that made the history intelligible. Intelligibility, no matter whether the communication is via language, music, emotional expression, and so on, means a great deal to Dr. Horowitz, and it is for him the first and foremost necessity in doing analytic work.

Although he did not directly refer the following pattern to his analytic work, it is characteristic of Dr. Horowitz that, once given a start in a subject, he then carries on and perseveres with it independently. For example, he took only a year of Latin but then continued to study and mastered the language on his own. At this point in the interview Dr. Horowitz reached over next to the chair behind the analytic couch and produced a copy of Plautinus on Military Strategy. Dr. Horowitz praised this text for its intelligibility in narrating the strategy and the cleverness of the generals of the distant past. He showed me the book and said he could do pretty well with the Latin, but you see there is the English on the opposite page.

Though he liked the details and the particulars of history, he liked more those courses that covered big sweeps of history and literature. He related the latter to his method of reading all of an author, so that he has long ago finished all of Trollope, and many others—often via the small individual editions he collects. There is always a small classic in his pocket. Of particular appeal to him was Charles Dickens as he felt close to the mistreated children who, of course, eventually became sturdy and heroic. This is, for him, one of the universal fantasies he said, since he was more favored than mistreated. He was the first grandchild and was indulged by six aunts and uncles on his father's side. They were somewhat better educated than his father, brought him books and introduced him to ideas. His father arrived in this country at the age of six and went to work at the age of eight. Dr. Horowitz is particularly fond of one aunt, the only one still alive, whom he talks to once per week. He visited her recently. She had trouble finding words except for the pet words that Dr. Horowitz's grandmother used for him. She asked her nephew to go for a walk so she could speak to him in

Yiddish, her childhood tongue. In that language she had no difficulty finding any of the words she wanted.

Dr. Horowitz's paternal grandfather also had rabbinical training but it, too, fell away in this country. The family was not religious, although they followed the rituals. Dr. Horowitz was Bar Mitzvahed and remembered most acutely praying for his maternal grandfather's health. The grandfather used to take snuff, claiming it cleared his mind and, Dr. Horowitz added, Oxford Dons did the same thing. Snuff rushes to one's head like horseradish. However, this use resulted in grandfather's cancer of the tongue while Dr. Horowitz was still a child. He realized then prayers were not successful.

It was in part this experience that made Dr. Horowitz want to be a doctor. He may have had this goal in mind at an even younger age, since there was an admired member of the family who was a doctor. He had a moustache, smoked cigars, had dark hair and looked like a wise owl. In any case his grandfather's illness turned Dr. Horowitz's attention to surgery, and he took a surgical internship.

In high school, however, Dr. Horowitz had read Freud's *Introductory Lectures* and was flabbergasted and excited. At the time, he was reading to blind children, and he developed what he called a low-grade fear of going blind himself. After reading Freud, he said, he was cured, as if by an interpretation that went deep into his heart. He understood that behind that manifest content of blindness there were other fantasies about what going blind meant. The transformations of anxiety and sexuality he read about were startling and exciting as though someone had looked inside him and come up with an explanation. It was surgery or psychoanalysis, and we are lucky that Freud won out.

He had wanted to go to Columbia College but when he went for an interview at the age of fifteen, the Admission Officer said he was too immature to enter. He then went up to University College of NYU and talked with the Admission Officer there about some research he was doing on the change of color in the eyes of Drosophila. The Admission Officer asked him whether he would like to meet the Professor of Biology. Dr. Horowitz was apprehensive since he had been told that this was the man who was the make-or-break-person in regard to admission to medical school, and was somewhat forbidding to boot. However, the professor was welcoming to Dr. Horowitz, who entered that college, became a biology major, and was elected to honors. He was accepted to The New York University School of Medicine before he ended his freshman year and started there after two years of college at the age of seventeen.

An arrangement had been made to further his interest in psychoanalysis. He was sent to Jack Frosch, a long-time teacher at Bellevue, who gave him the charts of five patients, told him to interview them, and return prepared to discuss them. Dr. Horowitz's only prior education in that regard was having read Freud's case histories. He expected to find, as he had in himself, something hidden beneath the surface; and so in Dr. Frosch he had his first mentor in psychoanalysis. At Bellevue he felt fortunate to meet somewhat older but very dedicated Residents whose interest in psychoanalysis was as keen as his own. Among these were Drs Arnold Z Pfeffer, Bernard Brodsky, and Joseph Cramer. It was Dr. Pfeffer who encouraged him to go into the Public Health Service where he could both get good medical and neurological training as well as do his military service, and that they might even promote his psychoanalytic training. This in fact happened. The Public Health Service stationed him at Staten Island and allowed him a year's residency at Bellevue while in the service. As he remarked, it was always of special meaning to him to have an older person show him the path and encourage him along the lines that person had followed, although, as he said, not to dictate to him.

He considered the Public Health Service one of the best periods in life. His interest in neurology was supplemented by being sent for neuropathology to Psychiatric Institute and serving on the Foster Kennedy

Service at Bellevue. He became the Deputy Chief of the Psychiatric Service at the Staten Island Public Health Hospital, where he was also Chief of Neurology. He was allowed to hire consultants, and once again added mentors. As before, he found the psychoanalysts wiser about life and more knowledgeable about literature and music than most of the other doctors. In this regard Dr. Horowitz is amused to recall the time he went to a business meeting at the New York Psychoanalytic Society and found no quorum in attendance; but the very next night at a concert in the Grace Rainey Auditorium in the Metropolitan Museum of Art there were some seventy members of the Society in the audience.

This essential part of the culture of psychoanalysis that Dr. Horowitz had already known unofficially, became official when he was interviewed for the Institute. He remembers being asked about and discussing what he had read in poetry and what he liked about the classics. He understood, since these were Europeans, that they were looking for someone who had the kind of educational experience and interests that resembled their own. Particularly he remembered discussing the Greek playwrights. The person most vivid in his memory in this regard was Dr. Henry Lowenfeld, who became one of his supervisors. There was a similar experience with Dr. Frederick Weil.

At the Institute at that time he was enthralled by the group jokingly referred to by Dr. Loewenstein as " Hart, Schaffner and Marx " after the well-known haberdashers. These were Hartmann, Kris and Loewenstein. Kris's talk about the creative imagination was "beyond delicious." Dr. Horowitz felt that he had finally found another intellectual home, but one in which he could also be useful. Looking back he remembers having the feeling that he had walked into a portion of the history of the Western Enlightenment, as if he had breached the walls of the ghetto to gain access to enlightened education.

The second theme in Dr. Horowitz's life and work after Intelligibility is History. The history of the patient, but also the history of our civilization, which he finds painfully missing from our current cultural environment. It is as though enduring aspects of our common culture have been forgotten.

His analysis, said Dr. Horowitz, was like a miracle. It started with transference; he had a dream prior to his first session that he was talking to his analyst in Yiddish the way he did with his grandfather. The prism of the past, as the light shines into the present, he considers the essence of analysis. Without origins in individual lives or broader elements of history there is no meaning. In that regard he found Ernst Kris an important mentor because he learned from him that all analysts should have training in medicine, on the one hand, and in early child development, on the other,

When Dr. Horowitz emerged from the Public Health Service, he took a position as the Chief of the Adolescent Service at Bellevue Psychiatric Hospital. He would not have left that job, he said, except for a recommendation by Dr. Fred Weil who told him that one cannot become an analyst without immersing oneself in psychoanalytic work. Dr. Horowitz was then moonlighting at a neurological clinic which was run by Dr. Ruth Loveland's husband. Having met her and knowing her to be a distinguished analyst, he thought she was the right person to ask for analytic referrals. She asked him what he was going to do in August, and he said go on vacation. She said, why don't you stay here, go on vacation later, and I will refer the patients that come during that vacation time; very shortly he had seven analytic cases, which began a practice that has lasted all these years. He immediately had many supervisors: Dr Herman Nunberg; Dr. Rudolph Loewenstein; Dr. Annie Reich, for whom he presented in the continuous case seminar; and intermittently Mrs. Berta Bornstein for his adolescent cases. He immediately recognized that no two analysts were alike and, as to be expected, they did not analyze in the same way. As he said, Freud told us that we had to use our own unconscious to understand our patients and after all, every person's unconscious is unique. There must, of course, be a standard at the same time against which these individual variations are measured. It was liberating to him then to understand that he could and would develop his own style of analyzing. He would be no one's disciple. There is also a rebellious side to Dr. Horowitz. His independence in his work was encouraged by his analyst, Dr. Arnold Eisendorfer. After the analysis, he and Dr. Eisendorfer met on occasion to discuss each other's cases. As he remarked, he was much fonder of him at that time than during the analysis since Dr. Eisendorfer was firm, strong and opinionated. However, he did leave room for Dr. Horowitz's differences, and especially important, was always interested in Dr. Horowitz's exposition of those differences. This was not a friendship, but rather two clinicians discussing their cases.

Dr. Horowitz retained his connection with Bellevue and held a seminar for residents for about fifty years. He required the residents to see their patients four or five times per week, unusual at the time, and then come back to talk about what happened between the doctor and the patient. Every member of the seminar participated. No one was left out. He did as Dr. Frosch had originally taught him. What did the patients say? What did you say and then what happened? From this seminar many candidates have come to the New York Psychoanalytic Institute.

Dr. Horowitz's reading, his immersion in great literature, continues to this day. He is lucky in that he never needs much sleep, he said, leaving him a lot of time for his favorite activity, reading.

An important stimulus for Dr. Horowitz began more than thirty-five years ago in Group Two of the Center for Psychoanalytic Studies (called CAPS) He remembers our first meetings with Dr. Robert Waelder. He knew he had a congenial mentor since Dr. Waelder was interested in Etruscan artifacts and whatever could be known of Etruscan History. He had read Dr. Kris's monograph on intaglios (incised engraved stones) and he collected some from a Mr. Lusting who had a gallery on Madison Avenue and who had once been Freud's dealer. This interest in antiquities, he said, is surely the same as his interest in the personal remnants of an individual's past. In his analytic work, in addition to his interest in the person's original love objects, he finds valuable insights in the relationship of the analysand to later figures in his life, including those who may be known only as historical figures.

Dr. Horowitz remembers the CAPS meetings very fondly. He disagreed with many of his colleagues there, but learned from each one, especially Dr. Charles Kligerman, who was under Kohut's spell, but was above all imaginative and intelligible. The special value of these meetings is the openness with which all of us could discuss our current cases with respected colleagues whose minds we admired. There was also, as a result of this meeting of minds, the referral of patients from one to the other, so that many members shared patients.

Dr. Horowitz gave as an example one of his own patients, a man who had a very complex sexual life, which took place mostly in the subway. The patient's father had died early in his life and the family tried to forget that period. Dr. Horowitz's patient longed to find a man underground and, having found a man and having had a sexual encounter with him, was then able to be potent with his wife; behind this, however, was the poignant experience of the loss of the father and the wish to be connected with the father who had once lived. The past is crucial in understanding the patient in analysis, In the course of analysis this patient found new ways to express himself metaphorically. The more he became reconnected to his dead father, the more intelligible did his communications become, both verbally and musically. (It is difficult to convey Dr. Horowitz's capacity for something more than what we know as empathy. It is as if he absorbs the patient into himself, a process which gives him an internal intuitive experience. He can thus translate this inner experience into an "intelligible" succinct observation, an explanation, or an illustrative analogy. This is not just a judgment in words but a form of capturing the patient's psychological communication and its sources.)

Incidentally, added Dr. Horowitz, one is given a great gift in being an analyst since one learns so much from one's patients—as he did about music and poetry from this particular patient..

Becker, W.A. (1923). *de Comicis Romanorum Fabulis Plautinus Maxime Questiones*. London: Forgotten Books, 2018.

INTRODUCTION TO SELECTED PAPERS

by Philip Herschenfeld MD

This book is a collection of papers written by a clinical genius. Many who were familiar with his work and teaching and supervision acknowledge this. He was not so involved as a theoretician, although in some of these papers you will find a keen understanding of theory and a useful description of the evolution of analytic theory, how one idea developed into another. Most of the papers demonstrate a deep, intuitive feel for what makes people tick and what intervention would be of most help to them. And helping was his stock-in-trade. He taught me that a therapist or psychoanalyst should always begin the initial session with a new patient, "How can I be of help? This is to communicate that the therapeutic relationship is not an intellectual exercise. It is not to prove some theory that you are fond of. It is solely in order to be of help to the patient."

Horowitz was known for his work with artists. Bernstein and Sondheim have acknowledged their work with him in memoirs and on the stage. He himself can be seen as a creative artist of psychoanalysis. He was able to mobilize his imagination and enter the inner world of the patient without frightening him or her but jointly creating a transitional space that facilitates insight and psychological change to which both contribute. This approach appreciates the potential creativity of the patient in a situation of the emotional safety. The psychoanalyst is facilitating development starting again. I think that this is a rare talent in our profession.

As my own analytic training progressed, it became time for me to take on a third supervised case. I had been working for a year with an interesting young man. He suffered from immense guilt and shame over his sexuality. He came from a strong Italian Catholic background and was a resident in surgery. He was insightful, committed to the therapy, and gay. I was assigned by my faculty advisor to consult with an older woman analyst as a potential supervisor. She was revered in the field. I felt privileged at the prospect of such a supervisor. We met and I presented what I knew about my patient, which was a lot. He had been quite open with me. My prospective supervisor asked only one question at the end of my presentation. "Is he very thin?" I said, "He is thin, but not very thin." Whereupon she dismissed him and me with a wave of the hand, "He is not analyzable." I thought that she had determined that because he was gay. But I never really knew; and I was too intimidated to even ask.

So, I returned to my advisor who asked if there was anyone else I might like to work with. I had very much enjoyed a class in Universal Fantasies that I had taken with Milton Horowitz. I was especially impressed with his erudition and his skill at telling stories. He had a wide ranging mind that took from case material, analytic literature, world literature and personal experience. He seemed affable, quite interested in all people and upbeat. I mentioned him and it turned out that he had time for supervision, and we met. I presented the same material to him, somewhat worried that I would be again told, "not analyzable." Instead, at the end of my presentation, I was told, "The only way to tell if someone is analyzable is to try to analyze him." And that approach characterized so much of what I learned over the years; it was Milt's practical way of being. "There is much that we don't know and can't predict. All we can do is try our best. And be honest regarding what we learn. If we learn that analysis was not the right choice for someone, we say so and modify our approach."

Here are some other of the principles I learned from him in over 35 years of conversation: "No dogma. We know much less than we think and must accept that in regard our patients and ourselves. We can only follow the data and meet the patient where he or she is. Every patient,, every analysis is different. Every analyst is different, and the analyst must understand how he or she is different. Each analyst and each patient has a unique technique for analyzing. Each analytic pair of analyst and patient is unique. We make mistakes. A patient will forgive any mistake except meanness. Shutting off our sensibilities through theoretical pre-conception is an assault upon the patient." Many of these ideas are demonstrated in the papers in this volume.

I realize as I write this that I have started with the story of how we began. Dr. Horowitz was a master storyteller. It must be related.

I had three excellent, but very different adult supervisors at New York Psychoanalytic Institute. In those days, I was able to remember every word of a session and write it down after the session for supervision. My first supervisor would listen carefully and at the end ask me what I thought. I would tell him and he would make a small remark and we went on to the next session. My second supervisor would frantically write down every word that I read, perhaps as a way to keep himself from talking. Then he made a few perceptive comments on what he heard or understood from that session. Milt would let me read for about 20-25 minutes, usually about two of my five sessions. And then he would say, "That reminds me of a case I once saw." And the rest of that day's supervision would be his presentation of a most interesting case or situation or analytic dilemma that directly related to my case. He told a story that was clearly illustrative of some aspect of my case. And I learned from those stories and still remember most of them. He had seen innumerable patients over the years, and he remembered them in detail. He remembered my cases in detail, years later. He had a phenomenal memory, but he did not think that that was a requirement for doing good analytic work. Milt, more commonly referred to as Muff by friends, (he always had a muffin in his lunch bag in grade school), did not write a lot, for someone who had so much to say. I think he saw himself primarily as a teacher and healer.

He was known for conducting second analyses, after the first one (often for analytic training) was not so therapeutic, for one reason or another. He was also a great teacher. He taught classes and seminars and post-graduate study groups. And he was a much sought after analytic supervisor and consultant. I have run into people from distant places who would come to New York for a consultation for himself or herself or for a patient. And he was a great reader of the classics. There are many references to great literature in his papers, all illustrating a point about a patient. In one paper in which he was particularly concerned about confidentiality, he illustrated the patient's conflicts through the life of Tolstoy who, he felt, had similar conflicts to the patient. But I guess writing was not such a priority for him. We have found about 30 papers to work with for this book. I was surprised that there were so many since he never referred to them. I think that this may have been out of an essential modesty. That modesty was a component of his insistence that our abilities to understand and to cure have limits.

Another story, told to me by the patient: The patient was an experienced analyst from far away who was having trouble with an event in his life. He heard Muff present at his own institute, was impressed with his clinical acumen, and called him for a consultation.

"How soon can you come to New York?

"I can be there Friday afternoon."

"See you then."

The analyst with the problem began talking. Soon, Muff said, "That's not a problem." He went on to a new topic. Again, "That's not a problem." And again, same thing. Finally, with the fourth topic, "That's the Problem!"

And they met weekly and spoke about The Problem over the course of months. Every time the visiting analyst got off topic, he was brought back to the issue. And it was mastered. (And he had a sandwich for the long-traveling colleague,)

How many of us would have such clarity and confidence to be able to say, "That's not a problem!" How many of us would have the ability to focus the laser like that in order to get the therapeutic job done?

Muff wanted, needed to make people feel better. He related this to his mother's depression and seeing his father come home some nights, realize that she was feeling poorly, and announcing, "Bessie, get your hat. We are going out to dinner!" And she would brighten up.

Let me say more about Muffs character. He did not gossip, a rarity in our field. We need to be silent so much of the time and I think that this failing comes from a need to sometimes talk and be heard. And we are interested in people. So we talk when we can. And sociologists tell us that gossip is an important vehicle for creating social bonds between the gossipers. But he just didn't indulge. Also, he was very understanding and accepting of human foibles. He did not condemn, but attempted to understand behavior. Except for when he was describing evil. He once described a woman who saved herself during the Holocaust by becoming a virtual slave to the family who took her in. "She was used as sexual toilet by the men in the family." The hatred he felt for them was palpable. And with colleagues, especially younger ones, he was supremely generous. (He gave me his custom made leather and chrome analytic couch when illness forced him to retire.) It makes me wonder about the necessity for such a sterling character in doing this work. Not everyone possesses such. I settle for the notion that our character flaws must not impinge upon the work. And that we must have the honesty to recognize when that does happen and return to treatment ourselves. Muff was a great proponent of analysts getting the treatment they needed- "We all have blind spots and if they effect the work, there is an obligation to do something about it. Not only the patient, but the analyst must also regress in the service of the treatment. If that regression threatens to express itself in action, return to analysis."

As you will find, he considered psychoanalysis to be a very intimate interaction between two people. A most unique and peculiar conversation. Every aspect of the conversation is fair game for inspection and introspection.

The papers included are as wide ranging as is our field. The topics include psychoanalytic education, tributes to valued colleagues [Martin Stein, Jacob Arlow, Leo Stone], various panel discussions, therapeutic process in analysis and adolescence. He considered adolescence the Dark Continent of analysis. It was often ignored in favor of mining the much more speculative, less remembered early childhood. "Adolescence contains so much pain that we remember little of it."

I joined him in teaching a course in Advanced Analyzability. The focus of the course was the failures of analysis in the cases of the candidates and the instructors. "Freud made most of his advances through studying his failures. We should have the courage to do the same and learn from our mistakes." He felt that successful people were not people who never made mistakes. They were the people who studied their mistakes so that they would not repeat them. He preached this to patients. Honesty with one's self was crucial. He was most honest with patients and colleagues and friends, but always in a way that, when possible, spared their narcissism.

The topic of Transference is paramount throughout his works. "Transference is a triumph of memory over perception." In his paper on "Narcissistic Contributions to Transference," he discusses the normal human tendencies to identify with our childhood caretakers and to project portions of our own minds upon those we love, respect, hate and fear. "Transference responses are ubiquitous and appear everywhere in life. The psychoanalytic situation is unique in that these universal reactions are allowed to flower, may be explored and sometimes explained."[1] The word "sometimes" is important. It expresses the limits of our abilities that we must accept as part of the work. "Boundary violations often occur when the analyst forgets the power of transference and imagines that the patient loves us because we are so nifty. None of us are that nifty and if you imagine that to be the case, return to your own treatment."

I have found these papers to be very useful in daily clinical work. I happen to be currently treating two men who are very different, but each has decided to divorce his wife of many years, mother of his children. Both men had carefully reasoned explanations (rationalizations) to support the decision. Then I read the paper on Men's Reaction to Menopause in Women and was able to fruitfully explore each patient's fear of aging and death. These fears were conveniently projected on their aging wives. This paper also goes into the history of cultural use of the witch, the old crone, for similar purposes.

The papers in this volume are not arranged chronologically. The first one, Hatred in the Analytic Situation, is perhaps my favorite. My own fantasy is that an entire curriculum of psychoanalysis could be based upon a close reading of this paper. (There is a Hebrew phrase that one traditionally writes in the flyleaf of a book given as a gift. "Turn it over and turn it over. For everything is in it.")

I hope that upon discovering the riches in this particular paper, you will be inspired to read all the rest. I doubt that you will regret the effort. And it is not such a painful effort. He writes in a plain, clear, understandable English. No jargon! His humanity and wisdom and scholarship are always on display.

---

1 Horowitz, M.H. (1996). Some Notes on Transference and Memory: A Tribute to Leo Stone *Journal of Clinical Psychoanalysis,* 5(2):197-211. p. 197. New York Psychoanalytic Association Symposium in Honor of Leo Stone, M.D., December 5, 1992. See also pp. 43–59 in this volume.

SECTION ONE:

Transference in Psychoanalysis: Opportunities and Obstacles

CHAPTER 1

Hatred in the Analytic Situation

INTRODUCTION

The Latin poet Catullus said:

> "I hate and I love: why I do so you may well ask. I do not know but I feel it happen and am in agony" (Carmina LXXXV)

We are often at a loss to explain the most powerful of the range of human emotions. Moreover, overwhelming love or hate is often experienced silently with little outward display: private passions are often so intense that they dare not be shared.

The psychoanalytic situation offers the opportunity to share thoughts and emotions, to attempt to express them, explore them and perhaps explain them. It also offers the opportunity to explore the difficulties in finding a mode of expressing idea and affect. The analytic situation involves two people in a strange intimacy conducting an idiosyncratic form of conversation and interaction. Both participants have needs, fantasies, thoughts and affects and resistances against expressing all or part of those intrapsychic and interpersonal issues which arise in a given moment of the "conversation" of analysis (Bernfeld, 1941). Each of the participants has a complex set of agendas and a mode of dealing with the immediate experience. Each of the participants has a "technique" of analysis.

We are often at a loss to explain the most powerful of the range of human emotions. Moreover, overwhelming love or hate is often experienced silently with little outward display: private passions are often so intense that they dare not be shared. At a point where the hypnotic situation formed for Freud the model of analysis, one might consider that "technique" was the province of the analyst doing something to a relatively passive patient. At those moments in the history of the psychoanalytic endeavor in which the patient was to choose the topic of discussion and attempt to convey thought and feeling by association, the patient became a full participant with his or her own "technique" of working. Furthermore, the recommendation that the analyst use his own unconscious as an "instrument in the analysis" placed both participants on a more equal footing and attempted to ensure that no two analyses would be the same.

Any discussion of "hatred" may well be extended to the more general issue of powerful affectivity in the analytic situation in both intrapsychic and interpersonal expression. I will present an extended clinical vignette in which hatred toward others and self-hatred stand in an interesting relationship, one to the other. Narcissism, that is, taking one's own self as the target of need, wish, impulse or fantasied organization of those forces, is a ubiquitous human capacity to deal with the vicissitudes of both love and *aggression*. Following the clinical data, I will attempt to focus upon the analyst's reactions to intense affect in the analytic situation and raise some issues of the analyst's working ego and the relationship of insight to the analyzing function.

Hatred, in itself, cannot be viewed as a pathological phenomenon. We all have a capacity to hate, and it undergoes a series of developmental vicissitudes not dissimilar to the capacity to love. To paraphrase a comment made by Anna Freud, we have to learn to be good haters as well as good lovers . The case material looks at some "miscarriages" of hatred, that is, where "hatred" is directed toward someone who is loved and needed—the extremes of ambivalence.

To introduce the clinical material, I would like to focus briefly on some of the structural and developmental issues implicit in the narrative of my patient's analytic work. Hatred toward a needed person is a danger; it presents the fantasy of destroying the very person one depends upon. There is a great tendency to deflect the hatred upon oneself to spare and protect the other. People vary greatly in their ability to tolerate strong affects in others or in themselves. This variability is not always on the basis of one's character. Life experience sometimes changes tolerance for affect intensities. For example, being a parent affects one's ability to accept emotional storms. On the other side, psychoanalytic inexperience makes dealing with certain clinical situations more difficult. Conducting our part of an analysis is a learned ability; the fewer the cases, the more surprises; the more surprises, the greater the tendency toward "emergency" reactions and counter-transference mishandling and breakdown.

Hatred is not an irreducible phenomenon. It may serve powerful defensive needs against feeling helpless or weak. It may cover guilt or shame. Hatred may convey a need to control or dominate or frighten the object. It may be connected to sexual excitement. Hatred is also a way to cling to the object through fantasies of revenge, a phenomenon best known to us in situations of divorce.

I will illustrate the major analytic issues involved by a long case vignette in the form of process notes of a single hour.

CASE HISTORY

The following narrative is extracted from the analysis of a 36-year-old man who had consulted me while suffering from a creative inhibition as a painter.

5

(The patient died of malignant illness some years after the completion of this analytic work. A major problem in reporting actual analytic data is always the problem of confidentiality, a problem not removed by any event, even death. The identifying material has been disguised but the process described is taken directly from my notes which were written at the end of each day)

Within a short period after beginning the analysis, the patient began to focus upon a more painful issue than his inhibition—a life of repeated losses currently made more vivid by an impending separation from his wife and two children . He felt crushed and humiliated after discovering that his wife was having an affair with one of his friends. The discovery of the affair filled him with the sense of shame and the feeling of being inadequate. This was connected with the description of repeated homosexual masturbatory fantasies since early adolescence; these fantasies enabled him to achieve erection with his wife. On a number of occasions his conscious fantasies led to sporadic homosexual experiences under circumstances uncannily paralleling the homosexual fantasy. This parallelism was unconscious to him; the conditions of homosexual encounter understood in the analysis were: the man was always older, the setting was dark and usually underground—the subway, a basement, The encounter in fantasy and reality was silent and dreamlike; it then led to an intense short-lived feeling of happiness followed by self-loathing coupled with hatred of the man—this sequence was unclear until the analytic work explored the details.

The patient was the younger of two children; there was a sister two years his senior. His parents were constantly fighting and painfully unhappy. Their fights centered upon his mother's continuous anti-Semitic remarks made to her Jewish husband, all taking place in a context of the mother's Nazi sympathies during the second World War. The mother had insisted upon her children denying their Jewish background. The patient remembered little of his father, for the early family group came to a crash with the father's death when the patient was four. The once prosperous family became desperately poor, they moved to a squalid apartment, changed their name to the mother's family name and shed all remnants of Jewishness. Only a bizarre ritual allowed brief glimpses of the past: a yearly picnic at the father's grave, always referred to by the mother euphemistically as a "day in the country."

Despite his pain and unhappiness, he would have glimmers of a joyous outcome. The idealization of me and the poignant child-like optimism served as bulwarks of defense against his ongoing misery. Throughout this period of analysis, it seemed to both of us that his life was one of unresolved mourning for his lost father, trapped in the underground grave and continually searched after. In the analysis he seemed to have found his father in fantasy, The open homosexual masturbatory fantasies receded (or seemed to recede) , he was divorced from his wife and soon fell in love with another woman. Some weeks after resuming analysis, following the second summer vacation, he became sullen and silent. His usual volubility, vivid capacity for visual imagery as well as words seemed to dry up. As we attempted to explore this shutting off of his words, he exploded with a fury of rage and hatred. "Dirty, filthy Jew, he shouted. "The Nazis were right, they should have killed all the Jews." He paused, "including me."

The flow of venomous hatred of me alternating with self-loathing went on for days, with unabated fury. My first response was one of surprise and shock at the unleashed volcano. This extraordinarily polite, well-mannered man shouted and gesticulated; after experiencing a few brief blips of irritation and anger after he shouted "Kike, kike, kike" my own mood took on a thoughtful quiet and profoundly sad tone, We were both responding to object loss—he in his way, me in my own way. I quickly understood that both responses were to a father's death; his was a 4 year old's childhood response, mine was a response echoing my mourning for father when I was 32 Though interpretation was not possible, I recognized that his previous affability served as a complex defense against terrible separation anxiety and severe castration anxiety (related to an earlier discussion of his circumcision);

he was enraged at having been deserted by his father, ashamed of having disowned his father and profoundly identified with his disturbed shouting mother. How was he to have access to what seemed a response to my vacation? And why this vacation and not the first? How to analyze those resistances which had shut off access to affectivity as well as memory?

The first order of business was to keep his anxiety in sight and not merely focus upon his hatred. Self-observation by the analyst in the analytic situation is a necessary ingredient of the work but not always sufficient. I have always had the opinion that consultation about difficult technical problems is a necessary part of ongoing education as well as ongoing therapeutic work. Psychoanalysis is no longer the work of the solitary pioneer; it is a collaborative effort between the patient and the analyst and between the analyst and other colleagues. I have never hesitated to talk over difficult problems with other respected colleagues, younger as well as older, and never hesitated to review certain issues with my own analyst. I had brief informal discussions about this continuing affect-storm with two colleagues: one a child-analyst with wide experience of early object-loss and the other a master of clinical technique who incidentally had elaborated. some ideas about anti-Semitism. Our discussions centered upon the transference situation, the problems of object-loss at age four, the problems of delayed and distorted mourning, and the role of age-appropriate sadism and hatred in the attempts at the mastery of trauma.

Slow careful attention to the immediate transference issues and careful analysis of minute aspects of resistance led quite unexpectedly to the following "good hour," to use Kris's term.

The session began with the patient in a grim mood, uncomfortable in posture on the couch, stiffened with ill-disguised anger. He began with a dream: "I'm on a rickety Ferris wheel with a woman. I fell out of my seat, caught by some wheels, I was crushed in the mud. I was screaming and I knew the screams were excessive and greater than the pain I was feeling."

He associated to the dream another dream which occurred during a nap following the previous day's analytic session. 'I l was running away barefoot—I was in an undershirt—it was in an institution—the door was open, and I ran away into a 5 & 10 cent store." (The central conflict of the previous day's material was about revealing a fantasy of his father or his father's body being hidden in a closet.)

He began to associate to the Ferris wheel which he could vividly picture. With some sense of amazement he remembered that he had a toy Ferris wheel which his father had brought home from a store that he owned. The patient had asked for a Ferris wheel not knowing what it looked like but having heard that his maternal grandfather had worked on a Ferris wheel at a seaside resort. There was also a family story that his maternal uncles had run away from an orphan asylum to find their father at this seaside resort. (Some months later this story of finding a father at a resort was associatively linked to the "day in the country" cemetery visits.)

I remarked that the two dreams were bound together in searching for a father.

He answered: "1 can't get a horrible picture of my father out of my mind—it's like the picture of Dorian Gray in that old movie--a portrait of Gray by Ivan Albright—sins and debauchery show up on the picture. Dorian Gray was homosexual. I feel horrible. I can see the house in which I was born; what I remember most right now are the closets, the attic, under the stoop-places where things were hidden. Oh God, the cupboard where I wanted to keep his body."

I said: The portrait is a living being, your father and you .

He continues; "In the dream running away from the institution meant running away from being caught in some homosexual act by my mother." He cries. "She didn't want me to love my father."

He picks up the element of being dragged in the mud. He remembers going to a church bazaar soon after his mother remarried . He was 10. "I took a chance on a basket of food." He weeps bitterly. "What brings tears to my eyes is that I won. My sister and I brought it home. We were always hungry then. Mother was in bed with her husband. I didn't get the reception I expected. (Silence for a moment.) I was afraid to be Jewish in school—the Jewish kids seemed to be driven to get high grades. My mother was always indifferent to grades. I thought that was a sign of great enlightenment ." (Silence.) "Driving myself was a way of secretly acknowledging that I was Jewish. (He cries again) "It makes me close to you. I think of a dark room, Father is sick in bed," (Silence.) "When I woke up this morning I thought I'll go to see that house this afternoon; now I'll really do it, maybe it will stimulate some memories. Going down in the mud reminds me of a vague memory of my father's car being stuck in the mud somewhere. I have a horrible image of being tied down and buried alive. Two bands tying me like the harness in a Ferris wheel. Then an image of being tied down to take out my tonsils. Another old movie, *The Fall of the House of Usher*—a woman in a coffin, chained in."

I said: "This continues the fantasy of yesterday. Father is buried alive. He didn't die but can be found underground."

You are hungry for "memories of him."

He weeps uncontrollably: "1 hated him for leaving me with Mother. Hated him. Hated him. (Silence) I am mortified that I have hated you so much. (Weeps for the remainder of the session.)

That afternoon he found the childhood home, visited some neighbors who remembered the family and recalled that his father died of "anemia." Though medically unsophisticated he then remembered hearing the words "aplastic anemia" in childhood.

The affect-storm of transference hatred receded into a more manageable affective contact with his anger and aggression connected to the hurt of being left by an adored father. His contact with me was restored without the initial over idealizing content. As this change occurred, the creative

10

inhibition vanished. It had been a punishment for his fantasied crimes of revenge.

The central issue of affective *resonance* was that my experience of sadness, as a response to his outburst of hatred, supplied an adult response to object loss where the patient re-lived the childhood affect of rage at abandonment. My response was based upon experience of object loss, his reaction was based upon *his* unique experience. Here, there was no direct mirroring of affect, but a consonance of response to the *situation of loss* occurring at different developmental levels. The consonance was at the level of *motive* and *not* at the level of manifest affective content. Hatred was not matched by hatred; his hatred was matched by my sadness. The analytic endeavor is designed to supply an understanding of the *unconscious* motives for affect discharge, to respond to Catullus' agony with our feeble attempts at enlightenment. In this clinical vignette we have a very small but crucial example of the operation of what Otto Isakower termed the "analyzing instrument," at work: my unconscious linked to my patient's unconscious in affective resonance, at different developmental levels.

Subsequent to this hour it was possible to examine the patient's fantasy that being enraged demonstrated strength while anxiety or sadness demonstrated weakness.

AFFECTIVE RESONANCE AND THE ANALYTIC SITUATION

Many clinical discussions about the appearance of intense hatred in the analytic situation make an unwarranted assumption that such hatred expressed by the patient will be met by intense hatred experienced by the analyst. Some of this has been viewed as justified by the reported work of Winnicott. Some of these discussions become muddy in their outlines when the clinical material does not come from an analysis but from a superficial psychotherapy and becomes more confused when the patients described are psychotic or severely borderline. I will restrict my remarks to data derived from the psychoanalysis of clearly analyzable patient.

The very design of the psychoanalytic procedure is to encourage a special form of reversible regression in both participants albeit different in form and function for patient and analyst. The quiet room, the recumbent posture, the attempt at free association all encourage this regression and are all reminiscent of the hypnotic procedure with which the history of psychoanalysis began. The patient is encouraged by the procedure itself to loosen some defensive controls and to do something closer to a creative work of art than it is to narrate a history. The reaction we conceptualize as transference (that is, the patient's inclusion of the analyst in the new version of the neurosis) stimulated by this regression. After having asked for anamnestic data in the initial phases of the interaction this new "transference" material allows the patient to *show* us what had happened in the past or had been fantasied in the past in a form of action. This re-living of pathogenic conflict (Bring) allows the full flowering of the "transference neurosis" as it was understood by Brian Bird and Martin Stein. Neurosis ceases to be seen as an archeological artefact; it becomes a living presence re-enacted on the stage of the analytic situation carrying with it a full sense of conviction that it is taking place at the current moment. Transference is an organ of memory that operates by re-creating new editions of an old plot and searching out new persons to play the old parts.

On the other hand, the analyst also encourages his own regression in order to exercise the analyzing function. Where the patient's regression is optimally across the board while preserving self-observing functions (Sterba), the analyst's regression has to be more selective. The analyst has to have access to his own unconscious, but *not* through re-enactment.

The analyst's access optimally is through *insight*, starting with insight into his own personality and searching for insights into the patient. Interestingly, insight into ourselves is more often achieved by the *continued* self-examination of our own experiences and fantasies and the related resistances to that scrutiny. With the patient we primarily focus upon his or her resistances (Freud, Gray) and rely upon the re-enactments and analysis of resistance to reveal memory and fantasy as demonstrated *in the present* and incorporating the analyst in their content. Throughout, the operative analyzing concept is *insight,* not merely re-experiencing. Whatever the therapeutic benefit of re-living pathogenic conflict, the analyst and the patient need insight in order to halt endless repetition and give a sense of meaning and control. That is precisely what Freud meant when he said "where id was, let ego be."

In this partly shared regression there is a special rôle for affect. The partial loss of control through regression permits and facilitates the upsurge of feeling, especially for the intense and passionate feelings of childhood. This is true for both participants.

THE ANALYST'S INSIGHT AND THE UNDERSTANDING OF POWERFUL AFFECTS

As I had mentioned at the outset, today, when we speak of "technique in psychoanalysis" some of us mean the intersection of two techniques; the psychoanalyst's method of approach to all the data of the analytic situation and the patient's approach to that data. Here we include the transference potentials and reactions of both participants and the vast range of affects which are part of recollections, acting-out, fantasies, dreams, rational plans, quite complex abstract thoughts, and creative experiences. Here, too, we understand that transference is an organ of for *both* members of the analytic effort. (The analyst has been through the process as a patient, we hope with successful outcome.)

In the past, certain unwarranted assumptions about the nature of transference led to an expectation that transference could be "resolved, " that is, analyzed away. We now know that transference does not disappear upon analysis, it remains as a potential throughout life, requiring fresh analysis (especially self-analysis) when old memories and their fantasy counterparts re-appear. Transference, as an organ of memory, has to undergo a change of function.

Here, the process of insight, so important in the personal development of the analyst, becomes crucial in the conduct of the work. The process of insight is the means by which transference reactions and repetitions might assert themselves *not* by full-blown elaborations but by signal "test-dose" phenomena. This fractional differentiation is a critical aspect of the analyst's technique. It should be noted that I am not speaking of "counter-transference"; rather I am referring to the ubiquity of transference response in all human beings, especially in conditions of regression. We have invited the patient into a regressive situation in order that pathogenic conflict might be *relived*, enacted, not merely narrated, and we participate in that regression in order to understand the patient's communications and affects. Freud had used the concept of regression in three senses: (I) regression in form from secondary to primary process, (2) regression in time: going toward the past and (3) regression from consciousness toward the unconscious,

Both analyst and analysand attempt to achieve this regression in the service of the treatment but with the significant difference that we expect the analyst's response to be aim-inhibited and measured, operating in the patient's interest, and monitored by the analyst's insight. On the other hand, we want the patient to have the widest untrammeled access to the content of those regressions, especially to their affective consequences.

Just as transference was seen by Freud to be the most important engine of the analysis as well as its greatest resistance, so does affect-laden analytic experience serve as the engine of insight as well as a resistance to insight. The organizing, integrating, and synthetic functions of the ego responsible for the construction of insights need affective fuel. This may very well be central to any aspects of insight relevant to early childhood before the development and organization of speech. The presence of those early experiences and their later developmental transformations are regularly re-enacted in the transference often accompanied by wide excursions of affective display, but they are unintegrated. When Freud first undertook some understanding of "hatred," he related it to experiences of "unpleasure," and he saw its subsequent development as connected to the complexities of libidinal and aggressive links to objects. Where those more primitive experiences and fantasies are connected to the destruction or disappearance of the object as well as to the state of unpleasure, later transformations are in the direction of sadism. Fantasies and impulses are then directed toward the control of the object and causing that person pain or humiliation. Here we see clearly the work of ambivalence; the major targets of sadism are the *ambivalently-loved* objects including the self.

There is no analysis in which some such hateful content and sadism does not emerge, and the analyst's insight into what facilitated the emergence in the current analytic work is necessary in order to provide the setting for the patient's emerging insight. Moreover, when the analyst does not react, in kind, to criticism or aggression the treatment may gain the impact of a corrective experience (Kris, 1956).

What is often difficult for the analyst is to not react to hatred with hatred, and not to become confused by the manifest content because it is so noisy and center-stage. The necessity of the analyst's controlling his or her reactions is more imperative if the patient's experience of hatred has been set off by some word or action of the analyst. The analyst, creating the condition of unpleasure, triggers the response. Here, we have to accept responsibility for our contribution to the reaction, but not act out our own response. Let me turn again for a moment to my clinical example. My contribution was to set off an experience of object-loss, my interpretive contribution about object-loss was to utilize my own affective resonance of sadness as a response to a father's death. My own response allowed for interpretations about the patient's age-appropriate enraged response to loss and frustration and set him upon the track of. completing an unresolved mourning which had been sequestered from his later development. Ultimately, his experiences of grief and mourning, now at his adult developmental level, allowed him to overcome his creative inhibition which was later discovered to have a withholding stubborn model linked to disorders of bowel-function. The related fantasies were about not giving up and losing the body contents; retention and inhibition allowed for *holding on* to that which might be *lost*.

Repeatedly experienced *grief* (instead of anger) was the analytic advance which led to my patient's insight, and symptom relief. The uncovering of his anal fantasies took place long after the inhibition had disappeared. The exploration of early fantasy can sometimes take place only in the calm of an analysis, not in its storm. But the storms prepare the ground. His hatred melted away in the pain of mourning .

MISCARRIAGES OF THE ANALYST'S INSIGHT IN THE FACE OF EXPLOSIVE AFFECT

Much of what I am about to report upon is the consequence of many re-analyses of colleagues, much supervision, and much self-observation. To repeat, the major hazard in confronting the enraged patient *is* the tendency to respond in kind. (This is quite exactly paralleled by the hazard of transference-love.) Response in kind is not merely reactive and reflexive.

In almost every instance where such reactions have been studied by me there is a sudden sharp increase in the tendency to use *identification* as a defense, The analyst has the impulse to behave as the patient behaves. This takes place not by some arcane process, but along lines well-known to us throughout the course of development. Identification can be a powerful defense against threatened or actual object-loss, the identification being a precipitate of the lost object-tie. It is a means of re-connecting to the object, to become congruent. Hatred threatens the object-tie, seems to threaten the very continuity of the analysis. It is an invitation to mutual acting-out in which the unconscious object-tie is not love but explosive sadism. This is a state of affairs well-known to us in certain disastrous marriages where two people are bound by hatred, and by certain disastrous stalemated analyses which seem to continue in mutual despair.

Now, individuals differ greatly in their tendencies to use identification as a defense. Some analysts, because of early life experiences, seem especially vulnerable. Here, I am thinking especially of those who sustained painful early object-loss in response to which there was inadequate mourning. Over-identification with patients' suffering, a kind of permeability to outside influences, and a tendency to discipleship to charismatic leaders are potential variations of this problem to which many of us are subject. The very nature of the work heightens this tendency and makes the requirement of insight even more urgent.

The nub of the analytic task is the simultaneous observation of the self and its functions as well as those of the patient *in the analytic situation*. This is an almost insuperable task requiring much personal flexibility and much knowledge. For the analyst to maintain some degree of objectivity in this effort requires full participation accompanied by exquisite self-observation; again, this is the analogous technical counterpart of Sterba's view of the "therapeutic split in the ego" needed by the patient. A balance must be kept between too great participatory identification with the patient leads to one set of problems, and too great self-observations bordering on narcissistic introspection leads to another set of problems. How to maintain balance bears some relation to the problems we have as parents and the problems we face as teachers in the three impossible professions .

THE IMMEDIATE HERE AND NOW AFFECTIVE EXPERIENCE AND ANALYTIC PROCESS

An extremely interesting way to view analytic data has been suggested by some recent scientific hypotheses in the spheres of fractal geometry and chaos theory. Its analytic application in simple form is to compare cross-sectional observations with longitudinal observations, that is, to compare a series of individual hours in the course of the work with our long-range view of patterns of the work over time. This comparison helps us establish individual concepts of *process*. Of special application to the topic of *hatred in the analytic situation* is to place the individual affective explosion as a moment in the process, a moment which is *not* a disruption of the process but intrinsic to it and eventually understood as a necessary component of the process. There *does* reside in each of us a potential for hatred, rage, revenge and destruction of others as well as a potential for love, care-taking and protection of the object. The merest inspection of the history of man gives testimony to the power of destructiveness in individual fantasies and acts of violence, and shared fantasies and acts ranging from horror movies to war.

The question is not whether such fantasies will appear but *when* will they appear and in relation to what circumstances within the analytic process. Of one thing we can be sure: these events are not random. As with all other aspects of human behavior, they are motivated, patterned, and repetitive and our task is to help the patient find motive, pattern, and stimulus for

18

repetition. Herman Nunberg, in a case discussion many years ago, said that the mere fact of being in analysis was an *unconscious invitation to remember* with the power of a hypnotic suggestion. We might add that one aspect of that unstated "unconscious suggestion" is not the "memory of recollection" but the "memory of repetition in action" especially in regard to the discharge of affect.

Moreover, we are not the neutral witnesses to that repetition; we invite it by our very presence. We become the target of old unfulfilled wishes and needs, included in the new version of the neurosis which Brian Bird described as the crux of transference neurosis. We lend ourselves to inclusion and by our actions and interventions help shape the way that reaction is made manifest. We do that by that which is appropriate to the work in the form of interpretive interventions as well as by the usual dumb mistakes that all human beings make. Here, it should be noted that not all interpretations are helpful and not all dumb mistakes are destructive . Often we cannot predict what consequences will follow our contributions to the process. What we can know is that the analytic method is complex and fallible and we are no angels.

THE ANALYST'S PROVOCATION OF HATRED

To narrow the field, let me cull out of my experience, and the experience of students and colleagues, a few characteristic circumstances in which the moment of explosive hatred appears in the process when stimulated by the analyst.

1. Any interruption of the analysis, vacation, holiday, weekend . This is accentuated if the analyst falls ill.

2.   Any intervention which is viewed as a "put-down," leading to some feeling of humiliation. However helpless-appearing, the patient is your equal and condescension at any level is a stimulus for rage.

3.   The breaching of a resistance, rather than its analysis, is viewed as an attack and rightly so. This was the essence of Wilhelm Reich character-analysis with all its military analogies of armor-piercing.

4.   Any seduction, either in the libidinal or aggressive direction, may well be a stimulus to attack as a means of defense. This includes seductions toward shared pseudo-insights as a means of feeling at one with each other. This may involve pseudo-insights about analysis in general, about the analyst's own *analytic world-view,* not about the patient's unique experience. The invitation to discipleship is then a forerunner of what Edith Jacobson termed the "paranoid urge to betray." The history of analysis and what had been termed the "psychoanalytic movement" is littered by disappointed disciples who turned against their former mentors with violence. That is one aspect of rivalries and splits in institutes and between various schools of thought which are as often about unanalyzed hatred and aggression in the transference as they are about true differences in points of view. (Moreover, analysts who have been disciples, rather than independent thinkers, are like those whose pseudo-insights have been for the purpose of *merger* with the hypnotist-analyst. Therapeutic effect collapses with disappointment, and this is transmitted to the next generation of patients.)

5.   The most commonplace of stimuli toward hatred in the transference I leave till the end because it is the most important: not understanding the patient's suffering and imagining that we do. Here, the most egregious element is not only the possibility of the analyst's insensitivity or stupidity, of which we can all be guilty at times, but the shutting off of our sensibilities by theoretical pre-conception. When we try to pigeon-hole patients into some theoretical structure, we invite their

righteous indignation. We have behaved as if we were authoritarian parents stimulating the child's hatred and rebellion.

SUMMARY

These notes have been focused upon the appearance of hatred and rage in the transference in the psychoanalyses of neurotic patients with problems of character. I have not tried to address problems of rage and hatred in patients with severe pathology nor of patients in other types of psychotherapies. I have tried to re-direct our attention from the manifest appearance of a profound affect to the sources from which it arose. I have introduced a concept of "affective resonance" in which the manifest emotional data of *the analyst's response* might be very different from that of the patient but directed toward an understanding of *similar motive*. In brief, I have tried to respond to Catullus' agony by attempting to find a method of answering *why* we feel what we feel. There has been offered a suggestion that sometimes insight might supplant agony.

REFERENCES

Catullus (57 and 54 BC). The Poems of Catullus, trans. Guy Lee. Oxford: Oxford University Press, 2009.

Bernfeld, S. (1941) The facts of observation in psychoanalysis. *The Journal of Psychology* 12:289–305,

Bibring, E. (1954). Psychoanalysis and the dynamic psychotherapies, *J. Amer. Psychoanal .Assn 2:745–770.*

Bird, B. (1972). Notes on transference: Universal phenomenon and hardest part of analysis. *J. Amer. Psychoanal Assn*. 20:267–301 .

Freud, S. (1933) New Introductory Lectures on Psycho-Analysis. *Standard Edition* 22:1–182.

Gray, P. (1973). Psychoanalytic technique and the ego's capacity for viewing intrapsychic activity.. *Amer. Psychoanal . Assn.* 21:474–494.

Horowitz, M,H. (1987). Some notes on insight and its failures. *Psychoanal. Q.* 55:177–196.

Isakower, O. (1963) The analyzing instrument: A faculty discussion, published in (1992). *J. Clin. Psychoanal.* 1:165-271.

Kris, E. (1956) .On some vicissitudes of insight in psychoanalysis. *Int. J. Psychoanal.* 37:1–11

Stein, M.(1981). The unobjectionable part of the transference. *J. Amer. Psychoanal.. Assn .* 6: 263–277 .

Sterba, R. (1934) . The fate of the ego in analytic theory. *Int. J. Psychoanal.* 15:117–126.

CHAPTER 2

How Character Shapes Transference

(1995). *Journal of Clinical Psychoanalysis* 4(1):45-52.

I

Thomas Carlyle is said to have dubbed history the essence of innumerable biographies. So too, the body of psychoanalytic propositions about character and transference is the essence of innumerable psychoanalytic biographies. As the data from these analyses have accumulated over the past century many of our explanatory hypotheses have been thrown into question and our questions have taken on increasing complexity.

Martin Stein, whom we honor here, has long recognized the complexity of the task, and his many papers on character and on transference have served to shake theoretical complacency and reductionism by focusing on unanswered questions.

The depth of the problem of character theory was first addressed by Freud in an unpublished discussion with his students later reported by Herman Nunberg (1955):

Character is a combination, or rather a synthesis of many traits, habits, and attitudes of the ego. Sometimes one trait prevails, sometimes, another. One may be tempted by this fact to evaluate a man's character on the basis of a single trait. Of course, this would not yield a true picture. In order to obtain a more accurate idea of an individual's character, we must consider it from several points of view—from the descriptive, genetic, structural, dynamic, economic and libidinal angles. Consideration from each of these angles will lead to different results. The ideal picture of a character would be gained if it were possible to view all these aspects simultaneously. Then we would have a metapsychological conception of character [pp. 303-304].

Freud's comment is worth a brief aside on the subject of psychoanalytic data gathering and theory formation. It was clearly the inspiration for Waelder's (1936) paper on multiple function, where it was suggested that all psychological phenomena would have to be studied from all the viewpoints mentioned. It is a method more closely related to the discipline of history rather than the disciplines of the physical sciences. Where history has increasingly placed reliance on the complexity of data and the consequent complexity of explanatory concepts, modern science has searched for spare elegance of concepts. In the sphere of the study of human behavior there is always a danger of premature reductionism without adequate data. This danger is compounded in the psychoanalytic endeavor where analytic data need to be acquired through the analytic method and not from anecdote or from brief psychotherapies. This is a special problem in the evaluation of data about transference acquired from methods where the phenomena are not adequately examined. The perspectives from other methods and disciplines are necessary for wider validation but will not substitute for accurate data gathering.

Let me return now to the topics of my comments: "character," "transference," and "shaping."

The concepts of character and transference are explanatory hypotheses which have been confused in much analytic discourse with description. They have been used in a kind of shorthand as if they were facts rather than attempts to conceptualize certain commonplace observations and their psychoanalytic refinements. They begin with the observation that human behavior seems patterned and repetitive. Certain further observations about the relationship between these repetitive patterns and the data of fantasy, daydream and sleeping dream, symptoms and affects, led to a hypothesis that human behavior was motivated. The röle in human existence of infantile helplessness and the need for the adult to care for the child, gave us a historical, developmental viewpoint which later illuminated why patients in analysis showed certain intense emotional responses to the analyst. The concept of transference was an attempt to explain these intense emotional experiences. The concept of character was an attempt to explain certain aspects of the repetitive patterning phenomena. Some observations suggested that character might have roots in the body, in the neurological organization; that is, in the "constitution," however vague that concept is. Certain other observations suggest that character is clearly responsive to developmental experience, evolves and changes in the course of development, and contains large elements of the processes of *identification* with others. Other observations suggest that certain elements of character serve functions of discharge of impulse and wish and other elements of defense, modulation, and regulation of the derivatives of the drives.

Those phenomena subsumed and explained under the heading "transference" may be viewed as aspects of the psychological organs of memory. Transference experiences seem to function as orienting devices in which the unfamiliar is made to seem familiar and in which the concepts of adaptation as used by Hartmann seem useful as explanation. (Here adaptation is used as a "fitting-in" concept and is not to be confused with the concepts within biology which have long been controversial.) What is presumed in the concept of transference is that certain early as well as later impressions received in the interaction with other people are viewed as taking place again. To this we may add that certain aspects of identification with those important people as well as other aspects of the self, are regularly projected onto others in the attempt to make the unfamiliar into something familiar. What is of interest is the regularity with which these phenomena are viewed as "real" and carry with them a full sense of conviction. What may have been, or was "real" in the past is now experienced as "real" in the present.

Now let me turn to the issue of "shaping," that is, the form that a given behavioral phenomenon takes. This may be analogous to what, in the psychology of dreaming, psychoanalysis has termed the "means of representation." It also bears some relationship to the concept of the "manifest dream."

Initially, Freud viewed the manifest dream as a husk; within its shell a kernel of more significant content was thought to reside, this kernel requiring interpretation after associations to the manifest dream were found. Thus, the manifest dream was seen as a disguise. Important in understanding the form taken was the concept of the "day residue," that is, a percept of the waking life which became amalgamated with present-day wish, fantasy, and childhood memory to form the dream images through a process prominent in sleep but not limited to sleep. This knitting together of disparate elements was also seen as integral to the formation of screen memories, symptoms, and even delusions. Various aspects of the process were termed as functions of the ego: the synthetic function (Nunberg, 1931) and the organizing and integrating functions (Hartmann [1947] and Kris [1956]).

It is, in fact, the shape or form that certain phenomena take that allows us to infer what have been called psychic structures. Shape and form are not mere husks, they are subjects well worthy of study and their study is rewarding. Of the infinite variety of such shapes and forms, each of us has a relatively limited repertoire of construction leaving a personal unique set of psychic fingerprints. Character structure, the repetitive nature of unconscious fantasy, and the tendency of unconscious factors toward discharge are among the limiting factors of finding "means of representation" for the contents of inner life.

Using the psychology of dreaming as a rough analogy, the nature of the analyst's personality, the patient's perceptions of the analytic setting (the office, the couch, the "ritual" aspects of recumbent posture, the request for free association), all serve as a kind of day residue organizing the patient's cognitive and emotional responses. The invitation to regression implicit in the procedure often leads to mild alterations in consciousness in the directions of sleep and dream and tends to revive experiences of the past and of earlier human relationships. As we study these phenomena with greater care we find that it is not only the earliest past and the earliest human connections which are revived, but aspects of the entire life history. Furthermore, it is not only that experiences with other persons color and shape what is termed the transference situation, it is also that large portions of the self are projected upon the analyst. All of this colors what I have called the patient's technique of analysis. Each patient has a *technique* of analyzing as well as the analyst having a technique.

II

The way in which character gives shape to the analytic situation and to transference phenomena may be illustrated by two brief clinical vignettes:

Mrs. A sought a reanalysis some years after a failed analysis had come to a halt and then trickled away in an ineffectual psychotherapy. She viewed herself as a hopeless case and the analysis had reproduced many failures in her life. She was one of those people with a propensity to snatch defeat from the jaws of victory. Her many failures were easily discernible as self-defeats, but in the telling of every instance of failure there was a strange smile which flitted across her face. As she described her expectation that another analysis would prove a failure, she grinned at me. She was disparaging of her former analyst as she was disparaging of her parents. An extended consultation process prior to starting another analysis allowed a clearer picture of her character. Severely masochistic, she was able to turn her suffering and failures into indictments of the malevolence and personal shortcomings of all the important people in her life. Within days of beginning a reanalysis she viewed me as stupid and inept, a sort of amiable clod that she could despise and who would be ineffectual as an analyst. Her failure in the second analysis would be my failure and she would tell the world. A powerful aim of her failures was to achieve revenge against her parents and their representatives. Imbedded in the midst of the masochistic character structure was a deeply unconscious sense of guilt about childhood sexuality and aggression.

Mr. B had also had a failed analysis prior to seeing me. Flamboyant and exuberant in manner and dress, he took over the situation during the first interview. He told me what was wrong with psychoanalysis and his first analyst. He hoped that I would be different and said that he was willing to give me a chance. He had a long history of phobic symptoms and behavior, potency disturbances, and promiscuity. His histrionic manner and impulsive behavior during his life since adolescence became reproduced in the analytic situation. He viewed the analysis as a con game and saw me as seducing him into compliance with the analytic procedure. He was continually reenacting a homosexual seduction by a trusted and beloved teacher when he was just entering puberty. His hysterical character structure, already formed in early childhood, was given new shape by the seduction and it was this early adolescent restructuring of character which became the manifest content of the reenactments in the transference situation.

III

Though at the outset of an analysis much of what we may surmise about the patient's character comes from anecdotal history, our view of the more proximate and immediate aspects of character achieves new vividness in the emergence of the transference neurosis. Here I use the term *transference neurosis* as it was used by Brian Bird (1972). Character becomes a here-and-now issue in that the preset patterning of behavior is manifest in every aspect of the patient's participation in the work. It goes without saying that the analyst's character operates in a similar fashion.

Many aspects of character seem rooted in the body and the image of one's body that forms part of the personal identity. This has particular relevance for sexual gender identity and its relation to character formation. The habitual forms of given reactions which we term character have a relative constancy (Fenichel, 1945); that constancy was said to depend on constitution, on the nature of the "instincts" against which defense was directed and the determinants set by the external world; that is, the effects of experience and culture. This is most striking in the development of morality.

The first psychoanalytic descriptions of character focused on the defensive response to impulse and fantasy. But character is not merely defense, it is also the way in which satisfactory solutions are formed in response to inner and outer demands. There are reassuring, energy-sparing adaptive aspects of character which should not be forgotten. These aspects also color the transference in the form of expectations derived from one's own self.

The two clinical vignettes were chosen because they contain very large elements of aggression; the relation of character structure to aggression must occupy our attention because the containment of aggression and the need for object-sparing often colors the transference. As Stein (1969) pointed out long ago, the psychoanalytic theory of aggression is not adequate for the elucidation of character theory. It is to be remembered that most of our theorizing about aggression centers on its relation to the sense of guilt and the need for punishment; it is a theory of the *intrapsychic* functioning of aggressive impulses and is inadequate for understanding aggressive behavior.

Furthermore, it is difficult to pick apart those issues relevant to "character formation" from those issues which are more specific to questions of superego formation. "Aggression" and "morality" remain thorny pathways to traverse in studying an individual's psychic functions, influenced by the aggressive titer and the moral stance of the analyst-observer.

Finally, I would like to address one specific issue of the role of identification in character formation and the subsequent shaping of the transference neurosis.

Nunberg had placed great emphasis on the identificatory processes in character (1955). There are aspects of character which seem to have been swallowed whole and provide a consistent gestalt of the identifications with the original objects. They are sometimes projected as a complete gestalt upon the analytic process and upon the person of the analyst. The patient assumes that the analyst is a sort of characterological twin. Sometimes, this projection is piecemeal. I include these styles as aspects of transference as I include all projections of the self in transference response. (I do not see the usefulness of making a distinction between displacements from earlier objects as transference proper and projections as mere externalizations.)

These identificatory processes are powerfully important in maintaining a tie to the original objects. With many patients we see that symptoms based upon identifications have object quality; to lose the symptom is like losing the object. For certain patients the character structure itself has object quality; to change or shift character also can represent object loss. To this I might add that early object loss and unresolved mourning have a powerful effect upon character and characterological attitudes, especially in attitudes of pessimism and hopelessness. For such patients, object replacement often seems more important than psychoanalytic change with its further threat of object loss at termination of the treatment.

Sometimes the fixity of character is to be understood as a conservative holding on to the old objects and to old modes of gratification, and defense serving a survival function. What we do *not* want to do is follow Wilhelm Reich's (1949) advice to "pierce character armor." We want to do that which makes life better for our patients. This may mean the recognition of analytic limitations and knowing when to be cautious.

The same resolutions of conflict which went into character formation enter into transference neurosis when propitious regressive circumstances are provided in the analytic situation. Interpretations seemingly directed toward one set of phenomena affect the totality of the process. Despite our best efforts, all analytic results are incomplete, but those best efforts have to be directed toward the most conspicuous patternings of behavior in the transference neurosis and the character structure which feeds it and is the template for it.

REFERENCES

Bird, B. (1972), Notes on transference: Universal phenomenon and hardest part of psychoanalysis. *J. Amer. Psychoanal. Assn.*, 20:267–302.

Fenichel, O. (1945), *The Psychoanalytic Theory of Neurosis*. New York: W. W. Norton.

Hartmann, H. (1947), On rational and irrational action. In: *Essays on Ego Psychology*. New York: International Universities Press, 1964, pp. 37–68.

Kris, E. (1956), On some vicissitudes of insight in psychoanalysis. *Int. J. Psycho-Anal.*, 37:445-455.

Nunberg, H. (1931), The synthetic function of the ego. *Int. J. Psycho-Anal.*, 12:123–140.

——— (1955), Character and neurosis. In: *Principles of Psychoanalysis*. New York: International Universities Press. pp. 303–320.

Reich, W. (1949), *Character Analysis*. New York: Noonday Press.

Stein, M. (1969), The problem of character theory. *J. Amer. Psychoanal. Assn.* 17:675–701

Wälder, R. (1936), The principle of multiple function: Observations of verdetermination. *Psychoanal. Q.*, 5:45–62.

CHAPTER 3

On the Difficulty of Analyzing Character

(1999). *Journal of Clinical Psychoanalysis* 8(2):212-218.

I

William Hazlitt in essay 21, "On Personal Character" (1821-1824), says:

> "No one ever changes his character from the time he is two years old …" (p. 230). Hazlitt's superscription to the essay is from Montaigne: "Men palliate and conceal their original qualities, but do not extirpate them."

As the psychoanalytic endeavor is now into its second century, we can look back upon an extensive scientific literature about specifically psychoanalytic views of character, often written with broad therapeutic hopefulness, but countered by a broad clinical therapeutic experience replete with limitations in effecting character change. The scientific papers and the analysts who write them offer multiple theoretical and technical precepts supporting their hopes, but many of our patients are disappointed, occupying the positions staked out by Montaigne and Hazlitt.

In these notes, I will not make any wide references to the literature, but will confine my remarks to the experience of my patients, the significant collaborators in this attempt to understand the seeming fixity and rigidity of character and character traits. I will also, to paraphrase Freud, attempt to understand the "resistance to the uncovering of" *character* "resistances." In this brief set of notes, I will try to differentiate some factors which permit psychoanalytic character alterations and many which mitigate against such change.

The vantage point from which these experiences will be described is entirely from the reanalysis of 24 patients, all of whom had been in prior psychoanalysis over extended periods of time. For the most part these analyses were with other analysts, though a few of the patients had been seen by me in the distant past. The previous analysts were from many different schools of thought, had many different therapeutic approaches. But the attempts to alter character provided significant obstacles, though symptoms might have been relieved and object relations may have improved as a result of the prior analyses.

The term *character* has been used variously by many authors and I will not attempt any restrictive definition beyond the comment of one of my patients many years ago: "That's who I am." One of the great early advances in psychoanalysis was the awareness that human behavior and the structure of the brain and mind, which were the underpinnings of that behavior, was *patterned, repetitive,* and *motivated.* Motive and function, moreover, were not to be attributed solely to mind and brain but also had to be viewed in a broad social developmental context. Despite some vigorous clinical denials, most patients come to some self-derived observations that, as in an album of family photographs (Hazlitt used the concept: "a gallery of family portraits"), they could see the characterological resemblances to parents, grandparents, aunts, uncles, and siblings. How much of that resemblance is genetically preprogrammed and how much is the consequence of identification with the child's observation of the traits of others, is still a matter of controversy. The rôle played by both love and hate in these identifications can be extremely variable. Folk wisdom tells us that apples do not fall far from their trees.

In a number of brief notes about "fantasy," "transference" and "character" I presented to this society in symposia honoring Jacob Arlow (Horowitz, 1992), Leo Stone (Horowitz, 1996), and Martin Stein (Horowitz, 1995) the central unifying factor was the relative stability, for a given individual over a lifetime, of fantasy, transference and character. These terms, in any event, are artificially delineated concepts, perhaps useful for purposes of discourse, but inseparable in each of us. We are who we are, capable of greater or lesser human attachments, having broader or narrower imaginative inner lives, having greater or lesser capacities to reach beyond the barriers to the unconscious aspects of our inner lives, and greater or lesser capacities to modulate our affects and regulate our behavior. What is so striking in clinical observation is how narrow, in most people, is the range between the greater and the lesser capacities mentioned. It is this relative fixity which helps define "structure" and reproducibility of attitude and response.

When we began with Freud to examine what we termed *mental structure* we were examining aggregates of functions which seemed to be related in the expression of wishes and needs, in their regulation in behavior in the world at large and in the development of ethical and moral positions which form the everyday aspects of society, and which the society then imposes upon us. The whole of human development starts with the infant's helplessness, the need to be nurtured and the inbuilt capacity for the perception of danger (i.e., anxiety) either from within or from without.

I will return to these issues of helplessness, nurture, and anxiety. I will preface my remarks by repeating a comment from a woman patient: "If I give up being like my mother, I cease to exist." Where the formation of character and identity is heavily dependent upon early identifications, to attempt to analyze character gives rise to multiple resistances designed to ward off profound separation anxiety. Character as a product of identification comes to represent, in the unconscious, the early objects and the safety afforded by that proximity.

"Character" as a psychoanalytic concept is a quintessential example of what Waelder (1936) termed "multiple function." In organized, sometimes conflictual, and sometimes confluent manner, sometimes adaptive and sometimes maladaptive, "character" provides preformed pathways for the expression of fantasy (both conscious and unconscious), the translation of that fantasy to action in the world or inhibition in the mind, patterned defenses against painful affects, and either facilitates or impairs object relations. I have viewed character as a template for transference. The röle of *self-observation* in the analysis of character is crucial; many people have a wide discrepancy between how they see themselves and how others see them. Many aspects of the *patterning* of characterological issues are not in the patient's awareness. In fact, we have focused upon this issue in making interpretations :to discern and convey to the patient "that which makes a pattern" in those clinical experiences meant to demonstrate that mental activity and behavior are not random and meaningless.

Where the psychoanalytic concept of the "ego" represents a locus in a schematic mental apparatus consisting of an aggregate of functions, this concept grew out of the psychoanalytic process and the need to explain such things as the *unconscious* nature of defense and resistance. The concept of character and its inexorable nature (unique to each individual) has been known to the world's poets, mythmakers, and novelists since recorded history. Achilles still sulks in his tent and Tom Jones will never be Blifil (cf. Hazlitt).

II

To attempt a global discussion of the entire field of the resistance to analyzing character (for both participants in the analytic process) is beyond the scope of a brief presentation. Instead, I would choose to focus on a special instance as illustrative of the whole, one which is frequent in reanalyses. Here, I speak of masochistic character structure and its special relation to unconscious fantasies of revenge. In a number of such analyses revenge upon an early object (more often the mother) is carried out upon the self, and suffering is the vehicle for accusation of the object. With a certain regularity, the transference situation acquires a perverse aura and the analyst is seen as the torturer, the accusatory figure of superego pressure as well as a loving nurturing figure. This is a crowning achievement of ambivalence in conjunction with the synthetic and organizing functions of the ego.

Everyone in the audience has seen such patients: despairing, in unbearable mental pain, silently or noisily accusatory of the analyst as the most intense color of the transference reaction. A recent talented supervisee, deeply honest in the work, "confessed" in the later aspects of the supervision that she dreaded seeing the patient who made the analyst feel foolish and incompetent. What the analyst was experiencing was the intensity of the repetition and reliving of the accusations the patient could only dream about making to the mother and never had the courage to openly express until now. The experience of both participants was actually an advance in the therapeutic process, one which required the most careful interpretation. Up to that point, the suffering was self-inflicted and silently accusatory, a martyrdom experienced with an almost beatific smile worthy of Saints Sebastian, Lucy, and Agatha.

The need and wish for revenge is one of the most dread of human fantasies, yet one of the most ordinary. Individuals can harbor wishes for revenge for a lifetime, and certain groups can harbor such desires for millennia. Sometimes this is cast by societies as a desire for independence and political autonomy but a virulent violence usually supervenes. Witness the Balkans where the Serbian Orthodox slay their own ethnic brethren who had become Muslim converts of their former Turkish overlords, an ancient ongoing battle which in the last century led to Byron's death. The war in Chechnya is a war similar to that described by Tolstoy in the novella *Hadji Murad.* Milton's fallen angel Lucifer vows eternal hatred and revenge upon God in *Paradise Lost.* Revenge is among the most durable of human desires, and fantasies of revenge carry with them powerful pleasures of gratification. Think of the shared motto of the Mafia and the Kennedys: "Don't get mad, get even."

What are the developmental predecessors of fantasies of revenge? My own clinical experience places two factors in the foreground, both of which may have simultaneous constitutional and experiential roots; first, a predisposition to anxiety; and second, a predisposition to shame and humiliation. Revenge fantasies are usually directed toward those who caused (or who are imagined to have caused) pain and injury either to body or mind, to those who caused fear and panic and to those who created shame and humiliation.

Remember that what began in the development of character theory as a concept of transformations or persistence of the drives shifted later toward processes of defense. This is probably best understood as a shift of emphasis; much of character structure remains linked to its drive-related fantasies from early life.

Where some analytic authors have seen the anxiety-prone and shame-prone patients to be viewed as narcissistic or borderline personalities, my own observations lead me to think of the narcissism as a secondary consequence, a defensive outcome, so to speak, of early constitutional difficulties which make the match between parent and infant more difficult.

Now the nature of human ambivalence is such that direct vengeance is much less rare than an indirect sort, in which one's own person (self) becomes the target of destructive impulses. In the theater of the mind the entire process can become self-contained. All of this internal strife is pushed along by the development of the precursors of the conscience aspects of the superego and its later jelling into a more organized superego structure. Prohibitions against aggression in the external world redirect the aggressive force back upon the self as an object-sparing mechanism. The object is protected, and the self suffers. What is pleasure for one system becomes unpleasure for another system of the mind. The pleasure of revenge is, for many masochistic patients, *more important* than the suffering caused to the self. This is the core of one major resistance to change: a relation to one's own self with all the excitement, power, and pleasure of that which has been termed *perverse*.

Here, the identification with the early objects which gave rise to an important aspect of character formation becomes self-contained sadistic perversion directed toward the image of the parent now taken in as part of the self. Self-torture and object torture are the same. No patient I have seen easily gives this up, any more than patients who achieve orgasm through organized fantasy easily give up that fantasy. We are creatures of habit.

In the analytic situation revenge fantasies sometimes show themselves in the patient's wish to defeat the analyst and the analytic process. Occasionally, we can catch a glimpse of this at the outset of work. Some years ago, a middle-aged man in the midst of a troubled marital situation (his wife was having an affair with a doctor), came to see me after a failed analysis. He told me that two well-known analysts had recommended me as having a good reputation; but, he added with a leer, he would have to ruin my batting average. A long analysis revealed that when he was a child, his mother had had an affair with his pediatrician, a fact repressed, revealed in a dream, and subsequently confirmed by the patient's aunt. The patient had become masochistic and hypochondriacal early on; and he had unconsciously manipulated his wife into an affair with a doctor. His ultimate revenge was to be upon other doctors. All was woven into his character structure and the dramatized acting out of experience and fantasy which substituted for memory. When he ultimately remembered that he had wanted (as a child) to tell his father but was prohibited by his mother, he said that he had known that all along. Even when the analysis succeeded he had to insist that it was no good since he had always known what the analysis uncovered and reconnected.

I have used the concept of revenge in the organization of character as an isolated example of the problem of resistance to analyzing masochistic character, a partial paradigm which emphasizes how the complex developmental conflict structures can be organized as a self-contained theater of the mind to be replayed over and over. When the analyst tries to interrupt the performance, the patient as author of his own script fights back. Neurosis itself is treated as a self-created treasure, a work of personal art which denies editorial intervention.

REFERENCES

Hazlitt, W. (1821-1824). Essay XXI. In: *The Plain Speaker*. London: Everyman Edition.

Horowitz, M.H. (1992). The durability of unconscious fantasy. *Journal of Clinical Psychoanalysis* 1:525–532.

——— (1995). Introduction to "states of mind," a symposium honoring Martin Stein, M.D. *Journal of Clinical Psychoanalysis* 4:7–9.

——— (1996). Some notes on transference and memory. *Journal of Clinical Psychoanalysis* 5:197–211.

Waelder, R. (1936). The principle of multiple function: Some observations on overdetermination. *Psychoanal. Q.* 5:4–62.

CHAPTER 4

New York Psychoanalytic Association Symposium in Honor of Leo Stone, M.D., December 5, 1992

Some Notes on Transference and Memory: A Tribute to Leo Stone

(1996). *Journal of Clinical Psychoanalysis* 5(2):197-211.

PREFACE

Leo Stone has enriched the psychoanalytic world as analyst, teacher, and as innovative contributor to our scientific literature. The psychoanalytic endeavor and its field of inquiry has been significantly enlarged by Dr. Stone's personality as well as by his writings. In fact, some of the shape and direction modern psychoanalysis has taken actually stems from his incisive and independent creativity. These notes focus on only one aspect of that work, Dr. Stone's contributions to our understanding of transference.

My brief tribute to his concept of "primordial transference" highlights the narcissistic aspects of the psychoanalytic transference situation. The narcissistic aspects to which I refer are not about the reactions of narcissistic or borderline personalities, they are about normality, about human tendencies to identify with childhood caretakers and then to project portions of our own minds upon those we love, respect, hate, and fear. Even the earliest relations to others contain aspects of the developing self.

Transference responses are ubiquitous, appearing everywhere in life. The psychoanalytic situation is unique in that these universal reactions are allowed to flower, may be explored, and sometimes explained.

TRANSFERENCE

Transference is a triumph of memory over perception. The concept "transference" was originally used by Freud as an explanatory hypothesis to account for the appearance of certain profound, insistent emotional states directed toward the psychoanalyst in the unfolding of psychoanalytic treatment. Its predecessors were hypnosis and hands-on suggestion. The patient's love, expectations of help, antipathies and hatreds, cooperation, and "resistance" were explained as having been "transferred" from earlier relationships to important figures in the patient's early life. Consider the conditions under which the phenomena described had appeared. A patient in the midst of painful symptoms is asked to enter a quiet room, assume the recumbent position, *not* facing the analyst, and to perform a task which must give rise to conflict: to say everything without editorializing. Regression, and the memory of childhood, is encouraged by the procedure itself, action is inhibited in the favor of speech, perception is limited in the favor of fantasies, projections, and some loss of social inhibitions. In the course of the free associations the patient's personal history tends to slip into the background and intense preoccupations about the psychoanalyst tend to appear. These events are so regular in appearance, in almost all patients, that the explanation "transference" has become, in popular speech, a *description* instead. We speak of "*the* transference" as if stating a fact rather than interpreting and explicating the mysterious.

However, when Freud and the early analysts carefully examined their clinical data they were quick to recognize that those mysterious emotions that sprang forth in psychoanalytic therapy were not artefacts; rather, they were commonplace everyday events which emerged in a facilitating atmosphere. The ordinary experience of "falling in love" was just such a commonplace. It was soon clear that "transferences" were indeed ubiquitous, but it was only in the psychoanalytic situation that they could be understood and explained by reference to the unique personal history of the patient.

Transference has been described as the patient's attempt "to revive and reenact, in the analytic situation, and in relation to the analyst, situations and fantasies of his childhood. Hence transference is a *regressive* process" (Waelder, 1956, p. 367; see also Nunberg, 1951). (It is an irony that some analysts, having induced this regression, then complain that the patient is "regressed," implying nonanalyzability.) However, the earliest events of life are not passively experienced and then reproduced in the analysis. We are all permanently altered by experience, and we change in relation to it; as Stone emphasized in a paper on resistance (1973):

The mental capacity for permanent representations and the processes of identification—indeed internalization in general—facilitate (and in turn are perhaps to some degree derived from) structure formation. Certainly, the earliest ego functions themselves include identification with the caretaking mother [1984, p. 133].

The analytic experience hopes to make *mobile* those structures which appear to be permanent. In the transference situation we do not merely displace experience from early to present objects. Having been transformed continuously by early experience, and having become the bearers of that experience, we unconsciously displace and project aspects of ourselves (including our identifications) upon the new object, either the analyst or some other person. We do not cease in our need to have wishes gratified; analysis can only provide new possibilities of gratification by adaptation to reality.

45

The difficulty of both patient and analyst in recognizing the identification with the early objects sometimes leads to incomplete interpretations in the analytic situation. Failure to interpret those identifications, as they *currently* exist, leaves the interpretations flat and unconvincing to many patients. It is as if we were speaking of an archaeological artefact of the distant past, rather than an ongoing living presence of the old object now internalized in the patient where the old experiences can be, and are, renewed each day. Interpretation must be directed toward the immediate and the available. Regression favors dreamlike processes of thought. By slight revision of the script and changes of cast we develop a new version of our mental theater. It is worth remembering that the original anamnesis offered by the patient is a blend of reportage and mythmaking; personal history is partly narcissistically determined and partly related to the wish to create some effect upon the new object—the analyst—and thus to include him in what may be seen as a work of art. When Freud compared his case histories to a novel, he was reporting the patients' presentation of a life history as well as his own; all of it was influenced by the shape of the nineteenth century novel and all bore some analogy to the secondary revision of the dream work; the need for intelligibility and emotional appeal were both in evidence.

Let us return for a moment to reconsider the transference phenomena as aspects of memory. The capacity for transference may be viewed as an adaptive organ of memory. As Freud discovered at the turn of the century, memory does not always reveal itself in the form of recollection. Memory through action and repetition in the form of acting out is ubiquitous, and transference may be viewed as an acting out of early wishes and needs in relation to the new representation of the early objects and containing early representations of oneself. All memory is contextual, containing myriad mosaic like elements, having resemblance to our concept of screen memories in their compromise like formations. There are no isolated object representations without self representations. To discern meaning of these aspects of memory requires the use of imaginative and poetic response similar to the *fantasia* described by Giambattista Vico in the eighteenth century. *Fantasia*, said Vico, was needed by the historian to make the past alive, and a similar poetic imagination is necessary for the analyst to make unique interpretations and to attempt to make unique reconstructions alive. There are no ideal childhood experiences, no average expectables to be used as standards, *only* the unique experiences of the individual. Furthermore, there are no ideal analysts to attempt understanding, empathy, and interpretation; there are no empathic virtuosi, only individual analysts using their knowledge, their personalities, and their own unconscious processes as instruments in the analysis. In this effort projections of the analyst's self may hinder or advance the work, depending on how these contributions are used and how relevant they are to the patient. The analyst's memories optimally appear as recollections, not as acting out as a distortion of technique. (Of special importance is the acting out of the fantasy of being a better parent than one's own mother or its competitive equivalence in relation to one's own analyst.) Memory, both for the patient and that analyst, may be enmeshed in self-deceit for reasons of both love and malice. There are self-justifying, narcissistically colored memories to prove oneself the victim of someone else's needs or desires. This is often seen in patients' "memories" or prior analytic or psychotherapeutic treatment, and is prominently part of reanalyses, where that issue of relatively recent "memory" or "memories" may be studied to advantage by that patient in order to understand memories of the past. The analyst is, of course, subject to the same narcissistic components.

It was an aspect of Freud's genius that he recognized a twofold quality of "transference." It could be explanatory of the genesis of neurosis, and it could become the greatest resistance to the explanatory task. What facilitated the "intellectual" aspect of the analyst's work was hindered by the "emotional" content of transference. All this took place in the partial abrogation of the sense of reality, where old memories and old wishes superseded current possibilities. However, not all aspects of current reality were ignored. In a manner similar to the use of the day residue in the work of dreaming to assure representability, analysts soon noted that patients were keenly perceptive in their judgments about the person of the analyst. Upon these reality hooks were hung prepared memories, fantasies, and portions of the self. In that sense, transference developments bore some analogy to Freud's explanation of delusions as having a kernel of truth as the nidus upon which there could be accretions of other psychological elements.

The concept of narcissism, derived from the psychoanalytic failures in the treatment of schizophrenic psychosis, widened our concepts of normality. Narcissism as an explanatory hypothesis hinged upon the psychoanalytic theory of the instinctual drives. Put briefly, the drives could seek out our own selves as objects in the search for gratification. We could love ourselves or we could hate ourselves. We could seek oneness with other persons or differentiate ourselves from others. We could magnify ourselves and others and conversely could diminish ourselves and others. Moreover, all these tendencies could take relatively stable shape or be in flux. Narcissistic regression in sleep or in illness was easily observable. But, more than the regression, narcissism became visible as an aspect of object choice. We could model object choice upon those who cared for us (the anaclitic model) or upon what we were, wish to be, or what we are (the narcissistic model), commonly with compromise of the two models as the outcome. Here, we must remember how much of ourselves is actually the product of early identifications.

The psychoanalytic transference situation, encouraging regression, repeats some of the conditions of childhood. Waelder (1956) described this succinctly:

The suffering patient comes for help and is in the position of a child turning to an adult.... He unilaterally is asked to be psychologically exposed putting him in the position of a nude child in the presence of adults.

Furthermore, free association shifts the balance between id and ego favoring regression [p. 367].

To this, I would add that the transference situation exposes all the patient's narcissistic vulnerabilities, all the tendencies toward shame and humiliation, and all the tendencies toward grandiose over-evaluations of the self and the objects. It exposes the contribution from the past of narcissistic aspects of object choice and how objects are viewed now in the present.

In the regressive atmosphere, memories as well as wishful representations of self and objects achieve new representation in relation to the reality of the analyst and the analytic situation. However, these revivals are not only about earliest infancy; rather, they are about the whole course of life. The need to protect one's narcissism can give rise to such phenomena as the "personal myth" described by Kris (1956) where many of the elements of the myth making may arise from later childhood and adolescence. Protective resistance maneuvers to preserve narcissism can enter into those grossly overall resistances described by Stone (1973) as strategic rather than tactical. Rebellious, negativistic elements from early childhood may achieve a new shape and representation from later adolescent rebellion. Increasingly we have come to understand that defensive processes and resistances operate not only against old memories, old traumas, and old fantasies; they also operate in the present against the exposure of narcissistic vulnerabilities associated with the old experience. This would seem to hold true for all of us. Those vulnerabilities are as true for us as analysts as for our patients. We too can create a fictive picture of ourselves in the rôle of analyst and envelop it by a ring of narcissistic protectiveness. We too can project portions of our own selves and our early identifications upon the patients.

ORIENTATION

All living animals need, as a survival mechanism, an ability to rapidly scan and assess the environment for potential danger. A similar need for the rapid assessment of reproductive possibilities is manifest in a form of rapid sexual scanning of the surroundings. There would also seem to be a similar rapidity of evaluation for aggressive, territorial, and rank-order aims. The capacity for what we term *transference* would seem to serve these rapid-scanning orientation purposes. It is to be emphasized that these processes seem to take place only partly within consciousness, but for the most part are unconscious.

We all attempt to locate ourselves in relation to the environment with varying degrees of appreciation of external perceptual reality and with varying degrees of distortion determined by wish, fantasy, and daydream. The rapidity of these unconscious determinations would seem to serve an adaptive function. (I will here leave aside current biological controversies about the term *adaptation*, and reserve it for the "fitting-in" concepts of Hartmann [1939]. Nowhere in this discussion does adaptation refer to giving-in.)

Using minimal cues from the environment we attempt to make the strange or unknown into the familiar. Picture again the analytic situation. The patient generally knows little about the analyst; however, little does not mean nothing. The patient has heard of the analyst, of his or her reputation, might have read something the analyst wrote, heard some gossip about the analyst, or know something of the analyst's history or family. At the very least, the analyst's voice, person, appearance, office, telephone manner all provide what in the psychology of dreaming might be termed the *day residue*. (This is an analogy, not an exact correspondence.) There is no blank screen of the analytic circumstances. The same factors apply to the analyst's assessment of the prospective patient. What is clinically striking is the frequency with which the two participants leap to conclusions. (One can only hope that the analyst has the process under some control.) In the attempt toward orientation, a phenomenon generally similar to the déjà-vu is set in motion, with the notable difference that the prior experiences slip into the background or seem to have no relevance. The patient experiences the strange analyst as a familiar person. This sense of familiarity carries with it a sense of conviction. The patient is convinced that he or she "knows" the analyst, and if questioned will point toward the day residue phenomenon as if it were proof. In a working day in which one sees eight or ten analytic patients there is a bewildering array of representations of the analyst, each only tangentially connected by these day residues. We can't be eight or ten different people, yet in a sense we are. The rest of the picture is constructed, like a dream, from memories, wishes, past perceptual realities, and past psychic realities containing pictures of important people of the patient's past, and pictures of the patient's own self, all of which tend to be unconscious. What is conscious is the sense of conviction that the impressions are true. Rarely is there a sense of skepticism about these "convictions." Upon analytic examination, the "convictions" about "truth" have a remarkable content: at some time in the past they were true about someone else or about the patient. They may also be true about the analyst, but the power and intensity of conviction usually comes from the earlier antecedents. What is important about the technical advice about not interpreting transference too early is not only that these phenomena are the engine of the analysis moving it forward, it is also that we do not want to dismiss the röle that the patient's perceptions of us (the day residue) gives to finding a means of representation of the emotions and attitudes that make up the emotional response to the analyst's person. Just as in the psychology of dreaming we are no longer willing to discard manifest dream content as a mere husk containing the real stuff, we cannot dismiss the conscious convictions in the transference.

What begins as an orientation phenomenon soon becomes a psychological structure. (Here again, "structure" is used in its familiar psychoanalytic context as behaviors which are patterned, repetitive, and motivated.) Those factors which in early childhood served the function of orientation, discerning the predictable "pleasurable" and the predictable "unpleasurable," miscarry in adult life when they are so rigidly structured that they lead to stereotypy of response rather than the flexibility needed for adult survival. It is clinically interesting to note how the uniformity, or lack of uniformity, of the parental responses in the patient's early childhood influences this process. For example, a mother with a mercurial temperament, always changeable and unpredictable, will lead to a specific transference confusion. By example of contrast, a parent with a consistently angry or depressive affect will give another more stubbornly consistent coloration to the transference. Initially in childhood the capacity for transference represents a *learning* from experience; this then tends to miscarry in adult life because it is the *earliest* experiences which serve as templates. Later experiences, even those described as "corrective emotional" experiences, tend toward only minimal modification of actual behavior (especially self-justifying behaviors) unless accompanied by insight into the origins of patterning. Here the emphasis must be placed on the maturation and development of ego functions as a consequence of the analytic interchange. The aim of the initial regression in the analysis is the reordering of development toward more successful mastery of internal conflict, as well as the increase in the capacity to alter one's own environment.

The transference potential which began in childhood as orientation devices and which then miscarry in adulthood as maladaptations may, upon the achievement of insight and in response to the analyst's real empathy, facilitate new and effective adaptation and health.

PROJECTIONS OF ASPECTS OF THE PATIENT'S PERSONALITY: THE SPECIAL CONTRIBUTION TO TRANSFERENCE

It is a relatively consistent aspect of human mental functioning that we search for the familiar. We do this as a way of orienting ourselves in relation to others, as well as to the material external world. Though the strange or exotic may represent opportunities for stimulation or adventure, the familiar provides an atmosphere in which there is some quality of reassurance. Even though the familiar might contain elements of unpleasure or pain, as we often notice in the phenomena of masochism, the familiar is associated with the relative *safety* of the known. As has been observed since the onset of the psychoanalytic endeavor, much of the human condition is determined by the long period of helplessness in childhood and the concomitant need to be cared for by adults. What Leo Stone termed the *primordial transference* hinges upon this initial helplessness and the need for others to satisfy our wants and needs. The primordial transference carries with it a profound and persistent need for orientation in the presence of the strange by searching for the familiar and *making* familiar that which *is* strange by way of fantasy and memory. As mentioned, some of this is accomplished by a sort of displacement from the important adults of the childhood past and some of it by projections of aspects of the self. Rapid assumptions are often made that the stranger resembles oneself, often without any basis or only minimal cues. This is visible in "transference" reactions in the psychoanalytic situation and outside it. People falling in love often assume, wishfully, that the love object is congruent with the lover; the rude awakenings of differences are then painfully disquieting.

As an aspect of having to create the "familiar," patients often *assume* that we share social outlooks, religious beliefs, and political positions. Global points of view, projections of the total self, and aspects of unique

53

personal history are grafted upon the analyst, often carrying a deep sense of emotional conviction, even if erroneous in reality. The conviction comes about because these issues *are* true, but they are true for the patient. The process is, however, unconscious to the patient who insists that the opinions are observations based upon perception, not projections from within. (The process I am describing is not the "projective identification" concept used by some analysts, where confusion of self and object seems to take place within the analyst and is "rationalized." It is to be viewed as a datum in the self-analysis of the analyst.)

But these global phenomena are only one aspect of what we are examining. Smaller, more discrete aspects of personality are regularly projected. It may be useful, for heuristic purposes, to divide these aspects from their presumed sources in the mental apparatus as viewed by psychoanalytic structural hypotheses, that is, derived from the id, the ego, or the superego. Fantasies, structured as compromises, may have predominant elements derived primarily from one or the other of the aggregates of functions we term *structures*. Thus, we can see as transference elements:

1. Assumptions of shared sexual or aggressive fantasies; this may be viewed as derived from the drives.
2. Total defensive projections of those fantasies upon the analyst as a denial of internal derivation of aggressive and sexual wishes; here the analyst may be seen as seducer, and the analysis itself viewed as an opportunity for gratification of earlier frustrations.
3. Projections of other forms of defense or resistance.
4. Defensive projections of transference may be seen by the patient as "countertransference" of the analyst.

The latter three phenomena may be viewed as contributions from the ego, particularly from its defensive function.

54

5.   Projections of superego functions in which the analyst is seen as punishing, humiliating, mocking, and shaming the patient.

Here too, what is often so clinically impressive is the deep sense of conviction with which these views are presented and acted out in the transference. However distressing to the patients, the analyst is made by them the object of familiarity. For them, we *are* the parents, and we *are* aspects of themselves, and they fight against the awareness of illusion of referring to the kernel of truth. The intensity of conviction derives from a species of truth both carried by the patient from the early important adults and having modified the mind of the patient through identification with those persons. To repeat again, we are not the passive bearers of experience, we are altered by it and reproduce those experiences repeatedly throughout life. In analyzing adult patients, we are *not* seeing the child of the past; rather, we are seeing an adult who had undergone numerous transformations. We see the panoply of an entire life and all its cast of characters transmitted by one complex personality. Moreover, we ourselves have a similar complexity, perhaps made understandable by our own analyses.

In all this, we are not speaking of pathology. Here we speak of the ordinariness of human experience in which both patient and analyst share common human tendencies. We view the present through the past, we view others through ourselves. Whatever I have said about the patient's transference tendencies holds equally true for the analyst; the capacity for transference is shared by all. Counter-transferences often contain large elements of projections of the analyst's self as reactions to the patient's person and to his or her transference. This is most conspicuous when the analyst has some strong opinion about a life decision of the patient. From ancient Rome we have been cautioned that "no one knows how the shoe fits except the wearer." We give advice or even think advice at our hazard and the patient's harm. Difficulty in clearly differentiating self from the other is an all too frequent adult human failing. At early stages of development that differentiation is often difficult and confused. The wish to be "as one" with the loved object remains throughout the life cycle. We are, for the most part, hopeless romantics.

PROJECTION OF DEFENSE AND PROJECTION OF THE NEED FOR PUNISHMENT AS SPECIFIC ASPECTS OF NARCISSISTIC COLORATION OF TRANSFERENCE

Two brief examples follow which illustrate the process.

Projection of an Ego Function of Defense

A young woman patient said to me, with an ingenuous air, "I know you don't want to hear the details." I had an immediate inner silent response, echoing the architect Mies van der Rohe: "God is in the details." The patient had projected upon me an unwillingness to listen to the richness of detail in her fantasy life because the details revealed the connection of her fantasies to me. She was frightened to tell the object of her wishes the detailed content of those wishes which had a sadomasochistic sexual coloration. She protected herself by insisting that I didn't like details, where it was evident that she liked to speak in blurred generalizations. In fact, she had some time previously accused me of "nitpicking" when I had asked her to repeat the content of a dream. She disowned her tendency toward generalization as an aspect of defensive isolation, since, for her, "details" contained emotions. Her view of me as a "superrational" being represented a wishful aspect of her defensive self controlling unruly emotion through an inner legislative fiat. Her obsessional-like defense was handed over to me; we were as two peas in a pod. To view me as different from her frightened her and made her feel "sick" and unsuitable for being loved by me. Her masochistic wishes were viewed by her as "weird" and had to be disowned. This attitude had an impressive childhood history; she grew up in a "superrational" household where affect was condemned, and she identified with her parents' demands. She became the bearer of those demands and handed them over to me. The entire process was "unconscious" in the sense that no connections were made until interpretation. Here it is to be understood that without interpretation, at some level, analysis would grind to a halt and even the transference could not achieve representation. E. M. Forster's injunction, "only connect," is particularly apt for psychoanalysis.

Projection of a Superego Function

A man, whose life had been characterized by self-induced failures in love and work, reacted to an exceedingly benign intervention as if he had been mocked and humiliated. (The intervention had pointed out the similarity between an event of the previous analytic hour and the content of a dream following the hour; its implicit unstated purpose was to note the day residue and that the dream had continued the emotions of the analysis in a special language.) He wanted me to apologize to him. "Say you are sorry," he repeated several times, reproducing and echoing an injunction from his mother that plagued his childhood. During the previous hour he had voiced a number of virulent complaints about Freud, about analysis, and about me. I had listened quietly, and he had thought and *not* said, "What a wimp" and wanted to punch me. This was an obvious unsaid remark to his father. He felt guilty fleetingly and expected punishment. He viewed my intervention as the punishment. He had projected the need for punishment upon me and also revealed his identification with his mother whom he blamed for degrading his father. His life failures had been contrived unconsciously so as not to surpass his father.

57

The transference situation was a projection of an aspect of his own self incorporating both his parents as well as his own person—a veritable trinity. (It is in superego functioning and its projection that the trajectory: outer-inner-outer can be most easily followed.).

These phenomena of the transference come to an astonishing crescendo during the terminal phase of the analysis, a period marked by recrudescence of symptoms, anticipated mourning, and a mixture of pleasurable and painful anticipation of the future. The revival of transference wishes and fears in both loving and aggressive terms is a way of holding onto both old object and old self representations. It is a magical mode of defending against separation anxiety by returning to the familiar past where even a painful familiarity represented safety. The old life was safe, the anticipated new life is viewed as dangerous. When translated into the social sphere, we have the essence of ancient liberal versus reactionary political arguments through the ages. When translated into the microcosm of psychoanalysis, we have a potential method for understanding the hostility with which new ideas are viewed. The excessive exercise of the transference templates actively prevents perceptions and forces individuals and groups to live in their histories rather than in the present world. It can make anachronisms of us all: however, through *insight*, we all have the potential for continuous growth.

CONCLUSION

Leo Stone's concepts of the widening scope of analysis were not only about the increased range of patients we attempt to treat analytically. He has also widened our view of the range of all analytic ideas, expanding our concepts of transference, resistance, attachment, and aggression. He has thus increased our therapeutic range and skills-

Inspired by him, in these notes, I have attempted a very small addition to that range. I have attempted to show that transference responses are not merely memories, they are current living experiences in which our identifications with early objects and projections of parts of oneself onto the analyst are regular events. Further I have suggested that a technical problem in achieving convincing interpretations about transference may hinge upon adequate understanding of the rôle of identification and projection in the current emotional tie to the analyst. We are the bearers of our experience, not merely passive victims.

The capacity for transference, which seems to have had roots in a survival mechanism of orientation and adaptation, regularly takes on maladaptive tendencies interfering with present-day life. Psychoanalysis offers the possibility of altering the maladaptation.

REFERENCES

Hartmann, H. (1939). *Ego Psychology and the Problem of Adaptation* (especially Chapter 3). New York: International Universities Press, 1958.

Kris, E. (1956). The personal myth: A problem in psychoanalytic technique. *J. Amer. Psychoanal. Assn* 4:653–681.

Nunberg, H. (1951). Transference and reality. *Int. J. Psycho-Anal.*, 32:1–9.

Stone, L. (1973). On resistance to the psychoanalytic process: Some thoughts as to its nature and motivations. *Psychoanal. Contemp. Sci*, 2:42-76. Also as Chapter 5 in *Transference and Its Context*. New York: Jason Aronson, 1984, pp. 119–152.

Waelder, R. (1956). Introduction to the discussion of problems of transference. *Int. J. Psycho-Anal.*, 37:367–368.

The Durability of Unconscious Fantasy

(1992). *Journal of Clinical Psychoanalysis* 1(4):525-531.

Jack Arlow, one of the more talented and prolific contributors to our field, has written on every major subject of psychoanalytic inquiry. What has characterized each of his papers has been a close adherence of his theoretical concepts to the directly observable clinical facts derived from the psychoanalytic situation. Every idea is linked to experiences of real people who do and say things derived from real circumstances. Arlow's explanatory concepts have consistently remained close to the experiential source, whether he speaks of neurotic symptoms, historical and cultural trends, or religious experience. As did Freud before him, he has extended the psychoanalytic endeavor to encompass the wide range of human experience through this close adherence to the directly observable. Thus, it comes as no surprise to this audience that Arlow's manifold speculations upon the concept "unconscious fantasy" are, in each instance, related to the evidence in word and behavior derived from daydream, dream, symptom, language, metaphor and behavior. Exquisite clinical description is the underpinning of his work.

The concept "unconscious fantasy" is an explanatory hypothesis for certain clinical facts. In one of the seminal papers in our field, Arlow (1969) presented a schematic relationship of a constant interaction of ever flowing daydreamlike activity with the data of perception, the two tendencies coming together, fusing, creating conflict, creating compromises, exerting a variety of expressive and defensive effects.

I would like to focus upon one small aspect of the concept "unconscious fantasy"; that is, the relative persistence in time of the unconscious fantasies of each individual. Over a long career, and with the experience of reanalyzing many patients, I have been struck by the fact that each of us has a *relatively few* major systems of fantasy, that they tend to persist for a lifetime, that they may undergo certain transformations in varying developmental epochs, and that they may lead to a variety of expressions in different developmental phases. Our few and limited fantasy systems are like mental fingerprints: they identify us and are distillates of the history of our lives. In a certain sense, they *are* our history, and they frequently determine our present and our future. They become available for study in the transference situation, that is, in relation to another person. Unconscious fantasy systems are not only about all sorts of old wishes represented as fulfilled, they are about the people toward whom those wishes were expressed; they, therefore, represent not only our histories of fears and desires; they also depict the history of our human ties. They *are* the history of our object relations.[2]

It is to be understood that this limited but durable set of fantasies is not only true for the patient, it is equally true for the analyst. Both participants in the analytic work are playing with stacked decks, and it is a central responsibility of the analyst that he or she knows *as much as possible* about the rôle played by unconscious fantasy in the personal determinants of doing the analytic work. I will return to this topic later.

Freud (1937) in "Analysis Terminable and Interminable" had pointed toward a set of problems inherent in the analyses of certain patients in which they showed evidence of remaining psychologically attached to early objects

---

2 Fantasies are not discrete and isolated; they exist in linked systems, their seeming discreteness being an artifact of the method of examining them in the analysis.

and to early modes of gratification. These tendencies are exhibited in fantasy and transference reaction. In the past half-century, I think, many of us have had the experience that this deep loyalty to the past is far more common than we had supposed. It may, in fact, be one of the underpinnings of the amazing durability of unconscious fantasy. It may also help us account for the old tendency toward transference in *new* situations, even after analytic attempts to understand and interpret transference reactions. We tend to want what we wanted, and from whom we wanted it.

Equally interesting are those who earnestly wish to deny old emotional loyalties and *betray* the past. They often wish to find new gods, and become rapid converts to new fads, the latest fashion in ideas and therapeutic methods; they discard parents, siblings, husbands, wives, and children. They go from analyst to analyst. It is not only that they might lack "cathectic loyalty" as described by Freud. (He described the analytic work with this group as being written on water.) They are actively and hostilely opposed to their own histories and often poignantly fail to recognize that behind the persistent rebellion and betrayal is the unconscious painful wish to refind the earliest objects and there to find some experience of satisfaction.

Fenichel (1945) had said that "As long as thinking is not followed by action it is called fantasy. There are two types of fantasy: creative fantasy which prepares some later action, and daydreaming fantasy, the refuge for wishes that cannot be fulfilled" (p. 50). The issue of creative fantasy had been approached earlier by Hartmann (1939) who saw an "auxiliary function of fantasy in the learning process. Though fantasy always implies an initial turning away from a real situation, it can also be a preparation for the reality" (p. 18).

Fantasy and wish have relative permanence in the life of individuals, either leading to pathology or contributing to subsequent development. Fantasy cannot be analyzed away; its derivatives, however, may be altered. In another paper (1987) I attempted to demonstrate that a specific unconscious fantasy, that of a phallic woman, had persisted throughout a patient's life giving rise to a variety of character structures, a brief period of transvestitism, and an eventual sublimation in the collection of art. In the analyses of a number of creative artists, early fantasy systems could be seen to fuel their creative efforts and energize their art. The fantasies here serve creative and adaptive functions.

In certain psychoanalysts, the analysis of their own unconscious fantasy enhances their capacity to understand unconscious fantasy in their patients. What Arlow referred to as the "community" of fantasy, that is, shared fantasies, enables us to understand both works of art and the productions of imagination. Thus, the capacity for poetic imagination may lead the analyst toward his own form of creativity in the work of interpretation. Not only can he call upon his understanding of his own fantasies, but the wider shared universe of the fantasies of others can be the "preparation for the reality" in Hartmann's terms.

If miscarried, the understanding of fantasy can also be regressively expressed in a wish-fulfilling turning away from reality, in taking the patient as a new version of an old object, and consequent countertransference disturbance of the analytic work. Why it will go one way sometimes and another way at other times would seem to hinge on a number of variables, not the least of which is the analyst's own grasp of insight into his own fantasy life. It is not enough to experience the derivatives of unconscious fantasy in an analysis, a process of insight is necessary for the analyst to have rapid cognitive grasp while in the process of analyzing others.

Nowhere is the rôle of unconscious fantasy life more dramatically displayed as having relative permanence in mental life than in masturbatory fantasy, the unique personal conditions for sexual excitement, and in object choice. It is not infrequently reported to us in the course of an analysis that internally operative conditions for sexual interest have remained essentially the same for most of a lifetime. For example, a woman in her forties entered analysis because she had just gone through her third divorce. Though initially described as all very different, each of her husbands was subsequently depicted as tall, thin, dark-haired, ambitious and insensitive. She was totally unaware that she had given this same set of characteristics as a picture of her much older brother. From adolescence onward she had had a conscious masturbatory fantasy which differed not in script but only in casting of characters throughout her life. In this fantasy, she, as a girl or young woman, is either initiated into a sexual encounter or she feels impelled to "service" an older tall dark man. During this experience, she must hold very still and not move while the tall dark man forces her to have an orgasm against her will. In the analysis, she rarely moves upon the couch and seems to be in a rigidly fixed posture only varying it by bending both legs at the knees upon rare occasion. Through a series of dreams and transference fantasies we learn that she was given repeated enemas by her mother when she was a child. She was forced to lie on her back in the bathtub, her knees raised, the enema tube inserted, and she was told to hold perfectly still while she felt she was bursting with pain, anxiety, and excitement. After some interpretation of subsequent fantasy in the transference, she remembered wishing that her father, a physician, would be the one to administer the enema for he would know how to do it better than mother. Her sexual wishes in childhood became displaced from father to her brother. She remembered wishing in early puberty that her brother would deflower her and teach her about sex. When she learned that a man ejaculates into a woman, she had the idea that she would "be very still" and "be good." Just as she had wanted to be the favorite child of both her parents, she wanted to be her brother's sexual choice and my favorite patient.

Lurking behind these fantasies was a hostile rivalry with all those that threatened her fantasied status as a "favorite." All was repressed except for the conscious masturbatory fantasy. It had been operative for a lifetime. In each of the marriages, she linked herself with a man who unconsciously represented her brother (who probably was the parents' favored child). She subsequently entered into an enraged rivalry with each husband and left them. This was repeated in the transference with frequent threats of abandoning the treatment if she didn't "get what she wanted." Her usual attempt to demean the analytic work was that she "could do it better" herself—a reference to her masturbation. Her fantasies had persisted for a lifetime, the conscious components never seeming to connect with the unconscious images of the original objects. Her conscious fantasies, much distorted by the defensive maneuver of *isolation,* had allowed some components into awareness while warding off other components. She had spent her life driven by factors out of her awareness while having the conscious fantasy of always being in control. This brief vignette helps illustrate my major point: unconscious fantasy, like screen memory, has structure, durability, and helps determine symptom, character, sexual excitement, and object choice.

Sometimes an organized system of unconscious fantasy seems to threaten the *possibility* of treatment. A woman who had been repeatedly told falsehoods in childhood about money, divorces in the family, and illness developed a persistent unconscious fantasy that all persons in the class of parents either misrepresented or withheld the truth. In multiple attempts at psychoanalysis she had failed because she disbelieved all interpretations. She presented herself as *consciously* skeptical. In the transference situation all interpretation was viewed as false, and she behaved as if she had never been told the things that had been gone over many times. This was particularly true of interpretations of affect. In this way she recreated an illusion of the familiar, a state in which she experienced a triumphant feeling of moral superiority in which she too could misrepresent herself as having *no* feelings. This was a form of depersonalization. It served the function of revenge. If not analyzed it would have derailed the treatment.

I would like to conclude by a brief follow-up, two decades later, of a case study I reported to the Kris Study Group many years ago. It is a case

Jack Arlow briefly noted in his paper "Unconscious Fantasy and Conscious Experience" (1969). This patient had developed an unconscious, extremely detailed identification with his mother who died when he was a child. From the label in her riding boots, "Made in England," he had invented a mythology of English origins which had been elaborately followed up by his attending a major English university and developing an English accent and mannerisms— and becoming homosexual as were many of his classmates. He was unconscious of the origins of his behavior in his identification with his mother. Having had a major resolution of symptoms, his analysis was terminated many years ago. Last year he returned to see me. He had had a life of conspicuous professional success. In recent years he had lived with a younger man, also a successful professional, in a very tenuous homosexual bond. Recently the younger man had left him to be married. The patient was both pleased and saddened. Exploration of the situation demonstrated that he had behaved as if he were the young man's mother, succored him, yielded to him in a passive homosexual relationship, and prepared him to go off with a wife—a set of conditions which he had wished for himself. The old fantasy, much analyzed, had again become unconscious and was acted out in a new way.

Unconscious fantasy and its connection with the early objects operates like a structure in the mind. It can change function, shift in manifestations, become conscious at times, but is part of us for life. It is integral to our personal history as well as our personal mythology. It is an organ of memory.

REFERENCES

Arlow, J. A. (1969). Unconscious fantasy and disturbances of conscious experience. In: *Psychoanalysis: Clinical Theory and Practice*. Madison, CT: International Universities Press, 1991, pp. 155–175.

Fenichel, O. (1945). *The Psychoanalytic Theory of Neurosis*. New York: W. W. Norton.

Freud, S. (1937). Analysis terminable and interminable. *Standard Edition*, 22:20–254.

Hartmann, H. (1939), *Ego Psychology and the Problem of Adaptation*, trans. D. Rapaport. New York: International Universities Press, 1958.

Horowitz, M. (1987). Some notes on insight and its failures. *Psychoanal. Q.*,56/1:177–196.

SECTION TWO:

Limits of Psychoanalysis

CHAPTER 6

The Fear of Knowledge

The 1982 Brill Lecture

INTRODUCTION

By Martin H. Stein

01/30/82

I have looked forward for many years to this opportunity to introduce you to my very dear friend, Milton Horowitz. I have admired him for years and am very grateful that he has been honored, and will honor us by delivering this year's Brill Memorial Lecture,

The dry facts of his career give only a hint of what he is, and what he has accomplished. A graduate of University College, New York University, and of the N.Y.U. College of Medicine, he has, along with his profound interest in psychoanalysis, retained close connection with general psychiatry, He has taught medical students and residents since 1953, and has achieved the status of Clinical Professor of Psychiatry at. the N.Y.U. College of Medicine. Remarkably, he has done this teaching of psychiatrists without in the least sacrificing his primary engagement in the practice and teaching of psychoanalysis. Many medical students and residents have received from him the impetus to explore further the intricacies of the mind—to seek personal analysis, perhaps to become interested in receiving psychoanalytic

71

training, for they have had the opportunity to observe a psychoanalyst, who, without compromising his standards, has remained a fine physician. His remarkable capacity for keeping abreast of' current developments in general medicine contradicts the stereotype of the psychoanalyst who in embracing his new found discipline, leaves medicine behind.

His active interest in psychoanalytic matters has by no means been limited to his very busy private practice. Having been trained at the New York Psychoanalytic Institute, he became in due course a training analyst, analyzing and supervising a great many fortunate candidates. He has acted, among other things, as Secretary of the N.Y.P.I., Chairman of the Curriculum Committee, Member of the Educational Committee and the Board of Trustees, and Fellow of the Board on Professional Standards of the Amercan Psychoanalytic Association. As if this were insufficient to take up his energies, he has taught both introductory and advanced courses at the Nev York Psychoanalytic institute and the Western New England Institute, as well as giving teaching seminars in Philadelphia and Chicago. He is also e long time active participant in the Center for Advanced Psychoanalytic Study in Princeton.

This is not all. Milton Horowitz is a man of the most extraordinary erudition, with that rare combination of high intelligence a memory so retentive to be occasionally awesome, great reading speed, catholic tastes and the enviable ability to get along with very little sleep. His interests are wide-ranging, to say the least, extending from classical literature and music to nouvelle cuisine. If you to know how to analyze a fantasy, what Plutarch said of Brutus, how to start your car on a cold morning, how to repair an antique chair, or how to prepare veal with white truffles a la Michelet (I don't believe there is such a dish, but if there is, he will not only have the recipe, but can prepare it for you!)—Horowitz is your man. I'm not fond of betting—I never win anyway—but if you do, don't bet with him on a question of determinable fact. One may always dispute matters of opinion; he's an excellent debater, but not necessarily infallible, I'm glad to say.

He has written discussions on a variety of subjects, virtually all of them valuable elaborations of original presentations, concise and to the point. They are the kind of discussions which lead the presenters to incorporate them into the final versions o! their original drafts. My own final drafts have been more than once improved by the benefit of his always meticulous research and original thought.

A special field of interest has been the theory of psychoanalytic technique, which he studied for years in collaboration in the late Dr. Rudolph Loewenstein, and which he has taught for years. The experience has been reflected in his formal teaching and supervision of psychoanalytic candidates at the New York Psychoanalytic Institute. He has been outstandingly successful in placing the raw data of the analytic session in a meaningful theoretical context, and thus to derive technical principles in a fashion which allows candidates to develop their own skills without being hampered by a too didactic approach.

He has written more extensively on a couple of subjects which are singularly appropriate. If I were indiscreet, I should have suggested that they were profoundly personal. One of them, entitled "The Erudite Nursling," might be claimed (by the indiscreet, of course,) to be more than a little autobiographical. The author in fact a very precocious young man, achieving graduation from college and medical school a mere youth, and he achieved academic and professional success at a remarkably early age—in a discipline in which faculty appointment are used all too often, to be made achieved the status of gray beard, at least figuratively. I have often wondered what he was like.as schoolboy–as I imagine a quite daunting little boy, if he didn't read Greek of four, it was only because he would have been more interested in other subjects, for example, attaining mastery of Yiddish jokes and a capacity for telling truly funny stories in a caricature of upper class British speech.

I know that his linguistic skills were employed tor weeks in translating tonight's lecture from that obscure middle-European dialect known as "psychoanalyse" into intelligible English—an essential but arduous task.

He. has entitled it "Fear of Knowledge." Wel! It's as if Sir Edmund Hillary, the conqueror of Everest, were to speak to us on his own fear of high places. He would probably do very well at it. So, Milton Horovitz is going to tell us about a fear, which, if personal, must have given rise to one of the most successful counterphobic adventures of all. My remarks are of course ad hominem, for which I make no excuse: this not an argument, but an appreciation of remarkable man whose knowledge of knowledge has for years aroused my open admiration and my secret envy.

I give you Dr. Milton Horowitz who will speak to. us on the Fear of Knowledge.

THE FEAR OF KNOWLEDGE
The 1982 Brill Lecture

Freud's tragic view of man centered upon an ancient awareness that we deeply yearn for the return of the past and fear the impossibility of its attainment. A continuous tension between the demands of reality and the escape of fantasy characterizes the mind of man. We want to know about ourselves, and the world, and we are afraid of knowing.

Poets and philosophers of past ages have spoken of the dread of knowledge. Thomas Gray ended an 18th Century lament on the lost innocence of youth by saying:

Since sorrow never comes too late,
And happiness too swiftly flies.

74

Thought would destroy their paradise.
No more, where ignorance is bliss,
'Tis folly to be wise.

Gray's thought, with its English rococo embroidery, reflected the stark caution of the *Ajax* of Sophocles:

"of woes thou knowest naught,
for ignorance is life's extremest bliss."

Euripides, Terence, Cicero, Martial, Montaigne, Davenant, and Pope all spoke of the same conviction that knowledge opened one's eyes to future sorrows and closed off some golden age of paradisiacal innocence protected by ignorance. Milton, in the greatest of English poems, paints the sweetness of Eden and the everlasting sadness of a *Paradise Lost* through man's disobedience.

The wishful desires to return to the Infantile past and the attempt to relive that past are not the concerns of poets alone. They are well known to psychoanalysis in the phenomenon of transference and in patients' fantasies of "cure." The wish for a terrestrial paradise in the consulting room, the fear of knowledge expressed in the phenomena of defense and resistance, the mournful fear of separation and death as part of the process of termination of treatment are regular manifestations of the "psychoanalytic situation."

Myths, legends, and sacred texts of many societies and cultures have warned humankind of the danger of knowledge.

How awesome is the Biblical version of the Fall of Man who tasted of the fruit of the Tree of Knowledge. How terrifying was the punishment of the chained Prometheus who had taught mortals the use of fire. The unquenchable curiosity which led to the opening of Pandora's box was said to have unleashed all the horrors to which we are heir.

To be curious, to know, to learn, to teach, to be inventive or innovative, to espouse one's own thoughts, have all carried with them threats of punishment and death, not only in myth but as products of almost all cultures since the beginning of written histories. Socrates *was* tried and killed; Galileo *was* silenced. "Curiosity killed a cat" is a frequent riposte to children's courageous inquiries and their infantile researches. That curiosity, intended or accidental, would lead to the *discovery of a gruesome secret* has been a common theme of literature. "Forbidden" or locked chambers appear in such diverse works as Perrault's *Bluebeard*, Grimm's *The Feather Bird*, and Charlotte Bronte's *Jane Eyre*. With some regularity, the dangerously curious person of myth and literature is a woman, *an Eve* who succumbs to the temptation to explore the forbidden. The blame cast upon the temptress woman for the release of evil and the gaze at horror appears puzzling; a German proverb cautions us, however: "Adam must have an Eve to blame for his own faults." (*Adam mus eine Eva haben, die er zeiht was er gethan.*)

And yet, mankind reveres knowledge and honors the learned. Knowledge is viewed as liberating, and curiosity the basic ingredient of science. Knowledge, invention, scientific and artistic creation have been seen as the pinnacle of man's achievement. Are we merely looking at the wide diversity of human thought, a variant of the commonly held idea that no two men think alike? Or are we looking at a tendency that exists in individuals as well as in cultures in which both the desire to know and the fear of knowing exist in conflict? Are we justified in comparing the history of culture and myth with the personal history of individuals? This question, which has dogged the psychoanalytic exploration of myth, remains open. Is there a validity in the utilization of myth, religious text, or chronicle in understanding the mind of an individual by analogy? Does an attempt at exploring the mental processes of individuals have any bearing upon understanding the *creation* of myth as an historical event? Though there is no need to assume a "collective" human mind for which there is no evidence, are we justified in thinking that the sameness of individual human concerns of life and death throughout the ages has given rise to repeated multiple examples of the individual similarity of response?

We might ask for example, "How does one critically read and understand a Biblical text?" as preparation for the examination of the story of Adam and Eve and their expulsion from Paradise—the result of their acquisition of "knowledge."

Franz Steiner suggested that there are various levels of approaching the reading of an Old Testament text:

> First, there are the implications of a given passage for a Semitic-speaking person of Asia Minor at the time at which … the cult … developed.
> Second, there is the meaning of a given passage for a person participating in the cult as one of its members.
> Third, there is the meaning of the passage for the body of persons whose business it is to supervise the cult and to maintain the purity of the text.

However, another dimension can be added to the examination of such texts, one which begins in the literalist fashion but transcends it, a method in which any text, ancient or modern, reverberates in the imagination of its hearer or reader, stimulating his own associative fantasies and memories. Its outcome is idiosyncratic. The mythologies of the past are not only historical texts, uniquely suitable for the period of their creation, but they are also *ideas or stimuli in the present,* often serving individuals as explanatory hypotheses or as "cautionary tales." It is the method of the ordinary reader who takes any story wherever it originated and attempts to understand it in his own terms .

The story of the fall of Man as narrated in the Book of Genesis, in its various versions, has the following general structure:

The two of them were naked, the man and his wife, yet they felt no shame. The serpent, the slyest of all wild creatures made by Jehovah, questions the woman about what she may eat and what is forbidden; she answers that God has told them not to eat of the tree in the middle of the abundant garden, or so much as touch it, lest they die. The serpent responds, "You are not going die. No, God to well knows that the moment you as eat of it, your eyes will be opened, and you will be the same as God in telling good from bad." The woman eats the fruit, gives some to the man; they both realize their nakedness and feel shame. God discovers their disobedience and condemns them to toil and suffer. God had wondered, "What if man, having acquired the knowledge imparted by the tree, should eat of another tree—the tree of life—and live forever?" He casts them out of Paradise, and they are destined to toil, pain, and death. The paradise, eastward of Eden, is lost to them forever.

Milton, in his *Paradise Lost,* gives words to Adam's remorse and homelessness:

> *.... since our eyes*
> *opened and indeed, and find we*
> *Both know and evil, good lost and evil of got,*
> *With bad fruit of knowledge, if this be to know,*
> *which leaves us naked thus, of honour void....*

The themes of sexual awareness, sexual knowledge, the development of shame, the acquisition of moral standards (that is, the capacity for guilt), the acquisition of knowledge in general, and the consequent expulsion from parental protection in an abundant Paradise are of far greater antiquity than the Biblical text. Various scholars have identified its sources in the Gilgamesh epic, with the Akkadian myth of Adapa, the Persian myth of

Meshia and Meshiane, a Cretan myth quoted by Apollodorus, and a Lydian myth quoted by Pliny (Graves and Patai, Speiser, etc.).

Viewed in a socio-political context, the story *is* a cautionary tale with an embodied threat, a story which demands both obedience and submission to authority, or the payment of the fearsome consequences of expulsion from protection, or the sentence of death. It has a familiar ring to the psychoanalytic student of child development; it Is an elaborated version of some of the childhood experience of each of us.

(The röle of myth-making in studying *origins* was beautifully explored by Arlow in his Brill lecture on Cosmology last year. Arlow's paper was a celebration of man's creative genius in elaborating hypotheses of creation and generation.)

Myth and religion are *not* twin aspects of the same subject, but certain themes are common to both.

Various scholarly interpretations of myth have shown two major trends: First, that these stories were a beginning of a progressive, essentially linear evolution of thought from primitive man to present day man. Here, myths are seen as child-like in structure. The second trend of modern myth interpretation is that these stories were explanatory expressions of a total view of life, authentic for their period and *for no other purpose,* i.e., that they halve no connection with the present.

To these views another perspective may be added by the psychoanalytic investigation of personal "myths" (Kris) of individuals in the present day, not only by study of their own explanatory expressions of their own life histories, but also by their perceptions of the mythologies of the past which form part of their social context. It is not uncommon to find among a *certain group of patients* elements of the story of the expulsion from Paradise as part of their personal psychology,. They fear the acquisition of knowledge as if it were a sacrilegious act, and they move through life unconsciously scanning what may be known, and what is to be avoided. They unconsciously fear the loss of attachment to those persons who nurtured them in earliest childhood or to those parental figures whose love and care they had much desired. They constantly fear the loss of the Paradise of the fantasied infantile past, even though that past may sound more like Inferno than Heaven. They avoid knowledge of their own sexuality, of the sexuality of their parents, of what the parents' personalities were "really" like. They may not know of other families, of the wider world, of other cultures, religions, and societies. Such information is viewed as a threat that might pull them away from their early ties and cast them adrift in stormy dangers. To remain in the Paradise of fantasied parental protection demands ignorance. The Age of Innocence *is* the Age of Ignorance. Its fantasied reward is perpetual imagined attachment to a protective mother or father.

A substantial number of analytic patients do not easily let themselves know of parental psychosis, criminality, sexual affairs, or homosexuality. Others may not allow themselves curiosity about parental financial affairs. Still others are not allowed to know about adoptions (including their own), illegitimacy, or the unmarried condition of their parents. Though sometimes in the category of shared secrets, these concerns are frequently simply forbidden knowledge. To know the forbidden is seen as an act of disloyalty which would make the patient a traitor and an "outcast." Loyalty requires silence; it is the "omerta" of neurosis, akin to the honor of the Mafia. In many families, and for many individuals, a family mythology evolves which prescribes exactly what may be known—a species of sacred text.

Smaller doses of this disorder are probably part of the life of each of us. The unconscious defensive battle against the awareness of *inner* conflict is perpetually recurrent. Conflicts about the perception of the external world take place ceaselessly, and our capacities to perceive and test reality may be variable and fluctuant, and easily subject to regression, whether in sleep, illness, or in variations of the willing suspension of disbelief necessary to read a poem.

To perceive, to be curious, to explore, and to know all have complex maturational and developmental beginnings. The human infant, born helpless, enters the world with an inborn set of neurological organizations which will mature according to a genetically determined program. The interaction of the infant's built-in maturational program with the behavior of the mothering and nurturing adults is the history of early development. A large number of investigators have focused variously upon the nature of the equipment, the quality of the nurture, and the interaction between the two (Mahler and coworkers, Piaget, etc.) .

The enhancement of the emergence of curiosity and exploration and the acquisition of knowledge, or its inhibition and discouragement, will follow an extremely variable course in the psychological "birth" of the individual. The "going-away-from" the mother and "coming-back-toward" the mother, both physically and psychologically, have been extensively described by Mahler and coworkers in what they see as a series of phases of the separation-individuation process. Learning and knowing about the external world (and one's inner world as well) proceed as the child develops mastery of the muscular apparatus, attempts control impulses, acquires language, and develops increasingly complex modes of thought. Throughout all this development, the child evolves some ability either to modify the environment or to exert some control over it. This control can take place either in reality or in fantasy. Individual variations in these capacities are very great. There are, as well, significant individual variations in the intensity of distress and anxiety which occur in a usual developmental sequence.

The developmental sequences of anxiety situations in childhood were described by Freud using the experience of separation as the central model. Earliest in the sequence is the fear of the loss of the nurturing mother, followed by the anxiety of the loss of love, anxiety about bodily, and more specifically, genital damage, and the distress of guilt.

The Biblical story of the expulsion from Paradise touches upon each portion of this sequence of anxiety situations. Its central model is also *separation,* and it points to *death,* the ultimate and inevitable separation. Death is the one certain piece of knowledge we all have about our own fate. Man, in his wishfulness, invents through myth and religion, ingenious fantasies of the conquest of death and a vast body of Imaginative pseudo-knowledge, in the attempt to achieve everlasting life and reunion with the dead. Many of these themes appear in the psychoanalytic situation in the form of symptoms and transference fantasies. Curiosity and its inhibition enter into the analytic study of almost every aspect of transference.

Let us examine a set of myths and stories about the fear of curiosity, stories about closed containers into which one looks at one's peril. The consequences of such curiosity carry the special menace of witnessing the horrors of mutilation, madness, and death.

The interaction of the themes of wisdom, daring inventiveness, knowledge, and teaching, all leading to mutilation and death, are incorporated in the myth of Pandora. As remembered by most people I have known and asked about this story, the myth is thought to be about a woman of insatiable curiosity which leads her to open a jar or casket from which all evils are let loose upon the world, save hope which remains. But the myth as it appears in ancient sources has a number of variant forms, all of which are consequent upon the Prometheus myth. Prometheus, one of the Titans, brother to Atlas, Monoetius and Epimetheus, is said to have surpassed all in knowledge, cunning and fraud. (The link between knowledge, glib inventiveness, and trickery appears repeatedly in such diverse mythical figures as Hermes and Odysseus, as well as the Norse god Loki); in all these stories the capacity for deception and verbal seduction is much admired.

Prometheus ridiculed the Gods, and even duped Zeus Almighty into accepting an inadequate burnt sacrifice of a bull's bones, instead of its flesh. To punish Prometheus and the Titans, Zeus took fire away from Earth.

Prometheus climbed to heaven with the aid of Pallas Athena, the Goddess of Wisdom. He stole fire from the chariot of the sun and returned to Earth. With the precious gift, he fired a figure of clay into the first mortal man. Zeus, provoked into greater fury, ordered Hephaestus to make a woman of clay, gave her life through fire, and sent her to earth with a box, jar, or casket supposedly filled with the richest presents. Pandora, whose name means "all the gifts," had been made irresistibly beautiful and had been given the arts of captivating and pleasing, as well as eloquence and splendid ornaments. When she presented herself to Prometheus (whose name means "forethought") he wisely ignored her. His brother, Epimetheus (whose name means "afterthought") could not resist her.

Without prudence, he took Pandora as his wife. According to Hesiod, a noted misogynist, no women existed before Pandora, and "tribes of men lived on earth, remote and free from ills and hard toil." Then, Hesiod says, Pandora appeared, took the lid from the "jar," and released "countless plagues to wander amongst men." Apollodorus and others say that Epimetheus, the dupe, opened the jar, releasing the evils. Even Elpis (Hope), which remains within, is seen as a potential evil, equated with the gambler's belief in luck which lures him on to destruction. Zeus, made still more furious and vengeful, has Prometheus chained to a mountain, utterly alone, tortured and mutilated by having a vulture peck at his liver repeatedly and endlessly. (Footnote: For the ancients, the liver was the seat of both love and bravery. A coward is still referred to as lily-livered; that is, bloodless.) As for mortal man (Prometheus' creature) Hesiod said he is to be endlessly tortured by the "sheer guile" and deception of women, the misery of toil, the dread of famine, illness, and old age. Man's fate leads him to death (Hesiod, *Works and Days and the Theogony*).

The rich and diverse elements of this remarkable story begin with an episode of parental insult—the slighting of Zeus and the mockery of the trick sacrifice conducted by the all-too-clever Prometheus. Similar to the story of the "fall of man," the Prometheus myth is about the challenge to authority and its dread consequences. Man's helpless puniness is starkly revealed to him. His creative urges are punishable as crimes.

Embedded in this tale is the striking image of Pandora's box (or jar or casket) and the intriguing issue of what lies within, and its potential for horror. "Gazing on in horror" has long been of psychoanalytic interest. Freud, in a remarkably lucid short paper on the head of Medusa (1922), demonstrated that the symbolic power of *that* image was related to the forbidden act of seeing the mother's genital and the unconscious horror of the possibility of castration. (To gaze upon the nakedness of the father is also forbidden in some cultures, as in the story of Noah's drunkenness.) Furthermore, in his paper on the *Three Caskets*, Freud had also described the choice among them, and the opening of those puzzling boxes, as a story of death transformed in the *unconscious* to a story of love; to choose the correct box was the pathway to securing the love of a beautiful woman.

But to look within the forbidden box has another consequence in mythology—*the fear of madness*. Here the theme of horrifying genital mutilation is presented in another form: the closed container is a metaphor for the mind. Madness is within. This may be seen in a myth taken from Apollodorus, that of *Demophon and Phyllis*. (Robert Graves considered the Demophon myth to be the older version of closed casket story from which Hesiod took his inspiration; Hesiod's Pandora story is colored by his woman-hating viewpoint.)

Demophon, the Athenian, returning from the war in Troy, touches on the Thracian coast, marries Phyllis, a Bisaltian princess, and becomes king. He tires of Thrace and Phyllis, and leaves her to visit Athens, supposedly to visit his mother. He promises to return in a year. Phyllis gives him a closed casket. "This contains a charm," she says. "Open it only when you have abandoned all hope of returning to me." Demophon, with no intention of returning to Athens or Thrace, sets sail for Cyprus. At the end of the year,

Phyllis poisons herself, and at that very hour curiosity prompts Demophon to open the Box. The "sight of its contents—who knows what they were?" drives him into lunacy. He flees wildly. In his panicky madness, Demophon is thrown from his horse and becomes transfixed on his own sword.

Here we see themes commonplace in mankind, themes that may be examined in the psychoanalysis of individuals: disloyalty, desertion, guilt, madness, and death. To look into one's own mind and examine one's destructive impulses—and fear of mutilation—is fantasied as leading to madness. The "closed casket" of the mind is described by a patient suffering with an obsessional neurosis: "I am afraid to look into my mind; it is like a sewer filled with disgusting filth. Once it is opened up, there will be no going back." Plagued by his fantasies of losing control of his infantile sadistic sexual impulses, he feared their emergence in the form of insanity as punishment. Insanity, for him, was an alternative representation of punishment by damage to his mind, as a substitute for damage to his offending genital organ. Furthermore, to be insane meant to be "isolated," "locked up in a hospital." all variations on the theme of separation.

Just as certain patients fear that knowledge of the external world means a separation from the fantasies of childhood bliss, many others are terrified of learning about the internal world. For them, too, the forbidden casket is the mind, the domain of thought, feelings, and impulses. Their fear of looking within may be matched by a fear in the transference situation of the analyst's curiosity, seen as a prying invasiveness. A patient with a wide range of hysterical symptoms had a number of transference fantasies of being intruded upon. She saw the analysis as invasive of her privacy and of her wish to 'keep some things" for herself. She had been given frequent enemas as a child by a mother fearful of the child's developing an illness and dying. The theme of an invasive and prying mother or nurse is a frequent one. In fantasy, the mother is blamed for the misfortunes that befall the child. The very circumstances of one's birth are seen as the mother's "fault." A young woman with a very much envied younger brother had the fantasy that her birth was premature and was the mother's fault. As a child, the patient had imagined that if she had been longer in the womb, she would have been a boy. This blame of the mother is matched by an observation in a children's playground. A three-year-old boy falls and scrapes his knee; he runs crying to his mother, hits her and says, "Bad Mommy." This, in turn, may be related to a number of concepts of neurosogenesis in which psychological disorder is seen, by some theorists, as almost entirely due to failures of the mother's emotional reaction to the child: "Bad Mommy." Could it be that the phrase "disorder of empathy" is merely a euphemism for "bad mother"? An evasion of seeing as the intrapsychic product of complex conflictual factors?

The woman, as temptress-and-witch, intruder-and-troublemaker, is derived from real experiences with real mothers, as well from infantile fantasies. The mother who. nurtures the child is also the one who "civilizes" the child by frustration, the one who helps institute "delay" in the carrying-out of impulses. It is the fantasied witch-mother who is misidentified as "woman" by Hesiod. She is the model for beautiful Eve, alluring Pandora, the horrid Gorgon Medusa, and for the Three Fates who are said to govern our lives. In varying guises these conflicting images of the mother appear in the transference, and may serve as the shadowy backdrop of still other transference fantasies.

The fearful inability to be curious or to show one's knowledge or excited interest occasionally appears in an interesting symptom-complex of *pseudo-stupidity*. Certain patients become seemingly stupid when knowing something or expressing curiosity would expose them to anxiety or to feelings of guilt.Fenichel had commented that psychoanalytic interpretations are nothing but attempts to give the patient insight or to show him connections where emotional resistances hinder his spontaneous understanding. But interpretations themselves sometimes expose the patient to the anxiety or guilt which he attempts to avoid. The *pseudo-stupid* patient may show inhibited sexual curiosity because of the warding off of intense voyeuristic Impulses and the symptoms may represent a simultaneous obedience to, and rebellion against, the parents who frustrated his curiosity. But pseudo-stupid patient is often the "wise fool" of fairy tales. As pointed out by Mahler, the pseudo-stupid child may unconsciously satisfy the inhibited curiosity by gaining access to that which would have been kept from a wiser child. A patient with a pseudo-stupid façade, on a several occasions simply opened the door into my consulting room while I was with another patient. She excused herself by saying that she thought I might be free, and that she didn't know the office procedure . She could understand her need to peek beyond the closed door only with the most careful exploration of the resistance value of her stupidity. The wise fool gains access to closed places.

Another variant form of pseudo-stupidity is seen in patients who utilize a special rationalization for not knowing, and who resist being taught by others. This rationalization is in the words "I need to find out for myself" and is exemplified by the character of Krook in Dickens' *Bleak House*. Krook never learned how to read; he didn't want to be taught because he could be taught wrong. This attitude was intrinsic to the psychology of a patient who had a severe reading inhibition. She could not read the literature of her scientific field because it might be wrong. She carried out a lifelong battle to prove to her mother that her own infantile researches into sexuality were correct and the mother's version of the *biological facts* of sexuality simply had to be wrong. A complex overlay of other developmental and conflictual factors gave this symptom a particularly dense texture, resulting in profound resistances against the interpretation of transference fantasies. To know the anatomical differences between the sexes may be frightening and forbidden to the child.

To be *unknowing* in order to evade guilt can be seen as a social phenomenon as well as a personal symptom. To "know" something often means to be a "'witness,'" and therefore to be culpable. Individuals and groups often take a position that says, "If I don't know that evil is committed, I am not guilty." A recent dramatic example of this phenomenon was reported by the German-born Harald Luder and his Czech collaborator Pavel Schnabel. Rhina in Germany was the only Prussian village before the war with a predominantly Jewish population. In 1938 its Jews disappeared. When the film-makers several years ago tried to investigate the fate of these villagers they were met by evasion, denial, and mass amnesia. The only evidences on the site of the town's Jews are a desecrated cemetery and a town record, some of whose pages are torn out. The current townspeople now all blame "Outsiders" for *Kristallnacht,* when the synagogue was burned, and the Jews beaten. The few Jewish survivors, however, remember the names of the townspeople involved. (This was made into a documentary film, "Now, After All Those Years.")

Less dramatic examples of "not knowing" to avoid guilt are frequent in the evasion of responsibility within families, particularly when death or some other grievous harm has come to someone. A patient who had caused the death of a family member in an automobile accident had histrionically feigned an "amnesia" which she came to believe. The guilt had been too painful bear without the solace of "not knowing" what had happened. We are often not able to tolerate our perceptions of the world around us, or of the world within, and we substitute wishfulness for perception. We see this striking in neurosis, and in its special recrudescence in the transference situation. This, of course, is not a discovery of psychoanalysis.

Two and a half millennia ago, Archilochus, the founder of ancient lyric poetry, strove to choose opposed the extravagant idealizations of the Homeric epics with the common-sense view of everyday experience. He said, "What men think is of like kind with what befalls them." In the view of this practical soldier, knowledge and thought were the products of changing experience, plain and simple, A hundred years later, Heraclitus countered Archilochus by another simple observation:

"What men think is not of like kind with what befalls them, nor does instruction help them to understanding; they imagine things for themselves." Heraclitus knew that man's thoughts and feelings did not necessarily correspond to observable reality; man invented explanations by wishfulness. "To fight against desire Is hard, " he said, "for it stakes the soul (i.e., life) on what it wants " (Frankl).

The history of Western philosophy and its branch of the study of knowledge—epistemology—is a continuing interplay of the concepts of ideal/essence, experience/perception, and wishfulness/invention. It has been a major accomplishment of Freud, and of psychoanalysis, that this interplay of forces has been made the subject of study in specific individuals by a shared exploration of the psychoanalytic situation. With Hegel and Marx, Freud understood that human beings do not have a fixed essence, that they change according to experience, and that to understand present experience, one would have to understand the history of development.

There was an important precedent to this viewpoint: Sir Isaiah Berlin, in his 1969 essay on "[Giovanni Battista] Vico's Concept of Knowledge," said that "Vico's claim to immortality [is] the principle according to which man can understand himself... and... his past—because he is able to reconstruct imaginatively (in Aristotle's phrase) what he did and what he suffered, his hopes, wishes, fears, efforts, his acts and his works, both his own and those of his fellows." Vico's "boldest contribution." says Berlin, "was that there could be a science of mind which is the history of its development, and in which "ideas evolve, that knowledge is not a static network of external, universal clear truths. . but a social process... [and] that this process is traceable through the evolution of symbols...."

What Freud became able to see, through his clinical experience, was that a central aspect of the study of human change and development was the particularized examination of symbol, dream, fantasy, wishfulness, defense and resistance. (This was coupled with the observation that many mental processes seemed to take place outside of conscious awareness, and could be inferred from specific derivatives in the analytic situation.) Freud credited the poets with the discovery of the unconscious; he saw his own efforts as merely the development of a method with which to study the unconscious. This study could extend from individuals to mankind in general. Freud made explicit what had always been assumed in our myth-making. Man's wishfulness and the capacity to bend and distort knowledge may be called into play by *fear* as well as by desire. That we "know" is limited by the process of defense as well as by the consequences of desire. The neurotic patient hopes for a distorted triumph of wishfulness over reality and expresses it in the transference.

The wish to avoid knowledge is no place more evident than in man's attitudes toward death, the final separation. To most children, the origins of life are mysterious, but to adults, death is the greater mystery. Death does not seem permanent to the young child; the dead person merely having gone away. Fustel de Coulanges, the eminent historian of the ancient world, said, "Death was the first mystery; it started men on the road to other mysteries." Franz Cumont said of Fustel de Coulanges's epigram that in no other people was there such a complete verification as in the ancient Egyptians. Nowhere else was life so completely dominated by preoccupation with death, and in the worship of Osiris, the god who died and returned to life. This inability to believe in the permanence of death, in biological non-existence, is found in everyday life in a phenomenon described by Freud as the "splitting of the ego in the process of defense." One sees with frequency patients have had a loved person die and who show a reaction which they believe in the death and simultaneously imagine that the dead person is alive. Death is unreal in that we can continue to dream of the dead as if alive or as if that person were living in another shadowy world, the world of dreams represented as an after-life, or heaven.

So dreadful is the word death, that in the English language there are hundreds of euphemisms for "dead" or " death." Certain newspapers will never use the words. Many people prefer such circumlocutions as: passed away, passed beyond, passed on, crossed over, home, carried to rest, removed to the divine bosom, answered the last roll call, in on the grand secret, yielded up the ghost or spirit, is asleep in the arms of Jesus, gone to a better land, or gone West. In all of these euphemisms the stark finality of death is avoided. The euphemisms function by either abstract or concrete circumlocutions, distant from the specific concrete image of the dead body. This is achieved by a process of defensive isolation and wishful distortion, usually implying a passage, voyage, or trip to another world. With some variations, the world to which the dead go is fantasied as a Paradise regained. It is often depicted as a world in which one is restored to the company of the dead. In certain mythologies or religions, the afterlife has a variety of forms depending upon a judgment of the moral worth of the dead person—some to Heaven, some to Hell. The need to regain Paradise and to avoid the horrors of Hell has impelled men to develop vast realms of pseudo-knowledge to insure their safe passage after death. The Egyptian Books of the Dead, the Eleusinian mysteries, Requiem masses, all were magical attempts to influence that fantasied journey. All require ritual repetition without liturgical deviation. The Eleusinian mystery religion, for example, focused upon the sorrow of the mother Deo (or Demeter) upon the disappearance of her daughter Kore (or Persephone).(The names Demeter and Persephone cannot be uttered in the ceremony,)

The mother's sorrow, search, and partial recovery of her beloved is said by Clement of Alexandia to have formed the central secret mystic ceremony. The initiates into the religion drank a sacramental cup, just as the Goddess drank in her sorrow. In its magic röle in insuring the return of the crops, they cried "Rain" to Heaven and "Conceive" to the earth. Aristotle said of the initiates that they "do not learn anything so much as feel certain emotions and are out in a certain frame of mind."They were excited, exhilarated, awed, joined with each other into a sacred band and comforted with a sense of' the return of the dead, both vegetation and human.

The extant descriptions by Clement and by Apulieus of such initiations and participation in a cult sound remarkably similar to certain. transference fantasies in the course of analysis. The analytic procedure is dealt with as a pathway to safety; the awesome emotion attached to the figure of the analyst, the "positive" aspects of transference providing an engine of suggestion that in creates a situation in which, in Aristotle's words, they do not learn anything so much as feel certain emotions. This is related to what was styled the "non-objectionable" aspect of transference, so admirably studied in a recent paper by Martin Stein where the resistance aspects of such "positive" fantasies were delineated.

A clinical experience will illustrate the problem. The case material is distinguished in the interest of confidentiality but, as you will see, this analysis was the springboard for this paper. A young man entered analysis because of a debilitating fear of death which had begun in his adolescence as a fear of syphilis and of cancer. In his attempt to conquer this fear, he became a physician with the magical expectation that to know about disease would protect him against it. Though he recognized that his own disorder was psychological, he avoided knowing anything about psychiatry except the little necessary to pass examinations. He began the analysis in a period of desperation, but with a remarkable skepticism. This soon was transformed into its opposite—an almost worshipful view. His fear of death was understood by me in part as the fear of his own sexual excitement, mixed with a fear of retaliation for wishing the death of both parents who preferred a younger brother. *His* view of entering psychoanalytic therapy was that he was being taken into a band of joined, embattled brothers. He frequently responded to my interpretations by saying that he had not really listened to the words but liked the sound of my voice. He had the fantasy of becoming an analyst, for which the treatment was a rite of passage. The "positive" transference was a defense against the transference revival of a mélange of libidinal, competitive, and destructive feelings toward me. He was terrified of his wishes that I would die on vacation and the fear that my death would leave him unprotected. He called my consulting room the "sanctum sanctorum," his version of a safe haven, where I would protect him against his impulses. He was afraid to know anything about me or to express curiosity about my life outside the room because he thought it would violate the rules of analysis, saying, "I'm not supposed to ask." He feared I would be angry if he knew anything about me. The analysis of the transference made him feel lonely and ashamed.

Many patients are fearful of their curiosity in the transference situation because of reactions against powerful voyeurism. But others are fearful of their curiosity because it *interferes with their attempts to relive the past.* They are unconsciously afraid that the analyst will be very different than the mother and father of childhood, and do not want to discover those differences. In effect, in their emotional responses in unconsciously insist that they *are* in the presence of mother and father. This wishful, partial constriction of the sense of reality may he elaborated into a grand illusion of transference The structure of transference is truly like an idiosyncratic edifice—a work of art. It attempts to knit past history with current perception, and attempts to recrate unconsciously the world of childhood.

Man has a need to reconcile consciously his wishfulness and pseudo-knowledge with current reality. This has contributed strongly to his greatest creative outbursts. Two of these accomplishments, seemingly widely disparate, may be singled out: the Gothic cathedral and Columbus's Discovery of America. Both are part of the history of the attempt at the recovery of Paradise.

Medieval man in the Western world, beset by famine, plague, invasions ,and endless warfare, immersed in endless toil, took comfort in the fantasy of *two* paradises, a celestial Heaven and a terrestrial Paradise. The "earthly blessed spot" was by popular Christian belief, located in the remote East of Asia, corresponding to the Scriptural story of being Eastward of Eden. The Greeks and Romans had placed the terrestrial paradise in the far West, in such mythical locales as a distant continent called Atlantis, or in what were termed the Fortunate Isles. The Western land, the Occident, was where the sun set or died (The Latin verb *occidere*—to cut down or kill—describes, the sun's setting,) This gave rise to the euphemism of "going West" to describe death. This ancient tradition of the Western paradise was popularly held in Europe, and the Fathers of' the Church waged war against this mythology. (Sabine Baring-Gould). When "Christopher Columbus sought and found Atlantis and paradise in the new world,... the theories of the Ancients and the Medievals met, for it was truly East of' Asia and West of Europe. Columbus wrote to the Catholic Monarchs of Spain, after first voyage, 'The saintly theologians and philosophers are right when they fixed the site of the terrestrial paradise in the extreme Orient...the lands I have t discovered are the limits of the Orient." Columbus, in 1498, repeated his conviction that the terrestrial paradise, located by Saints Ambrose, Isidore, and the Venerable Bede in the East, had been reached by sailing West.. To search for that Paradise was not a mere fantasy, it was one of the engines of the Age of Exploration. This search as important spiritually to Catholic Spain, exulting in its recent victory over Islam, as was its need for greater dominions to supply its economic wants. Columbus's reasoning was a triumph of what Nunberg styled "synthetic function of the ego."

The concept of the rediscovery of the terrestrial paradise as an actual enterprise and an actual place, not a myth, had been presaged by another earthly *representation* of heaven. Suger, the Abbot of St. Denis, friend and counselor of Louis VI and VII, in the twelfth century, was inspiration for, and essential architect of, what became known as the Gothic Cathedral at

St. Dinis, then later at Paris, Sens, Chartres, and throughout France, there arose a series of breathtaking structures pierced by spectacular stained-glass windows representing the celestial City of Light, the depiction on earth—in a tangible structure—of the image of Heaven. Here was to be found the salvation that would pen a path to a Paradise, where one could yearn for sweet death to provide everlasting life. Here, to Medieval man, was more than symbol: the Gothic cathedral was a *gateway.* Entered from its Western portals, the Eastward or *oriented* altar pointed to Paradise.

The fantasy of a safe haven, or a holy place or sanctuary full of repose and grace, is a not uncommon *transference fantasy,* often connected with fantasies of confession of "sin" and forgiveness. For the patient to unmask these fantasies as unreal is both difficult and painful. To abandon solace sears the soul. The terminal phase of analysis is akin to a period of grief and mourning. To avoid ending the analysis, many patients experience a return of symptoms as a last-ditch attempt to remain within the fantasied parental protection.

The task of psychoanalysis is to face the truth of one's own inner life and the path for that exploration is the *analysis of the transference.* Truths may be sought, or pseudo-truths invented. The reality of a life that leads to separation and adult autonomy with its resultant loneliness may be faced, or a make-believe Paradise invented on Earth or in Heaven. The work of analysis is slow and painstaking, analogous to Francis Bacon' s concept of the advancement of learning:

> When industrious persons, by an exact and scrupulous diligence and observation, out of monuments, names, words, proverbs, traditions, private records and evidences, fragments of stories, passages of books that concern not story, and the like do save and recover somewhat from the deluge of time.

How distant from ritual repetition is the industrious psychoanalytic assemblage of tiny detail, *never* the same for any two human beings. What we attempt to rescue from the deluge of time is a *unique* personal history of the development of personality. With that insight we hope that the endless problems of life may be faced realistically and not through neurosis.

Bernard Knox, in examining Sophocles' *Oedipus the King* (1982) says,.

> "Oedipus did have one freedom… the freedom to search for the truth… this is perhaps the only human freedom, the play seems to say, but there could be none more noble."

Few men and women are of the heroic stature of Sophocles' Oedipus, and few can unreservedly pursue that search for truth and show an unwillingness to be deceived by wishfulness. Neurosis and the invention of personal myth *are* the more usual consequences of our being afraid. We tell ourselves stories to calm our fears and quash our curiosities. We limit our knowledge in obedience to threats, real or imagined, from inside ourselves or from outside authority. Myth, ritual, religion, and ideologies comfort mankind, but woe to the disobedient.

To be curious, to search, to know oneself *are* perhaps the only human freedoms, but there could be none more noble.

REFERENCES

Aristotle (322 BC). *Complete Works of Aristotle, Vols. 1 & 2*, Jonathan Barnes, ed. Princeton: Princeton University Press, 1984.

Bacon, F. (1605). *The Advancement of Learning*, CreateSpace Independent Publishing Platform, 2017.

Berlin, I. (1969) Vico's Concept of Knowledge. In: *Giambattista Vico: An International Symposium.* Baltimore: Johns Hopkins Press.

Cicero, M.T. (55 BC). *On the Ideal Orator,* trans. James M. May & Jakob Wisse. Oxford: Oxford University Press, 2001

Columbus, C. A Letter from Christopher Columbus to the King & Queen of Spain, 1490's. Narrated by Robert Gworek. Audible Audiobook. Chicago: Audible.com. SonicMovie.net, Chicago: Wood Media, Wollcott & Sheridan, 2013.

Davenant, W. (1651). *The dramatic works of Sir William D'Avenant,* eds. James Maidment & W. H. Logan New York: Russell & Russell, 1964.

Dickens, C. (1852). *Bleak House.* London: Penguin Classics, 2003.

Euripides (407 BCE). The Bacchae. In *The Bacchae of Euripides* by C. K. Williams New York: Farrar, Straus and Giroux; 1990.

Frankl, V.E. (1946). *Man's Search for Meaning.* Boston: Beacon Press, 2006.

Freud, S. (1922) Medusa's Head. *Standard Edition.* 18:273–274

——— (1938) Splitting of the Ego in the Process of Defence. *Standard Edition* 23:271–278.

Fustel De Coulanges, N.D. (1873). *The Ancient City*, transl. Faith Bottum. South Bend, IN: St. Augustine Press, 2023.

Gray, T. (1747). Ode on a Distant Prospect of Eton College. In *The Poems of Thomas Gray,* London: Forgotten Books, 2012.

Hesiod (700 BC). Works and Days. In: *Theogony and Works and Days,* transl. Martin Litchfield West. Oxford: Oxford University Press, 2009.

Knox, B. (1982). Introduction. In: *The Three Theban Plays by Sophocles* transl. Robert Fagles, ed. Bernard Knox. New York: Viking Adult.

Kris, E. (1956) The Personal Myth—A Problem in Psychoanalytic Technique. *Journal of the American Psychoanalytic Association* 4:653–681.

Lüders, H. & Schnabel, P. (dirs.) (1981). *Now - After All These Years:* Documentary Film. Frankfurt am Main: Pavel Schnabel Filmproduktion.

Mahler, M.S. (1942) Pseudoimbecility: A Magic Cap of Invisibility. *Psychoanalytic Quarterly* 11:149–64

——— (1963) Thoughts about Development and Individuation. *Psychoanalytic Study of the Child* 18:307–324.

Martial (86–103). *Epigrams with parallel Latin text,* trans. Gideon Nisbet. Oxford: Oxford University Press, 2015.

Montaigne, M. de. (1570–1592) *The Complete Works,* transl. Donald M. Frame. London: Everyman›s Library, 2003.

Piaget, J. (1957). *Construction of Reality in the Child.* London: Routledge & Kegan Paul.

Pope, A. (1711). Essay on Criticism. In: *The Major Works,* ed. Pat Rogers. Oxford: Oxford University Press, 2009.

Sophocles (5th Century BC). *Ajax.* Sir Richard Jebb, Ed., London: Bristol Classical Press, 2004.

Stein, M. H. (1981). The Unobjectionable Part of the Transference. *Journal of the American Psychoanalytic Association* 29:869–892

Terence (166 BC). Andria (The Girl from Andros). In: *Terence The Comedies,* Trans. Peter Brown. Oxford: Oxford University Press, 2010,

CHAPTER 7

Some Notes on Insight and its Failures

(1987). *Psychoanalytic Quarterly* 56:177–196.

ABSTRACT

Many patients who had been in a prior psychoanalysis or psychotherapy have a view that "insight" has not been useful to them. The previous treatment has often been condensed into a screen memory serving a variety of functions. An attempt is made in this paper to explore problems of the effectiveness of insight and its relation to a range of ego functions, transference issues, and related fantasy systems.

A striking number of patients who had been in one or more psychotherapies or psychoanalyses had the opinion that they knew "all about" themselves and that the knowledge had not done them any good. They were very skeptical about future psychoanalytic investigation of their continued sufferings. With some regularity, they tended to view "insight" as useless, and many of them wanted to be referred to someone who would deal with "current" problems and not with the "past." Careful investigation of such patients' knowledge of their autobiographies was disappointing to both patient and consultant. Their "insight" seemed sparse, fixed in structure and content, and tended to be limited to a few historical events early in life. Often the "insight" focused on either a single external event or a few events which were viewed as catastrophes. It was difficult to get any fullness of detail, and the "insights" often seemed two-dimensional and trivial. Full of contradictions, the narratives were told, nevertheless, with conviction. Repeated attempts at further exploration led to a stereotyping of response.

A related and similar state of affairs may be seen with certain other patients during an ongoing analysis. The patients complain that knowing about themselves is of no help. Their "insights" seem to be personal clichés (Stein, 1958). Of all the potential rich tapestry of intrapsychic experience revealed in the analysis, some patients seem to have chosen a few details of history, almost always of external and interpersonal content, and created a simple explanatory formula. It is of little heuristic advantage to view these phenomena simply as intellectualizations used for defense. Nor can we pass them over as artificial obsessional symptoms developed in response to inexact interpretation (Glover, 1931). The awareness of he complexity of intrapsychic experience, of the multiplicity of conflicts arising out of long developmental vicissitudes, all seem pushed aside. The "insights" are simplified reconstructions of personal history resembling genetic interpretations and only rarely have dynamic content. When dynamic issues are presented, they, too, tend to be formulaic, for example, "My depression is repressed rage."

These stereotyped "insights" bear a structural resemblance to screen memories, and they may be demonstrated to serve a wide variety of functions. They are rubrics or chapter headings of experience and fantasy. Like other screen memories in which a sequence of conflict, defense, and substitution involving a compromise takes place, these "constrictions" offered by the patient are built like a neurotic symptom and serve functions of both resistance and discharge in the current analytic situation. Freud's (1899) analogy between screen memory and symptom led him to question the very nature of childhood memories. He asked if we have any memories *from* childhood or only memories *relating to* childhood. Furthermore, he wondered if childhood memories *emerge* or are they *formed* retrospectively. Similar questions may be asked about the content of our patients› sparse «insights.» But are these responses so different from those experiences of insight developed in the transference situation which lead to significant structural and functional change? Are they as useless as the patients claim, or, like screen memories, do they contain a world in a grain of sand?

A series of recent papers has illuminated many aspects of the problem of insight. Abend's (1979) study of patients' fantasies of "cure," Arlow's (1981) contribution on fantasies of pathogenesis, and Stein's (1981) paper on unanalyzed aspects of positive transference have all pointed to the problems posed by insufficiently examined fantasy systems. These papers have all clearly indicated the need for increased technical refinement in the exploration of the fantasy structures of the analyst as well as of the patient. Therapeutic preconception colors technical behavior.

The rôle played by the analyst's interpretive interventions in establishing insight is paralleled by the study of the patient's own capacity for self-observation, discovery, and integration. Here, we may focus upon the development of the patient's analyzing and integrating functions and the consequent expansion of the autonomous ego.

The growing experience of re analysis allows the issue of insight to be explored in the current transference situation by the analysis (and resistance to exploration) of previous transference situations. The problem of recovery of memory and patterns of memory touches not only on childhood but on the relatively recent past. Screen memories are not only about childhood. It is usually difficult to acquire any useful picture of what happened in a prior analysis. Sometimes largely forgotten in a manner analogous to the forgetting of a dream (Stein, 1965), the only available residue of the prior analysis may be a formulaic statement serving as a recent screen memory.

Patients in re-analysis often tend to be dismissive of these memories and offer varying degrees of resistance to examining them, focusing instead upon the person of the previous analyst. Frequently, the patient tells an accusatory anecdote in which the analyst was discovered to be "imperfect" and the patient's narcissism was wounded. Another version of this problem has been repeatedly seen by me in supervisory situations where a prior psychotherapy has been "converted" into an analysis with the same analyst. Here, difficulties are often encountered in the search for what had transpired during the psychotherapy. The prior treatment may be trivialized or dismissed, or it may be sequestered and even treasured. Access to the prior experience may be shut off by resistance on the part of both participants. The prior psychotherapy seems to become a walled-off foreign body.

Re-analysis and study of the previous treatment experience offer a special opportunity to explore the function of insight. A complex clinical experience, presented in vignette, outlines the major problems. In this example, the focus is upon the phenomenon of clichéd, reductionistic "insights."

Two years after the completion of a five-year period of psychoanalysis with another analyst, a thirty-two-year-old woman asked for a consultation. She announced at the outset that she knew all about herself and that it had not helped. She had recently interrupted a love affair with a man two years her junior. She now felt depressed and angry. She provided very few details of her recent life, and her anger soon focused upon the previous analyst. She viewed him as well-meaning but unperceptive. When asked what she had learned about herself in the analysis, she gave a few sentences of cliché formulation and capped it with a statement of closure: "That's it!" Upon reflection, she was startled that she knew and remembered so little. Her self-knowledge centered upon the birth of her younger and favored brother and, in her words, her "supposed penis envy." These sparse comments were meant to serve as an explanation for her depression, low self-esteem, career inhibitions, and difficulties in love. She found her "insights" to be of no particular use, although she believed them to be true. In the subsequent period of re-analysis, the patient found that her synoptic view of the previous treatment was indeed analogous to a précis-like fragment of a forgotten dream. In a manner resembling the dream work of condensation, a few elements came to represent the entire experience of the analysis.

This screen memory of the analysis and the recent past was based upon screen memories of her mother's pregnancy and the brother's birth. This façade defended her against awareness of earlier experience of childhood eczema, thumb-sucking, and difficulties in bowel training, all of which contributed to elaborate fantasies in which damage at the mother's hand was a repetitive feature. The initially offered insights resembled highly condensed inexact interpretations. She became able to recall her behavior in the prior analysis where she had great difficulty in free association, rarely remembered dreams, and had long periods of silence. She now viewed herself as a poor self-observer despite an adolescent tendency toward introspection. This introspective phase became characterized by her as wallowing in self-pity. She remembered how much she had liked the first analyst during most of the treatment. However, the ending of the analysis had been an angry re-enactment of the disappointment in love experienced with her mother. This was accompanied by an unreported fantasy that she was replaced by a male patient. Her life history had been re-enacted upon the stage of the analysis, but she had not provided the analyst with sufficient data with which interpretations might be made.

The analysis of the transference in the first analysis took place in the transference situation of the second analysis. The seemingly sterile intellectualizations were in fact like "emblems" of a rich life history and an elaborate masochistic fantasy life. In the day-to-day analytic work, she demonstrated what we both came to call "reductionism" as a resistance. Dreams were presented in a few words, the experience of the prior day in a few sentences. This laconic style became the subject of long exploration, and its origins seemed to be in fending off what she felt were her mother's intrusive questions. In her work, we recognized a parallel process. Though gifted as a writer and capable of inspired beginnings and story outlines she was unable to elaborate upon plot structure. Here too, she had re-enacted early conflicts and fantasies by condensation and "reductionism." Her seemingly useless "insights," demonstrated to be a product of a process analogous to the dream work of condensation, could now be re-expanded into colorful detail. Her inhibition in writing seemed to melt away.

The vignette illustrates some major issues that need to be examined in future studies of insight: first, those ego functions—especially self-observation—necessary for analytic work; second, the childhood antecedents of specific defensive tendencies; and third, how fantasy and acting out shape the transference and the potential for transference interpretation. What follows are some sketches of ideas about this wide subject.

THE STRUCTURE OF INSIGHT

Kris's (1956a) paper on the vicissitudes of insight presented us with a wide spectrum of problems to be studied. He described insight acquisition and its miscarriage in both defense and in drive discharge. Moreover, he sought to link experiences of insight with infantile prototypes. A centerpiece of Kris's work was his aphoristic idealization: "the good analytic hour." This rare phenomenon where a multiplicity of elements seem to fall together into a creative entity (often seeming pre-prepared) was viewed by Kris as a triumph of the integrating and organizing functions of the ego. Thinking old thoughts in a new way and thus leading to new thoughts bears a suggestive similarity to the process of scientific theory formation.

The oscillating flow of data from present to past and back again in fused new forms reminded Kris of what Anna Freud termed the telescopic character of memory. The acquisition of insight, the processes of memory (Kris, 1956b), and the need for causality (Nunberg, 1931) are seen to be interrelated. The "good hour" is a rarity, an ideal toward which we strive. Even the "almost good hour" is not frequently experienced, and such creative bursts do not appear as often as the more usual ebb and flow of tiny bits of insight. Here, as in other aspects of analysis, we must depend more on the quiet establishment of patterns rather than blinding revelations.

At the beginning of this century, when symptom-formation in hysteria was Freud's central model of psychoanalysis, the recovery of memories of traumatic experience was the major technical task. Insight and recovery of memory were then synonymous. Freud's initial environmentalist hypothesis was of a single-event trauma and repression of its memory, to be cured by a single-event specific memory and its attendant affect achieving consciousness. The complexity of the individual's history of drive development, of ego development, and of object relations with representations in multifold fantasies and conflicts make us aware that we cannot single out specific simple causes for the patient's current behavior (Arlow, 1981). Nevertheless, both analysts and patients are attuned to the Lorelei of "specificity" and the lure of "reductionism."

The analysis of my patient with the laconic style may offer some perspective upon the infantile roots of this problem. She was of precocious verbal ability. The earlier described model of being unwilling to answer her mother's questions led to the study of the patient's own insatiable curiosity. She asked endless questions and wanted what she called "explanations." She recalled being irritated by her father's overly detailed answers and pleased by her mother's terse responses. The question of how babies were born was "too complicated" for her, and her father's biological version was "unbelievable." However, her mother's answer: "Babies are born in the hospital" was very satisfying since it corresponded to her own fantasy that the doctor would open her mother's belly-button and the baby would emerge. As she grew older, she developed a life-long aversion to "science" and a love of fiction and poetry. Poetry was especially pleasing because of the economy of representation and the quality of ambiguity. Her development of language and cognitive functions bore a close relationship to her style of defense. She claimed that she was bored by details even about her own life. Any interpretation offered to her that was longer than a single sentence caused her to be irritated and restless. After several years of analytic work, her heightened capacity for self-observation and new interest in detail led to a process she termed "discovery." She would find by herself issues that had in the past been the subject of the analyst's interventions. She did not want to be "told," she wanted to "find." She developed a sense of wonder at the intricacy of her mind and the complexity of her development. Her initial total focus upon events surrounding her brother's birth became viewed by her as analogous to a Japanese "haiku": deep observations stated in a few syllables. In this example, we may examine the complex interplay between a wide range of ego functions: perception, self-observation, memory, language, the need for causality, and those organizing and integrating functions which make for meaning, intelligibility, and structure,.

Kris (1956a) had described the process of insight following the crumbling of resistance structures. The ability to reconstruct the past psychoanalytically as a pathway to insight involves not only the function of memory but a wide range of other ego functions. How ideas are laid down in memory will depend upon the stage of ego development in which they occur and upon the subsequent stages in which they retrospectively acquire new meanings. Memory traces primarily visual in content seem to have a different structure and fate when compared to memories after the consolidation of speech. The ability of the child to use accurate sequential ordering of perceptual data may be a variable acquisition. This capacity seems necessary for a reality-oriented sense of causality. The concepts "before" and "after" are integral to the sense of reality. Some of the telescopic aspects of memory seem to depend upon the confusion of what is "before" and what is "after." The source of the confusion may be developmentally as well as defensively determined. The use of inductive and deductive logical methods have their consolidation in late latency, but some individuals' development of cognitive functions may follow highly individual timetables. Children who have had markedly skewed development of the functions of abstract thinking and concept formation show special difficulties in the analytic process in adulthood (Kafka, 1984). Learning difficulties in childhood may be the consequence of a neurobiological disorder which manifests itself later in an analysis in the inability to make sense of one's experience.

Where in the past we have examined individual differences in the functions of defense, now we are alerted to the further study of individual differences in a wider range of ego functions. Language development, auditory memory, concept formation, and logical narration are not uniformly spread among individuals, and significant maturational differences of these abilities can be noted. In analytic work, skewed aspects of development will then require the more extensive examination of intrasystemic conflicts in the ego. What we have globally designated as integrating functions of the ego may now be more profitably studied as a group of subfunctions. To create an entity from disparate data turns out to be an extremely complex task.

Kris (1956a) had placed three interrelated ego functions as central to the unfolding of insight. He referred to the "control of temporary and partial regression, to the ability of the ego to view the self and to observe its own functions with some measure of objectivity, and to the ego's control over the discharge of affects" (p. 450). Exploration of these functions may lead to therapeutically induced change or may demonstrate fixities which preclude analytic progress. Wide variations exist in these "analytic" functions, that is to say, functions which break down psychic data, so that they can be reassembled in new configurations. Freud had been of the opinion that the analyst can only analyze and that the synthetic functions must be left to the patient; this view was echoed by Kris when he said, "We cannot guide patients in their 'synthesis', we can, by analytic work, only prepare them for it" (p. 453).

However, our greater knowledge of childhood development of ego functions offers us a new opportunity. We can more minutely examine the patient's modes of thought in the analysis, see characteristic patterns of narration and their relation to resistance, and explore fluctuations between free association and purposive thought. Certain specific conflicts in latency and prepuberty impair the development of logical thinking on the conscious level and integrating functions on the unconscious level. The study of insight is the closest that psychoanalysis has come toward developing a learning theory based on strictly analytic evidence. The rôle of the development of cognitive ego functions in latency and prepuberty has been relatively neglected in the analysis of adults. The tendency to look to earlier and earlier developmental phases in the search for pathogenic phenomena has seemed to have greater lure for analysts than has the much more accessible postoedipal period. Yet it is the ego-developmental consequence of latency and prepuberty that may make analysis possible or create such ego restrictions as to preclude analysis.

Superego development in this phase may also determine what can be seen, what must be kept secret, and what may be spoken. Even "how" something is said may have the stamp of latency superego development. It is the period in which euphemism and cliché develop and in which spontaneity may be severely inhibited by superego demand and by the need for peer approval as well. It is the developmental phase in which many children are taught "think before you speak," which one of my patients could recognize as the anlage of what Sterba (1934) described as the therapeutic split in the ego. As a child he had to learn to give thought to the consequences of his words; action was to be preceded by reflection. He had the experience of simultaneously feeling and thinking and yet observing himself long before he came to analysis. The process had high moral value for him and was related to his father's moral standards and expectations of civilized behavior. Here, the röle of late latency in the processes of identification and superego formation aided the analytic work and simultaneously served as a resistance to spontaneity. We see similar results where the capacity for self-observation in certain patients is the outgrowth of identification with the analyst's observing functions, but is also immersed in libidinal and aggressive conflict and consequent fantasy formation.

Insight falters when the patient is intolerant of temporary and reversible regression. Self-observation becomes constricted and inhibited. In certain clinical states characterized by the fear of loss of control, the necessary analytic regression is warded off. A clinical example follows.

A young woman with a conspicuous phobia of crossing bridges and multiple fears of loss of control of both sexual and aggressive impulses began her second analysis with a series of facile rationalizations about her distress. Her pseudo-explanations had the tone of pronouncements or dicta. Some had antedated the first analysis, and some had come out of interpretations made to her. She was afraid to use the couch, hesitant at attempts at free association, and remarkably unobservant about herself. She could not tolerate going to plays or movies, nor could she read novels. She read only for information. She had, as a child, found stories too exciting and was more comfortable with facts. Hyperactive in early childhood, she had been aggressive and given to temper tantrums. She could not examine her own behavior in the analysis but became a condemning observer of the behavior of others. Her condemning attitude was projected in the transference, and examination of her transference fantasies led to the understanding of a pattern: she could not tolerate being in a situation whose outcome was uncertain. She could not read if she did not know how the story ended, and she was fearful of what her thoughts would expose. Her fears of loss of control and of horrid consequences had multiple meanings in a wide range of fantasies.

As the analysis of her fantasy life progressed, her symptoms receded. She was more able to associate and to observe her inner life. The clichés fell away in favor of her examination of her transference fantasies of violent sexual content and her concomitant fears of retaliation. However, this newfound ability showed frequent reversal, with the anxiety of having "gone too far." Insight was fluctuant and easily reinstinctualized. The insight would lead to self-condemnation, a phenomenon which seemed linked to negative therapeutic reaction. She would then fall back upon intellectualization, and there remained a significant limitation in the ability to sustain insight. Though she experienced profound symptomatic relief, there were gaps in her "analyzability." Though I was tempted to fall back upon the concept of "excessive strength of the drives," I found that a non-explanation. The patient was satisfied with the therapeutic result, but significant areas of her development remained murky at the termination of the analysis. Regression "in the service of the ego" remained elusive to her.

The inability of certain borderline patients to tolerate feelings of shame may lead to special difficulties in self-observation. Such a patient came to see me shortly after ending a long analysis. She seemed unable to describe anything about the treatment and could not give a coherent account of what led her to seek the treatment in the first place. She could talk about the analyst and described her with great vividness as a motherly woman with ample breasts. She then remembered lying on the couch in silence listening to the slightest sound from this woman who was much admired. The patient was afraid that she would be silent in a new analysis. In an extended consultation lasting some weeks, she described a series of events in which shame was the central emotion. She began the analysis with trepidation, slowly discovering that her difficulty in self-observation in the previous analysis was defensive against her sexual excitement in the presence of women with large breasts. She felt humiliated by exposing this interest. As a small child she had watched her mother nurse a baby sister, and she wanted to be fed as well. She asked her mother for a suck and was rebuffed. This was the model for many diverse episodes of shameful response. Violent fantasies of revenge toward mothers and babies, analysts and patients, were hidden behind her excitement. During the subsequent analytic course, the arousal of conflicts in the transference which contained components of shame or guilt regularly switched off her self-observation, leaving her silent and feeling stupid. At such moments all the previous work of insight seemed as if "written on water" and disappeared, only to reappear as interpretations centered upon her shame. As with many other borderline patients, her grandiose self-representations and expectations and their discrepancy with her actual personality made her specially vulnerable to shame.

In many patients, the inability to modulate affect discharge is a substantial barrier to the process of insight acquisition. In my experience, it is significantly more difficult to effect analytic change in patients' intolerance to shame or guilt than to modify their anxiety responses. This corresponds to the not infrequent clinical link between moral masochism and disorders of self-observation. In life experiences moral masochists are often oblivious to the consequences of their wishes and actions. Life is always surprising them with new pain. The unconscious nature of the need for punishment and the fantasies which stir that need present us with some of the most profound resistances to analysis. In this setting, negative therapeutic reaction can grind the work to a halt. Freud's technical suggestion that the unconscious guilt of the moral masochist must be made conscious is notoriously difficult to achieve. However, unless those pathogenic fantasies which lead to superego condemnation are made conscious, the self-observing functions necessary for insight may remain paralyzed. Here, the task is rarely accomplished by the analysis of situations outside the transference setting. Sadomasochistic fantasies with the need for punishment seem only to be accessible when the object of the fantasy is present in the form of the analyst and the impulses have a vivid immediacy. Perhaps fantasy, affect, object, and self-observation need to be sharply confluent in order to lead to understanding. Fortunately, the analytic situation provides a unique opportunity for both achieving that confluence and permitting interpretation.

THE RESPONSE OF INTERPRETATION AND THE PROCESS OF INSIGHT

The analytic procedure is a joint undertaking between patient and analyst. We ask the patient to attempt the process of free association not because we literally expect uncensored data but because we await the inevitable conflicts to which the request gives rise (A. Freud, 1936). Those conflicts themselves become the subject of the analysis in the study of resistance. However, without the analyst's interventions, of whatever sort, the process soon comes to a halt. The analyst's interpretations (particularly those directed toward resistance) assist in modifying the patient's censorship and allow greater correspondence between associations and the primary process. The shared scrutiny of the transference situation permits the analysand more accurately to relate present to past and to see the dynamic value of fantasy and behavior in the analytic setting. Interpretation tends to heighten the self-observing functions by providing new tools for the task. But it is the patient's specific response to interpretation that will be decisive; merely to provide him with new tools does not mean that the patient will use them to build his own structure.

Interpretations, by their very nature, are merely provisional explanatory hypotheses. Whatever our own sense of conviction of the "correctness" of an interpretation, it must remain tentative as we await the patient's response. No one should be disappointed by the limitation on the part of the analyst.

Accuracy is determined by the patient, not by the immediate response but by the process of conflict to which interpretation now gives rise. Therapeutic efficacy is among the least reliable of indicators. Thanks to Glover (1931), we have been aware that inexact and poorly timed interpretations may lead to considerable symptomatic relief. The inexact interpretation may function as an analyst-induced artificial symptom aiding defense or permitting drive discharge. Such a response tends to take on a fixed and stereotyped quality. The "process" stops, does not broaden or deepen. The interpretation has been swallowed whole.

By contrast, there is another realm of response. Here the issue is not merely one of acceptance or rejection, increase or decrease of resistance, or the patient's attention to the whole or to parts of the intervention. Instead, we might focus on the events and the patterning of the process that ensues. (The very method of hearing the interpretation may depend upon the analysis of a range of ego functions.) It would seem, from certain successful analyses, that responses to interpretation leading to useful insight undergo continuous revision both during the analysis and following termination. Continuous revision allows for the patient's own discoveries and is linked to the patient's own memories and reconstructions of his or her biography. The analysis of broad structures of resistance allows the patient to become a discoverer both of personal history and of new resistances. Insight tends to grow as resistance analysis becomes a shared task and not something the patient experiences as imposed by the analyst.

The process of discovery and insight may expand after the formal termination of the analysis. Spontaneous revisions of memory may be part of this post-analytic phase. A young woman psychotherapist saw me in extended consultation several years after the successful completion of an analysis with me. She was confronted now with a series of conscious conflicts between her career and the needs of her children. In the course of several meetings she reported that about a year before the consultation she had been watching her children play "nurse and doctor" by decorating themselves with Band-Aids. She suddenly remembered a detail of a childhood experience that surprised her. She recalled a minor childhood injury in which she had been very frightened. Her family physician reassured her and calmed her fear. She realized that she had identified herself not with the doctor's person but with his reassuring manner. She had long been aware of the rôle played by the doctor game and sexual curiosity in her career choice, but the rôle of identification with a helpful calm adult turned out to be decisive in her career. Here, identification served not only defensive but adaptive needs. The memory was a new one and had never appeared during the analysis. Here too, the insight grew in usefulness. The process begun in the analysis continued in self-analytic response containing identifications with the analyst's analyzing functions, not with his person. Review of these post analytic issues led to a creative resolution of her career conflicts and an opportunity for greater closeness to her children.

THE VULNERABILITY OF INSIGHT TO REGRESSION

Insight is a fragile acquisition, easily subject to regression and dismantling. What is seen clearly today becomes murky tomorrow. Easily forgotten, it is often reclaimed at another time. One cannot expect a linear progression in personal hypothesis formation any more than one can believe the myth of linear development in the unfolding of scientific theory (Kuhn, 1962). What makes for this unstable vulnerability in what has been analytically learned?

Neurotic repetition of behavior as examined in the transference is not a mere automatism. Old behavior patterns are repeated because old circumstances leading to that behavior are re-created in a living form. The repetition is not exact but is modified to the new reality of the transference. The reactions to the analyst as the object of fantasies (and their drive origins) push insight forward and pull it back. Insights help expand the autonomous sphere of the ego, but newly generated fantasies toward the analyst emerge in the wake of insight. The autonomous sphere contracts with the new "re-instinctualization" of the analytic situation. Insight opens the path to fresh dangers leading to new waves of defense. The new acquisitions, instead of being reassuring, evoke new anxiety and insight is again masked.

A brief clinical example illustrates this common problem of ebb and flow of insight. A young woman with an obsessive fear of hurting her children had a series of transference fantasies in which she saw me as erratic and crazy. With much difficulty she was able to talk about her mother's severe mental disturbance and the alcoholism which was a family secret. She could see the displacement in the transference and her own identification with her mother's instability. The new insight soon succumbed and was swept away as the patient became depressed and thought I was angry with her. She felt guilty about exposing her mother, having told me what she wanted to tell her father in childhood. Upon the analysis of this specific conflict of loyalties engendered by "telling" mother's secrets with all their oedipal phase implications, her insight into displacement in the transference reappeared. She could again see me as helpful and not like her mother. Interpretation and partial insight may lead to new conflict and stimulate fresh waves of defense, focusing upon the transference.

The transference situation and the analysis of resistance are not only the major sources of data leading to insight, but they may also be the chief source of new resistance to the development of ongoing processes of insight. Insights are then lost, to be discovered anew by examining newly exposed resistances and new transference fantasies.

CONCLUSIONS

There is no one path toward insight. Each patient must traverse a personally unique method, and that journey will be determined by the structure of the neurosis. The same forces which govern conflict and compromise formation in symptom, dream, and screen memory will govern insight formation if artifacts are not introduced by the analyst by technical manipulation or rôle playing. Each patient has formed a developmentally idiosyncratic style of conflict resolution, and part of the analytic work is to facilitate exposure of its patterning and origins. Bibring (1954) described the analytic process as one in which the pathogenic conflicts are re-experienced on the conscious level. His comment underscores the view that psychoanalysis is a data gathering method which utilizes the transference to inform both present and past. Part of the technical difficulty in conducting an analysis is to create what Kris termed a "climate" for the transference to unfold according to the patient's own psychic structure. In the appropriate "climate" each patient's analysis is unique and different. Central to the optimal "climate" is the necessity of the analyst's not clouding the picture by therapeutic preconceptions and premature diagnostic categorizations. We come to understand the individual structure of neurosis by analysis and not by initial anamnesis. The natural corrective to global conceptualizations by either analyst or patient is the piecemeal revelation of shared analytic work. In a general way, where the transference is pushed from within and develops with relative spontaneity (depending as little as possible upon the technical behavior of the analyst), the sense of conviction about historical origins in the past and dynamic repetition in the present is strong. (Here, the "past" includes the entire longitudinal developmental history. This may include prior analysis.) Insight developed in this setting becomes part of autonomous ego functioning and is not easily destroyed. It is the consequence of shared conscious experience in the present, illuminating the past. It is characterized by a simple descriptive fact: no two cases sound alike.

In contrast, where insight hinges primarily on the analyst's behavior and interventions, deep conviction about the "present" situation may develop, and the patient often contrasts this with a picture of the distant past in which a limited and specific theory of pathogenesis predominates (Arlow, 1981). Often, this is a theory of parental mistreatment and is contrasted with analytic care. Insight in this setting may depend upon the maintenance of the transference connection and is object bound. It is unlikely to become autonomous and is likely to take on a fixed symptom-like structure. Nevertheless, it may be powerfully therapeutically effective. The structural change it may effect can often be understood as a shift in identifications. In several such cases that I was able to study in re-analysis, the patient identified with the personalities of the analysts and not their analyzing functions, a process which leads to discipleship or enmity but not to autonomy. Discipleship gives a strange uniformity to case histories. Discipleship also poses special problems for training analysis. In this setting distortions of "insight" are not so much related to the establishment of a meaningful psychoanalytic autobiography as they are to a reverence for a meaningful therapeutic experience. The analytic process described by the patient is not about what the patient learned but what the analyst did. The story that evolves is not about autonomy but about object-bound fantasies.

Even where no manipulation of the transference has taken place, we often observe limitations upon the autonomy of insight. The most common example was described by Stein (1981) in his study of the unanalyzed residua of "acceptable positive" transference. The positive relationship to the analyst may serve as a defensive screen behind which lurk fantasies and impulses. Because one can live more easily with love of the object than with destructive impulses, it is aggressive conflict that is often behind the screen. Though the capacity for transference is never analyzed away (Pfeffer, 1963), we need to be aware that unanalyzed but re-enacted transference fantasies tug at insight and cause it to wither. The termination phase always shows us that old forces are still alive, partly changed in structure and function, but alive, nevertheless. We remain the bearers of our history. Conviction and insight come with the "alive" quality of that history. Past experiences are not archaeological artifacts in a psychic museum. Sometimes that history is too unbearable and cannot be sustained in consciousness. The same psychic raw materials can generate both adaptive autonomous insight and varieties of pseudo-insight used for defense. Where the thorough attempt at the analysis of transference and of the wide range of ego functions may lead to the expansion of the ego, failure of transference analysis tends to lead to frozen restrictions of a range of ego functions. We have an opportunity to examine the very apparatus of personal learning. Re-analysis or "better" analysis gives us a unique opportunity to question and refine our technique and its effectiveness in helping patients make sense of their lives.

REFERENCES

Abend, S.M. (1979). Unconscious fantasy and theories of cure. *J. Am. Psychoanal. Assoc.* 27:579–596.

Arlow, J.A. (1981). Theories of pathogenesis. *Psychoanal. Q.* 50:488–514.

Bibring, E. (1954). Psychoanalysis and the dynamic psychotherapies. *J. Am. Psychoanal. Assoc.* 2:745–770.

Freud, A. (1936). *The Ego and the Mechanisms of Defence.* New York: Int. Univ. Press, 1946.

Freud, S. (1899). Screen memories. *Standard Edition* 3.

Glover, E. (1931). The therapeutic effect of inexact interpretation: a contribution to the theory of suggestion. *Int. J. Psychoanal.* 12:397–411.

Kafka, E. (1984). Cognitive difficulties in psychoanalysis. *Psychoanal. Q.* 53:533–550.

Kris, E. (1956a). On some vicissitudes of insight in psycho-analysis *Int. J. Psychoanal.* 37:445–455.

———— (1956b). The recovery of childhood memories in psychoanalysis. *Psychoanal. Study Child* 11:54–88.

Kuhn, T.S. (1962). *The Structure of Scientific Revolutions.* Chicago: Univ. of Chicago Press.

Nunberg, H. (1925). The will to recovery. In *Practice and Theory of Psychoanalysis: A Collection of Essays.* New York: Nervous & Mental Disease Publ. Co., 1948 pp. 75–88.

———— (1931). The synthetic function of the ego. In: *Practice and Theory of Psychoanalysis: A Collection of Essays.* New York: Nervous & Mental Disease Publ. Co., 1948, pp. 120–136.

Pfeffer, A.Z. (1963). The meaning of the analyst after analysis. A contribution to the theory of therapeutic results. *J. Am. Psychoanal. Assoc.* 11:229–244.

Stein, M.H. (1958). The cliché: a phenomenon of resistance. *J. Am. Psychoanal. Assoc.* 6:263–277.

———— (1965). States of consciousness in the analytic situation: including a note on the traumatic dream In *Drives, Affects, Behavior, Vol. 2. Essays in Memory of Marie Bonaparte* ed. M. Schur. New York: Int. Univ. Press, pp. 60–86.

———— (1981). The unobjectionable part of the transference. *J. Am. Psychoanal. Assoc.* 29:869–892.

Sterba, R. 1(934). The fate of the ego in analytic theory. *Int. J. Psychoanal.* 15:117–126 .

CHAPTER 8

On the Fate of Unconscious Fantasies: Experiences in Middle Life

When Karl Abraham in 1919 wrote a brief paper about the analysis of patients of "advanced age" he was speaking of those in the fourth and fifth decades of life, that is those in their thirties and forties. His clinical note suggested that for those patients for whom the onset of neuroses was relatively recent, analysis was a feasible procedure even in those over fifty! To put Abraham's ideas into perspective we must remember that the average life expectance (in the US) in 1920 was *54.1 years* and then the current life expectancy is *74.7* years when patients consult us *now* middle age is much more likely to mean 50's and 60's and their expectations for longevity now stretch into the eighties.

Furthermore, though a considerable number of middle-aged patients come to us complaining of discrete neurotic symptoms, a far larger number consult us because of something which might be characterized as a "wish for a full life." Something seems missing, old ambitions seem unfulfilled, personal powers have failed or are failing, physical health seems undependable, and romantic and sexual expectations become embroiled in new conflicts. The patients want something more than mere relief of anxiety or depression; they went the fulfillment of old wishes. Often they feel infuriated with the expectation that they will be denied the "full life."

Some years ago, a 56-year-old woman, disappointed in her career, her marriage, and her children, consulted me about beginning an analysis. She summed up her needs in a single plaintive query: "I've taken care of everyone, now who will take care of me?" The complaint had an entirely familiar ring. I had heard *almost the same words* from a number of other patients in middle life. Her poignant and anxious question *was* in fact the beginning of her analysis. It was a rubric or chapter-heading which organized a life-long fantasy of being an unappreciated unrewarded caretaker and rescuer. Behind this meagre surface, seemingly unrelated to her immediate life-situation, was on entire autobiography in fantasy. In a manner analogous to the dream-work of condensation, her cry for help expressed a central fantasy which had depicted the infantile relation to her parents, revealed an important masturbatory fantasy of adolescence, and described her character structure. The details of the unfolding of a complex structure of interwoven fantasies was the subsequent work of many years.

The central idea presented in this brief communication is that unconscious fantasy is remarkably durable, relatively fixed in structure, variable only in conscious expression end derivative, and notoriously resistant to alteration. This finding of the durability of patterned behavior has been a consistent one throughout the history of analysis.

It was part of the mythology of the earliest hypotheses of the theory of psychoanalytic therapeutic results that the process of defense could be abrogated. Furthermore, in the twenties, Franz Alexander, viewing the superego as a "parasitic" organ, thought that it could be *abolished* through analysis. Subsequent analytic work, especially that of Hartmann, Kris, and Loewenstein, demonstrated that the functions of defense were necessary for health and equilibrium and were not the consequence of psychological disorder. Furthermore, the functions of ideals and standards in the superego have been demonstrated as necessary for personal and social coherence. The sense of guilt is quantitatively two-edged: both a source of pain if excessive, and a guardian of self-esteem if experienced at minimal signal-level, The individual capacity for guilt glues the social fabric together, and is the unseen backdrop to the jog and pleasure of social coherence. The superego cannot be abolished; it can be analyzed and understood.

Now, too, we can see fantasy and wish as having relative permanence in the life of individuals, either leading to pathology or contributing to subsequent development. Fantasy cannot be analyzed away; its derivatives, however, may be altered. *Nowhere is the issue of persistence of fantasy more poignant that in the ananlysis middle-aged patient.* Many such patients have the idea that this is *their last opportunity* to make their wishes come true.

What do psychoanalysts mean by the terms *fantasy* and *unconscious fantasy?* Fenichel (1945) said: "As long as thinking Is not followed by action it Is called fantasy. There are two types of fantasy: creative fantasy, which prepares some later action, and daydreaming fantasy, the refuge for wishes that cannot be fulfilled." The issue of creative fantasy hod been approached earlier by Hartmann (1939) who saw on "auxiliary function of fantasy in the learning process. Though fantasy always implies an initial turning away from a real situation, it can also be a preparation for the reality…"

Daydreaming is often visual and pictorial in its form and magical in its representation of wishes and desires as being fulfilled, or anxieties as being realized. As early as 1915, Freud had recognized that certain fantasies were not accessible to consciousness but that they produced derivatives. They were "preliminary stages in the formation both of dreams and of symptoms." From the analysis of dream and symptom we are able to infer the existence of highly organized pictorial and verbal concepts, and representations of self and object and of Impulses and wishes in relatively stable structures. Perhaps the most striking evidences of these patterned organizations of wish, self, and object appear in those derivatives we have designated as *transference response.* The patient is given the opportunity in the analytic situation not merely to talk about these derivatives but to experience them in their most peremptory affect-laden forms. The transference situation is the neurosis made all the more *alive* and *present*. It offers a special opportunity to give *more accessible form* to fantasies which had been unconscious or had been given distorted and unrecognizable form in symptoms.

The simplest way to present the life-long rôle of fantasy is by specific case illustration from an extended analysis. The patient was a 54-year-old man who had been extremely successful in business but whose personal life was chaotic and painful. He saw himself as having a lest desperate chance at having the life he had always wanted. A physician friend had suggested to him that he take some mood-alleviating medication and perhaps seek some psychotherapy. Both suggestions were rejected by the patient, who wanted a psychoanalysis with the conscious fantasy that such a procedure "would be a complete overhaul."

He had been married shortly after graduation from college. His wife had been a campus beauty queen. He described her in great detail as willowy, long-legged, long-haired, self-possessed, and cool in manner. They came from grossly disparate social backgrounds, he from an upper-class, prestigious but impecunious family, she from a brutal alcoholic rural-poor background. Her great beauty and Intelligence had always appealed to teachers, and she had escaped into a world of achievement. She had latched herself to the patient because she viewed him as a "winner." By winning her, he felt victorious over his college rivals and wag excessively proud of her good looks. He was pleased to show her off to others, proud of her talents as a hostess, and saw her as an asset to his business ambitions. Much of his euphoric pleasure in possessing her come to a crash about a year after the marriage when she confessed to him that her seeming sexual pleasure was an elaborate "act." The "act" had had several consistent elements, central to which was her dressing in black underclothes, black stockings and garter belt, all of which had to be worn during the sexual act itself. At first the patient thought this had been her interest, but he soon become aware that the costume had obligatory fetishistic meaning to him and that he could not achieve erection without her dressing up. After her confession of her sexual anesthersia, he became morose, and she began to drink heavily each evening as they attempted to have some sort of sexual life. He soon took to buying sexual costumes for her. When on business trips, he would bug black underwear for her and lovingly finger it when he returned to his hotel room, masturbating with the fantasy that he was making love to her. As he told this narrative he recalled that he had masturbated in adolescence while clutching a pair of his mother's silk panties that he had taken from the laundry room at home. The marriage became more and more painful for both. The birth of a number of children made the internal pressures of the marriage worse. The wife's alcoholism increased, her language became coarse and her behavior violent. She went in and out of institutions to "dry out" and was euphemistically described as having a "little alcohol problem." The children were sent to boarding schools. The patient missed them. He and his wife lived in a state of sullen misery. He grew increasingly ashamed of her and of himself. He entered a number of brief affairs but found that his potency was absolutely dependent on the fetishistic costume, and he found it difficult to secure cooperative partners. As he got older, his sexual interest and abilities underwent a serious decline and he felt hopeless.

About a year before the consultation he had met a woman who interested him immensely. She had been a childhood friend from a family very like his own. She was very plain in appearance, somewhat overweight, and with thick legs and ankles. He was astonished that he felt excited by her unprepossessing features. He had many day-dreams about living with her but could not bring himself to leave his sick wife.

About a month after the analysis began, to his surprise end mine, he completely broke down and wept uncontrollably, covering his face with his hands, and turning to the wall. He said that he was a horrible fraud, that he had been keeping a dread secret from me and that he felt desperately ashamed. He seemed crushed and spoke in e whisper. Since meeting his old friend something changed In him that made him feel that he was "going insane" and this "something" was a "compulsion" that he tried to put out of his mind. It only occurred while on business trips. He could not speak of it for several days but made elliptical allusion to his shameful compulsion. With a conspicuous act of courage, he told me that he had had an image of his friend in the black underwear and had gone out to buy some for her. He bought the largest size available in the shop, returned to his hotel room and immediately put It on accompanied by an excitement he had never before experienced, masturbating repeatedly for hours. On a subsequent trip he had purchased a dress, a coat, high-heeled shoes and an expensive wig. In each shop he told the salespeople that he was buying the item for his mother. On his last trip, he had dressed himself in the entire costume, made up his face with lipstick and eye-shadow. He wanted to appear on the street and be noticed by someone. He went through the same wild excitement. He debated whether he should call for room-service and let the waiter see him. He masturbated repeatedly in front of a mirror and fell asleep in a state of complete exhaustion. He awoke, still costumed, with a strange sense of peace and an accompanying idea that he had lost his mind. This event was the actual precipitating cause for his seeking the analysis and the wish for the "restructuring" of his personality. This "restructuring" fantasy was a derivative of the unconscious wish to be made into a phallic woman. Parallel with his conscious wish to change his life was an unconscious wish to undergo another sort of change.

The analytic work was characterized by a deeply ambivalent but clinging transference response. There was extraordinary anxiety at even brief separations, but only if those separations were initiated by me. He had been unaware consciously that separation caused him any distress whatsoever. Well into the analysis, he reported a memory in association to a dream. He saw a child standing in a hospital crib and after a moment of wonder realized that the memory was of a child in the crib next to his own during a hospitalization of many months about the time of his third birthday. He had never remembered anything about this hospitalization, nor was It ever spoken about in his family. He had had e number of bouts of excruciating abdominal pain and fever. What had started as a hospitalization for suspected appendicitis had extended for months until spontaneous resolution of the symptoms, The essential corroborative information for this memory was eventually supplied by the patient's aunt. When he returned home he was described as not recognizing or responding to his mother. Subsequent to that time he had remained extremely attached and close to her. He was docile, well-mannered and described by his father as "too good." From about his tenth year, he shared an interest in sports with his father. He became an excellent athlete, surpassing his father in golf and tennis. He imagined that by staying fit he could ward off illness and death. In early puberty he often looked in the bathroom mirror with his penis tucked between his legs imagining what a woman looked like naked, He then surprised himself by letting his erect penis pop out from between his legs. Prominent in his most shame-laden transference wishes were sudden obsessive Ideas that ! should see him as a woman and be astonished. He wanted an external confirmation that his fantasies could be made real.

It required little in the way of interpretation for this patient to recognize that from early in his life he had hod an unconscious fantasy that there was such a creature as a "phallic woman" and then the fantasy had been expressed in a number of derivatives in object-choice end in behavior. His wife and her long willowy body represented one form of the phallic woman fantasy and his friend with her piano legs represented another form. It did not require much interpretation, either, for him to be aware that the fantasy had helped solve anxiety about separation and about bodily intactness. The most dramatic derivative in the transvestism was that he was safe from separation anxiety; he had become a *self-contained entity*, man and women, a woman with a penis who needed no one else. He had undone the early infantile separation from his mother and even when alone in a hotel room, he seemed not alone. The wish to be seen in public, like the transference fantasy, was to confirm that a phallic woman could exist.

The rivalry with other men, the demand for success, the choice of women, the fetishistic compulsions, all exploded in middle life into the dramatic symptom of transvestism. To those familiar with reported cases of the effect of the persistent fantasy of a phallic woman (Fenichel, Lewin, Bak), all of these events seem familiar. Whet is so unusual Is that they all took place in the same patient at successive stages of his life. The late appearance of transvestism without prior cross-dressing is also remarkable.

What Is of special interest Is that we can trace in this analysis the precipitating events for the shift in each phase of his development. In each phase, the phallic women fantasy, which remained unconscious, served as motive power for fresh derivatives in fantasy and behavior. Driving the entire process was the central rôle of separation anxiety. The early separation experience sensitized this patient to later experiences of anxiety of bodily damage. At each step he attempted to control that anxiety by new methods, using an old template. When he arrived at the analysis, his "loss" of his wife through her depressive and alcoholic illness, the departure of his children, and the gradually evolving conscious awareness of his declining powers had pushed his behavior in a regressive direction. He came to be aware that he was not as sharp as he used to be about business issues, and that he had e lesser grasp in remembering names. The small inevitable inroads of age had been denied but had stimulated further regression.

The analysis had a felicitous result. The insight into the rôle of separation anxiety was the most decisive therapeutic event. The external situation could be altered. He divorced the wife, married the old friend, and decided on a lesser involvement in business. He experienced both his awareness of his declining powers and the end of the analysis with a sense of mourning. His happiness with his new wife and his restored potency, without obligatory fetishistic requirements, have given him a more genuine and reliable sense of self-esteem. An unexpected fresh sublimation appeared: he has become deeply immersed in the collection of art which he pursues with the professional elan which characterized his business life. In the shadow of his collecting was the remnant of his fetishistic interest. Connoisseurship has replaced perversion, He was particularly Interested in sculpture end its *tangible* qualities. When I last saw him, he commented that his transvestite symptoms seemed "like a dimly-remembered nightmare, all pale and washed out." He had seen a Broadway play about a transvestite; he felt moved and sympathetic, but though he recognized something of himself, it, too, seemed far away.

His new wife shares his artistic interests. Their collection can be exhibited by both of them. All the fantasy elements that went into the neurotic and perverse distortions are still there but they have been rearranged and have led to a very different outcome.

What is the applicability of this very dramatic case report to the more general problem of the analysis of patients of middle-age? It is simply this: old fantasy and fantasy-systems ore never extinguished. They have a remarkable persistence and they may be manifest in a variety of forms throughout the life cycle. More often than not we are accustomed to seeing the persistence of the derivatives themselves. That is to say, we are accustomed to seeing the chronic repetition of symptom and character trait, and by their clamorous quality these derivatives of the underlying fantasy take our attention. But *symptoms* are not pathogenic. Biological constitution, conflict, disturbance in object-ties, alteration of ego-functions, and their representations in fantasy are the sources of neurosis. It is the persistence of unconscious fantasy that must constantly claim our attention as analysts. Symptom and character trait are the consequence of underlying pathogenic predispositions. Fantasy is rooted in the constitution, In bodily and emotional needs, and In the life history. Fantasy is, in fact, the record of that history.

Of all the wide range of potential fantasies each individual patient seems to have only a *few* systems of fantasy. These persist for a lifetime. They manifest themselves in a variety of derivatives and tend to be expressed in the analytic situation in wishes in the transference. Such needs and wishes, rooted in the body and bodily sensations, are the clinical data which underlie those explanatory hypotheses of psychoanalysis which are termed "the drives."

Among the first psychoanalytic views of the persistence of relatively permanent, that is "structuralized," fantasy systems resulting in behavior, were the concepts of *character* stated by Freud and elaborated by Abraham. Anna Freud, in a seminal paper, described a beating fantasy carried out over years as If it were a novel. She demonstrated that a basic fantasy could show protean manifestations. Derivatives of unconscious fantasy have subsequently been shown to be manifest in conscious daydreams and masturbatory imagery and in symptom, character, object-choice, and transference manifestation.

The circumstances of middle life, and our opportunity to examine them psychoanalytically, give us a newly-discovered mental landscape: *middle-age as a developmental phase.* In middle age, as in other developmental phases, basic fantasies are re-worked in a phase-specific manner leading to certain phase-specific manifestations. The *form* they take is often highly rationalized and presented as seeming reality. For example, middle-aged woman, fearful of her loss of sexual attractiveness, agitated by her scanty menstrual periods and approaching menopause, frightened of death, had a passionate Interest In much younger men. She gave a highly plausible view that younger men were more sexually vigorous, had better bodies, made her feel more youthful and put her in touch with younger people. A sturdy resistance was mounted against any examination of these ideas; they were presented as simple realities. With reluctance, she examined this view. Behind the seemingly realistic story was a life-long fantasy of being a boy like her adored younger brother who had always claimed her mother's love. This fantasy had been expressed in a variety of vastly different forms throughout life. A wishful self-image had been transformed into an object-choice. One may tentatively generalize that the manifest form that is taken by underlying fantasy is phase-specific and highly subject to rationalization.

Recent work by Abend and by Arlow have presented us with the ideas that theories of cure and theories of pathogenesis have their origin in unconscious fantasies. These concepts have their own phase-specific content in patients of middle life. Though each patient has a unique life experience, unique memories and unique fantasy systems, culture and society provide some final common pathways of representation and expression. (Heinz Hartmann once said that culture provides a pathway for the discharge of the drives.) Most conspicuous of these modes of representation of the fantasies of pathogenesis, in middle life, the röle given to object relations and the röle given to work. Current symptoms were often blamed upon e troubled marriage (or lack of marriage) end upon boring work. Change of lover end change of job are often equated with cure. Cure is seen as taking place in the external world end not In the realm of the mind. As a means of achieving that cure, a vary frequent fantasy is the wish for a powerful emotional catharsis in the presence of e loving parent-analyst. Fantasies of rebirth with new parents often stand behind the wish for corrective emotional experience.

A special and powerful phase-specific resistance to analysis in the middle-aged patient is the frequent *trivialization* of neurosis. Though such trivialization may take place throughout the life-cycle, with the denial of suffering and of serious disorder, middle age provides some special paths of expression. Here, too, insistence is placed upon changing the external reality and minimizing the need for treatment. If treatment is sought, it, too, is trivialized. If analysis is suggested, a frequent response is, "I'm not as sick as all that; I need is a little help with current problems." It is very frightening to arrive in the sixth and seventh decades of life and realize that one has not solved of lifetime of trouble. Gently helping the patient to examine a life of fantasy and its consequences is a challenging diagnostic and therapeutic task.

REFERENCES

Abraham, K. (1919). The Applicability of Psycho-Analytic Treatment to Patients at an Advanced Age 1. *Seled Papers on Psychoanalysis*. New York: Routledge, 1988.

Alexander, F. (1925) A Metapsychological Description of the Process of Cure. *International Journal of Psychoanalysis* 6:13–34.

Freud, A. (1923) The Relation of Beating-Phantasies to a Day-Dream. *International Journal of Psychoanalysis* 4:89–102.

Freud, S. (1916) Some Character-Types Met with in Psycho-Analytic Work. *Standard Edition* 14:309–333.

Hartmann, H. (1939) Psycho-Analysis and the Concept of Health. *International Journal of Psychoanalysis* 20:308–321.

—— Kris, E. & Loewenstein, R. M. (1946) Comments on the Formation of Psychic Structure. *Psychoanalytic Study of the Child* 2:11–38.

CHAPTER 9

IPTAR Lecture: Revenge and Masochism

In a recent Freud Lecture on *Revenge*, I hoped to demonstrate the ubiquity of revenge fantasies resulting from early developmental wounds to infantile narcissism. Helpless at birth, we would all die if not for the nurture received from the all-powerful adults around us. The power of adults endows them with the ability to cause each of us varying levels of frustration of our wishes and multitudinous narcissistic mortifications to matter how thoughtful and loving our caregivers are. Our early object-needs and self-needs are the forerunners of later conflict.

My awareness of the relationship between narcissistic defeat, early rage, revenge fantasy and masochism was brought to dramatic attention by the re-analysis of a patient now deceased. I have lived long enough to mourn the loss of many former patients and can now feel freer about reporting some clinical vignettes to illustrate the clinical hypotheses. In the Freud Lecture I had used illustrations from literature especially from the revenge plays of Sophocles, Euripides, Seneca, Calderon, Corneille and most especially the Elizabethan plays culminating in Shakespeare's Hamlet where, at the final curtain, we have seen a stage littered with corpses.

Tonight, I want to talk about revenge centered upon the self. Let me start with one of the most famous of Greek plays, *Oedipus Tyrannos*. In brief, Laius, the father of Oedipus, had been told by the Delphic oracle that his son was destined to kill him. The child's feet were pierced with spikes, and he was exposed on a mountain-side to die. Found mutilated by a shepherd, he is delivered to a royal court. Named for his mutilation, Oedipus or swollen-foot, he later kills his father at a cross-roads not knowing the identity of his victim. He marries Jocasta, the victim's wife, and has children by her. When he later discovers the nature of his crime he pierces his eyes and blinds himself. Jocasta, hoping to console him, tells him he has only done "what other men dream of. "

Now to an analytic experience of revenging self-damage and doing that which other men only dream of.

Clinical vignette:

An extremely intelligent creative man came to me after two failed analyses. Skeptical, yet still hopeful, he had heard from a consultant that I had an extensive experience of re-analysis. Smiling broadly, he told me about the two failures placing much emphasis upon the last experience. He had gone to an older woman he viewed as an expert, and had remained with her for many years without any improvement but with a sense of enslavement to her. Much acquainted with literature he saw himself in the position of Samson with Delilah. When he was with the analyst he felt alive but furious, often expressing his rage by silence. When he was away from her, he felt a dull overpowering loneliness having given up much of his social life which now narrowed to a tunnel-vision in which the analyst was the central focus. He had become her masochistic prisoner, negativistically rejecting her interpretations and other interventions but unable to leave her. It should come as no surprise to this audience that he was reliving in the transference his enslavement to his mother of which he was unconscious. His complex revenge fantasies centered upon never succeeding and never making his parents proud of him. His current aim was to prove the impotence of psychoanalysis to help him or anybody else.

For reasons known only to his analyst, the complex nature of his transference was interpreted, in a sense, only at the edges. His masochistic revenge was to fail and to subsequently tell another analyst of the repeated failures of inadequate damaging parenting. He had multiple dreams of various dream-personages apologizing to him.

Having had many patients who had multiple analytic failures, I have remained deeply aware of how revenge and masochism have been deeply entwined. Embedded in this entanglement is the most profound unconscious pleasure of the fantasy of pay-back. In the Freud Lecture, I had commented on an idea I first heard from Lawrence Kubie which he incorporated into a paper on ideas of reversal of generations: "when I am big and you are little." This is a variation on the theme of "identification with the aggressor." In the patient I am describing the aim is the humiliation of the inadequate analyst who is then condemned and consigned to public humiliation, a repetition of the patient's childhood. However, this must be perpetually re-enacted; otherwise, deep loneliness intervenes.

At the conclusion of *Howard's End* E.M. Forster adumbrates the principle of only connect. Masochistic revenge and masochistic exhibitionism (remember Saint Sebastian is depicted as smiling while exhibiting being pierced by arrows) are a means of remaining connected with the earliest objects of desire, the parents of infancy. I am indebted to Leonard Shengold for his repeated emphasis on suffering as an object-tie. Psychoanalysis early linked object-ties to love, nurture and need satisfaction and only later did Freud recognize masochism and beating fantasies as strong as chains adamantine (Spenser's *Faerie Queene*) to the objects of desire. This came with the recognition of the universality of ambivalence. Libidinal and aggressive components are part of all object-connectedness. Seduction of the object is a universal wish whether libidinal or aggressive.

Children want to revenge themselves on their parents and parents want to revenge themselves on their children as well as gratifying their libidinal demand even if in sublimated form. The same components enter into every analysis. The unfinished business of childhood is a part of every transference reaction. By the term transference I do not mean only a displacement from the past onto the person of the analyst. I mean, with Brian Bird, a view of transference as a kind of ego function, an orienting mechanism in which unconsciously we scan the whole world looking for the familiar. This is true not only for us as *patients* but also as *analysts*. I do not like to use the term "countertransference" implying that we react to the patient and the resultant transferences .I prefer to think of us having our own persistent "transferences" in or out of the analytic situation requiring our constant self-observation and constant self-analysis. We cannot act out the grandiose perfection the patients expect of us and project upon us. We are extraordinarily fallible and potentially subject to the same sorts of revenge fantasies as the rest of humankind.

We are called upon to remember that many symptoms and many character traits are indissolubly linked to the original person with whom they were unconsciously associated. The resistance to analyzing the symptom or character trait can be linked to losing the original object with its consequent sense of revived anxiety and the usual conscious concomitant affect of loneliness. What starts out in life as "separation-anxiety" undergoes a change of function and change of affect-representation. Loneliness is its common adult form as it had been in childhood partly repaired by an imaginary companion, a teddy bear, or a pet animal. Remember too that for children the usual affective component of what has been termed primal-scene fantasy is feeling lonely, left out. I challenge anyone in the audience who has ever had a seriously self-mutilating masochistic patient who did not carry out the self-stimulating mutilation in a state other than that of painful empty loneliness. (I, of course, am *not* including among these patients those that have organically determined brain diseases involving disorders of D1, D2, dopamine receptors.)

Let me return for another moment to discuss loneliness. Current psychiatric and psychological usage pays little attention to affects other than anxiety and depression. That may be because there are some drugs targeted toward anxiety and depression. There are many more affects, particularly those associated with shame and guilt, which claim our attention all the time. Think of popular usage, think of all those who say they are "dying of shame" as well as those who are "dying of heartache." I will return to this later when I speak of hypochondriasis as an object-related self-directed painful aggression bearing some of the marks of a revenge fantasy and often mediated by identification with a hated hypochondriacal parent.

In each of my comments so far there is the shadowy image of a parent or other caregiver from whom the patient cannot bear to be parted, a person whose torture would be enjoyed unconsciously by the patient as long as they were not separated. Let me turn my attention for the moment to the paradigmatic fantasy of masochism made famous by Freud in the paper "A Child is Being Beaten." Emphasis has been characteristically placed upon the libidinal connection to the father, the wish to be the loved parental favorite, the masturbatory genital pleasure of the fantasy and the röle that both parents may have played in the genesis of the fantasy. For the moment I would like to shift our attention to the rivalry and competition with the beaten child and the vengeful pleasure in the physical mistreatment of rivals. This is closely related to the pleasure I have reported in revenge plays with their specific visual pleasure and in reading murder mysteries and their complex relationship to guilt and absolution.

The beating of the rival, often in the form of spanking, is deeply pleasuring to the to the patient, made only more intensive by the fantasy of the rival's ultimate humiliation. Think of Iago's malignantly duping Othello into killing Desdemona and his exulting pleasure in causing such downfall.

Think of the malignant pleasure taken by the electorate in savoring the defeat of certain candidates in an election and not being satisfied with defeat but desiring degradation and even death for the defeated. Think of the murders daily committed out of jealousy and unrequited love.

Revenge fantasies can easily shift their target from the hated rival, and hated caregiver, to the self when the need for object-sparing requires that though revenge is needed, the target can be varied. Suicide can be substituted for murder. Man, the tool-using, story-telling animal, is capable of exulting in blood, his own as well as others. To anyone who has ever been to a bull-fight at the Fiesta of San Isidro in Madrid, who has ever listened to the collective gasp as the first enormous Miura bull comes roaring out like a locomotive train into the ring, who has ever heard the roar as the matador kills the bull or who has cried out when a matador has been gored, knows the pleasure man is capable of in watching cruelty and the infliction of death. Gladiatorial combat did not end with the fall of the Roman Empire.

In a private conversation with Dr. Rudolph Loewenstein during a long collaboration he told me that the most difficult patients for him to treat were those consumed by the need for revenge. Seemingly devoted to the pain and humiliation of others, they were also the most vulnerable to searching out their own pain and humiliation. In a landmark paper on masochism in 1957, Loewenstein had added to Freud's concepts of the origins of masochism and the importance of beating fantasies in organizing those fantasies. Loewenstein's added contribution was a broad developmental set of ideas later acknowledged by Novick and Novick (1987) giving a much broader picture. A 1976 contribution by Jacob Arlow on "The Revenge Motive in the Primal Scene" provided a vital bridge between the narcissistic mortification of primal scene experience or fantasy and the persistent drive for vengeance on both father and mother.

In Loewenstein's contribution he notes, with Freud, that to "seek physical or mental suffering to achieve, be it consciously or not, sexual gratification...

138

. seem to contradict a basic characteristic of the human mind: the trend to avoid pain and unpleasure. " To that I would add that through masochism, the object-tie to the parents trumps the biological tendency. For some pain is the road to pleasure by linking current sensation to past objects. Like neurosis in general, masochism is an anachronism: the patient partially lives in the distant past not in the present. The patient tries to recreate the distant past by displacing it to the present, not just with the analyst. In a sense the patient does not have a past history: it is present here and now. To give up the past means to give up not only the parents but to disavow part of oneself. This includes the threat of losing portions of one's developmental experience in which identification with parental injunctions gave rise to what has been conceptualized as an organ of the mind: the superego and the ego ideal. Adherence to induced standards of behavior and the shame and guilt resulting from failures of such adherence were conceptualized by Freud as the glue which bound civilization together. In a sense this meant that the internal relationship hinged on amount: some shame and guilt were socially useful, too much was resultant in individual pathology and suffering. Masochism finds a pathway to unite suffering with sexual pleasure. Masochism is an object-tie useful to pre-disposed individuals to allow them to be attached, to connect. The patients I have seen to be most suffering are the unattached, the unconnected. They are the ones most vulnerable to self-directed fury, to intense self-hatred, the lowest self-esteemed and the ones most directed to seeking out failure in life. They correspond to those viewed by Loewenstein as the most difficult to help toward reasonable health. Such patients are almost inevitably hypochondriacal and are always having the fantasy that punishment and death await them.

Clinical vignette:

A mature woman of very good intellect and physical attractiveness had a relatively fixed idea that she was stupid and ugly. Possessed of both a deep sense of inferiority and a grandiose conviction of superiority she criticized her husband, children, friends and colleagues. High on what she termed her "shit list" were several prior psychotherapists and analysts. Nevertheless, she returned again and again to ask for help. She showed a remarkable hysterical pseudo-stupidity. She seemed profoundly unaware of her identification with a critical condemning mother who seemed to hate her husband and children. The patient longed for the mother's love which was only apparent when the children were ill. Hypochondriasis was an invitation to the mother's love which had been doled out in tiny homeopathic doses. The patient's low self-esteem corresponded to the mother's estimate of her. All of this was dramatically repeated in the transference: all unconsciously acted out and all resistant to change by the pseudo-stupid stance. The whole of the past history was dramatized in the patient's symptoms and her suffering. The transference was the stage upon which these events were acted out.

The importance of transference re-enactment as an aspect of the therapeutic process cannot be overemphasized. Many patients, afraid of the dangers of intimacy, want to avoid analysis and its intensity of contact. They are instinctively afraid of the reliving in the transference since they have already had that experience in other failed relationships including marriage. With regularity they often voice a preference for limited psychotherapy where they hope to tell a story, ask some questions and get some answers. They often find therapists to collude with them in what Isakower called "psychoanalytically disoriented psychotherapy."

The intensity of the transference situation stimulates reliving. It is not for nothing that we arrange the regressive atmosphere of the psychoanalytic ritual: recumbent position on the couch, the analyst partly out of sight, the request for free-association all promote regression. By the way, when we ask for free-association we should not expect it. Rather, we should expect silence, and gaps in the data which represent resistances (and their intrapsychic counterparts: defenses). As I have repeatedly stated, we want to see and hear a life relived with us, not a story told to an undiscriminating audience. This is long, slow, painstaking work on the part of both members of this strange conversation (Siegfried Bernfeld), a conversation in which the gaps are as important as the content, a conversation which illustrates how the patient's mind works and how the analyst's mind works.

Part and parcel of this strange conversation is the desire of the patient to quit and run away: the process of defense illustrated by flight from the unpleasant. What we hope to achieve is self-knowledge through connection to another person ultimately leading from the analyst to a real object of love .A loving husband, wife, lover is the analyst's hoped-for collaborator. A satisfactory sexual relationship is the best therapeutic agent for masochism, an intermediate step often playing out a masochistically-tinged game rather than a real torture, and a playful fantasy of revenge against another person, rather than punitive self-torture. The intermediate transitional object is almost invariably the analyst who is often denigrated in the terminal phase of the work. Most gratifying of all is the patient's decision, like the white knight in Alice in Wonderland, that this was "all my own invention" or even more dramatically: "I've known this all along" as if nothing had been unconscious, and the analyst's interpretations were mere clichés. The patient's fantasy of a cure through love is sometimes achievable as a result of an analysis which makes a real love possible in the real world, not the infantile wish of seducing the parent or the parent substitute.

Nor can the analyst really offer the possibility of a substitute mothering and soothing. Some years ago, our London colleague Clifford Yorke gave a paper to a discussion group of which I am a member. It was to throw into question the work of a number of colleagues advocating the creation of a special environment suitable for re-development. Most memorable of what he said was: "What good mother would be content to seeing her child for 50 minutes five times a week?" Love needs to be continuous through good times and bad—24 hours a day. Analysis can make it possible for the patient to be loving and lovable to a suitable person. Analysts do not need to be loved by the patients nor the patients to be loved by the analysts. *Transference love is a vehicle for the analysis, not the goal of analysis.* Incest is not the goal of development, independence is.

ON THE ROLE OF TRANSFERENCE IN SELF-DIRECTED REVENGE

As I have emphasized before, most revenge fantasies are closely tied to the important figures in the child's life: parents and siblings. As such they become the substance of subsequent object-ties and are lived out in the transference. A spurious connection between positive loving transference and therapeutic outcome has been made by many colleagues, especially those who place being loved as high on their personal agendas.

Ernst Kris in his excellent paper on the vicissitudes of insight taught us, in speaking of the good hour, that insight often appears in the midst of a dark mood, where the issue is not the valence of the mood (positive or negative) but the intensity of the mood. For certain patients, to view the analyst intensely and negative is akin to being admitted into an inner sanctum of family life: a position of honor.

This sometimes allows for the reversal of direction of revenge fantasies back from the self and toward the original objects. Transference fantasy is the vehicle for such change of target, Transference, central to the data-gathering of analysis, receives powerful stimulus in the patient's reactions to interventions and interpretations; they may feel humiliated, stupid, childish, and filled with rage re-stimulating revenge fantasies, now toward the analyst. "History" becomes alive and contemporary, and affects are electric.

REVENGE AND SUICIDAL FANTASY

Having an experience of over five decades has taught me to treat all suicidal fantasies with great seriousness. I have never yet had a patient commit suicide though many have had the idea. One should have wide experience in treating patients with manic-depressive disease to differentiate patients with a potential psychosis from those whose fantasies have a neurotic basis. The concept of revenge may exist across the diagnostic spectrum but a hysterical wish for revenge against a parent or lover is structurally different from the desperate urge for the relief of mental pain seen in the psychotically depressed even though some revenge fantasies might exist across that spectrum, and might even appear in very ill or aged persons who want to remain in control of their own fates.

Very young children often hold their mothers responsible for whatever happens to them. For many years, in fair warm weather, I used to eat my lunch in Central Park in a children's playground watching the children at play. One day while watching a three or four year old play in the sand-box, the boy slipped on the concrete edge and scraped his knee. Crying, he ran over to his mother, seated near me, and hit her. Blaming of the mother for every pain exists for some people throughout a lifetime.

Clinical vignette:

A young woman who had been born prematurely had a fantasy when in adolescence that if she had been born full-term, as had her brother, she would have been born a boy. She imagined she had been "untimely ripped"

143

from the mother's womb but blamed her mother. When later in adulthood she thought of divorce from her brother-like husband she blamed her mother. When she had a suicidal fantasy it was to blame her mother and me for not "doing enough. " This was designed to induce guilt in mother and analyst. The fantasy was told in lugubrious fashion but with a strange smile conveying pleasure. (By the way, I suggest to analysts that one's chair should be placed in such a relation to the patient on the couch so that the patient's face can be seen.)

Clinical vignette:

A young man beset with a jealous depression centering on his girl-friend had an ominous fantasy of committing suicide to punish her. As the fantasy flowered he was watching her weeping at his funeral. When I said "Tom Sawyer" reminding him of such a scene depicted by Mark Twain he had a complex response of laughter and slightly wounded narcissism. His depression lifted immediately. He was identified with a depressive guilt-making mother. The tendency to transmit guilt through the generations is well-known and part of many cultures and families. The wish to induce guilt in the analyst is to include the analyst in a family milieu. It is a mode of attachment. Even in the midst of destructive fantasies of death, the need for attachment shows itself. Even in the midst of the fantasy of the punishment for the unloving, there remains the wish to see the agony of revenge in the victim's face.

MASTURBATION AND REVENGE FANTASIES

One of the consistent problems of the psychoanalytic endeavor from its onset has been the resistance to revealing crucial and often treasured secrets, some conscious and most of them unconscious. A characteristic secret, enveloped in shame, is the relationship of some of the most cherished fantasies to masturbation. Here, I am not speaking only of childhood masturbation but of contemporary masturbation where the stimulating excitement often includes the image of the analyst. It is not the actual masturbatory act that is the center of shame but the identity of the incestuous characters.

The beating fantasy much discussed in the psychoanalytic literature is almost always accompanied at some point by a masturbatory act. Very often the rhythm of the beating is the rhythm of the masturbatory act rising in intensity as the patient approaches orgasm. Sometimes to heighten the excitement and prolong the fantasy, the patient puts a temporary halt to the process only to resume with renewed intensity until orgasm seems to take place without the patient's control. The closer the cast of characters approaches the analytic situation, the more intense is the shame and the more likely the patient will withhold the information. What is conspicuous is that the adult who is imagined as beating the child comes closer and closer to resembling the analyst whether depicted as male or female. Though originally described by Freud and by Anna Freud as being modelled on the father, many patients model the fantasy on the mother. The closer the resemblance to the analyst in the actual masturbation, the more intense the shame and the greater the resistance to exposure. However, the more the analyst is depicted, the more the rival children resemble the analyst's other patients, the more intense the excitement and the more the masturbation becomes akin to a beating.

Two clinical vignettes:

a. A woman patient, envious of other women patients and filled with fantasies of revenge, would come to orgasm when she would spank her vulva.

b.   A male patient would describe his masturbation in the midst of such fantasies as "beating [his] meat," otherwise referring to masturbation as merely "jerking off, " a more benign reference.

All these fantasies achieve very heightened representation, and the more they stimulate heightened defense, the closer the transference fantasies seem in the midst of such conflict one patient would writhe on the couch, in contrast to his preternatural stillness at other times. The patient's stillness represented an attempted control over overwhelming excitement while turning it into its opposite: a state of suspended animation.

THE SELF-CONTAINED UNIT—SUBJECT AND OBJECT UNITED THROUGH

Freud's early paper on narcissism was one of the great nodal points in the development of psychoanalytic explanatory hypotheses. Put in its simplest form it suggested that though we had become accustomed to thinking of love taking place between two people as in the romantic poetry of the past (*The Song of Solomon,* the love poetry of Sappho and Catallus, the romantic traditions of courtly love as sung by the troubadours, Shakespeare's sonnets, Goethe's *Wilhelm Meister,* etc. etc.), it was also possible to conceptualize love of one's own self. This later gave rise to a concept, in relation to aggression, that one could take one's own self as the object of one's own aggression as in the model of primary masochism. What had been sadism toward the object could be turned back against oneself thus sparing the needed object from harm even though that person was hated. This fusion of forces gave self-directed hatred an overpowering strength. Self-directed sadism could now be viewed as an attachment of the self to the object available in periods of isolation and loneliness. The transitional object of early childhood is replaced by total attachment to the self for more or less time depending on external circumstances. The boundaries between inner and outer worlds are porous and where either love or hatred cannot be expressed in the outer world they can always be expressed to ourselves either intrapsychically or upon our own bodies. The most prominent of the bodily expression of this ambivalence is of course in masturbation. Here the self-contained quality is often heavily-populated by characters from the outer world.

Clinical vignette:

A woman masturbating with a vibrator-dildo says to herself, "Take that, bitch. " This, upon investigation, turns out to be part of a primal-scene fantasy of her father saying that to her mother. This was unlikely to have been seen or heard but was imagined since she was a little girl. It is not a rare clinical experience. Masturbatory fantasy has a creative dramatic aspect and can be a forerunner of creative work in literature and theater.

As I have mentioned elsewhere the telling of fantasy to the analyst draws the analyst into a privileged family cycle and has to be treated with delicacy and respect—it is closely related to listening to a child's secret. It is at the heart of intimacy, akin to the intimacy of lovers, easily wounded and hesitatingly told.

As reported by me in the Freud Lecture this week, fantasies of revenge are ubiquitous; they are not in themselves pathological but are capable of achieving pathogenic power. We all have them and under terrible stress we are all capable of turning revenge upon ourselves. Remember E.M. Forster's injunction, after a painful lonely masochistic life: "Only connect."

SELF-HATRED AND MASOCHISTIC REVENGE

One of the more pernicious symptoms of self-hatred and masochistic revenge is the intense hatred of one's body and one's appearance, a set of ideas of almost delusional intensity accompanied by feelings of utter conviction. Such fantasies are extremely difficult to analyze and are almost never amenable to any reassurance. They bear some relation to convictions about stupidity—hysterical pseudo-stupidity being extraordinarily ego-syntonic. These almost intractable attitudes are sometimes allied with severe hypochondriasis, mentioned before. Central to all such symptoms is a hopeless conviction of not being lovable. Hovering in the analytic shadow is usually an image of an angry mother, disapproving and critical. This is not necessarily a true portrait of the mother.

Clinical vignette:

An extremely well-dressed, well-groomed woman in her 40's had made several attempts at analysis with little success. She had also had several plastic surgical procedures without any satisfaction with the results. In her past many people had commented upon her resemblance to her stylish, pretty mother. The mother, ill-tempered and selfish, was steeped in her own narcissism and viewed the patient as an extension of herself. Never satisfied with her own appearance, she was always dissatisfied with the daughter. They shared a common sense of distress that they "hadn't a thing to wear, and they couldn't do anything with their hair." This attitude has appeared in many of my patients, often accompanied by complaints from them that men don't suffer from those feelings.

In their past experiences, this has often been interpreted to them as feeling envy towards fathers and brothers differently anatomically equipped. Such interpretations have only sometimes led to any insight, not because they were incorrect but because they were insufficient. With this patient, her hatred of her mother was experienced as hatred of her resemblance to that mother and her identifications with the mother's superego. Her mother's complaints that she was a "rotten brat" became concretely incorporated into fantasies that she had "rotten" organs, a "rotten" body and a consequent hypochondriasis. Severely punished for masturbation, she became convinced that she had damaged herself irreparably and sought reassurance through promiscuity. Actual sexual experience never convinced her of her having any value. Though consistently frigid, she went through repeated attempts at seduction of her several therapists and analysts, male and female. Her pseudo-erotic acting-out in the transference provided the data for the interpretation of her fantasies. Revenge upon her mother was achieved by what represented an indictment of her mother's sadism by telling her physicians a bill of particulars of having been ruined by her proud, socially-prominent mother. The patient was living proof of the mother's wickedness. She often compared herself to renaissance depictions of St. Sebastian—smiling beatifically while penetrated with arrows.

Hypochondriacal attitudes with revenge as a motive betray their object-related connections by a variety of attitudes toward doctors and other health-practitioners. These people can be revered, despised, accepted, cast off in sometimes astonishing array. Drugs of various kinds, herbal remedies, acupuncture, massages are all ways in which to maintain a human connection, often with the predictable outcome of disappointment, failure, and indictment of the ineffectual. Particularly vulnerable to such complaints are hairdressers. Some patients have come to my office in hysterical tears after a haircut.

I would now like to return to the symptomatic fantasy of being hopelessly ugly or stupid and the relation of such fantasies to early images of parents or other caretakers.

A child's appearance is often a determinant for the responsiveness of adults. For those who have had experience in hospitals, orphan homes, adoption agencies and similar institutions, it is no surprise that beautiful, curly-headed blonde children drew the greatest attention. It is currently a commonplace of experience that many women want to achieve that situation by dyeing their hair blonde and having plastic surgical procedures to give them child-like features. These observations allow us to see concretely the social contribution to these phenomena.

Another contribution to social relevance is body weight. A society obsessed with both obesity and thinness presents opportunities for revenge in the behavior of adolescents and young adults. In this setting, one's own body becomes a laboratory in which revenge can be exercised. A number of anorexic patients regulate their food intake by the wish to torture their parents. Conversely, a number of children become obese by the desire to provoke their parents to endless concern about food intake. Such fantasies can be very easy to uncover in analytic work, but they are extremely difficult to change. The object-relatedness is all important and can be easily reproduced in the transference. It is a very easy trap into which the analyst may fall. Sadistic glee toward the analyst and fantasies of magical control can also be seen in patients who toy with the idea of suicide, particularly as blackmail. However difficult clinically, it is a therapeutic boon when such behavior involves the analyst. The "here-and-now" phenomenon becomes dramatically played out, and, however difficult, the inclusionary involvement of the analyst becomes subject to analytic scrutiny in an intense fashion. The revenge motive can sometimes emerge clearly and consciously. The conventional psychotherapy setting, once or twice a week, is not usually suitable for such exposition; it is insufficiently intense.

HATRED OF THE SELF AND MASOCHISTIC EXHIBITIONISM

The need to present oneself as ugly and repulsive is often mimicry, another fantasy of the living depiction of a "bad" parent with whom the child is identified. Sometimes this "uglification" of self is to insure the depiction of having been ruined to the point where no love would be forthcoming from the world. The agency for such depiction is frequently in this culture, via hair and clothes. (The preponderance of such patients I have seen have been women.) Sometimes this can be achieved by a claim for attention via ugliness, a variant form of exhibitionism.

Clinical vignette:

A basically attractive woman made herself conspicuous at her job by having her hair butchered by her father's barber, who knew little about women's hair. She wore baggy, shapeless clothes of drab camouflage colors and a bedraggled coat with a ratty fur collar. None of this would have been remarkable if not for her being in the fashion business. She told me one day that she would not be noticed wearing fashionable clothes in her business, so she arranged to "look like something the cat dragged in." It also served, with her haircut, as an indictment of her father, who never encouraged her femininity. This was dramatically turned around by coming to a session with her hair fashionably styled, wearing a beautiful dress, high-heeled shoes and swathed in perfume. She ignored any intervention that it was done for me, insisting upon a fantasy that another physician in my building was my consultant or supervisor and it was done for *him*. He represented her oblivious father to whom her attractive femininity could be proved by seductive display. Only after much working-through of defense could she admit that part of the behavior was targeted at me. For months she was in conflict about either appearing attractive or hiding in camouflage. In a dramatic session in which she revealed her exhibitionistic adolescent wish to show her father her breasts and the resultant wish to hide her breasts could she reveal the extent of her erotic transference.

Analysis of these fantasies allowed her to take pride in her attractiveness. Her analysis ended with finding a man who loved her, deflowered her, and married her. She quickly had a number of children, vowing to be a good mother unlike her own mother, who had disdained her as a rival.

BONDAGE AND MASOCHISM

A frequent source of intense pleasure for some patients has been the fantasy, and the action, of being tied up or immobilized during sexual encounters. This can be either active or passive or both. I have also seen this phenomenon in several patients as a solitary masturbatory phenomenon. One patient, on occasion, accompanied the self-bondage by a gesture toward self-strangulation as an attempt to heighten sexual excitement; as we know, this procedure has occasionally caused death. Bondage phenomena are always (in my experience) accompanied by elaborate fantasies about controlling the victim, sometimes loved, and preventing the victim's escape. Alternative fantasies sometimes are to prevent being harmed by the bound "slave." (Michelangelo's bound slaves, now in the Louvre, illustrate this phenomenon.)

Two clinical vignettes:

a. A woman fearful of being hurt in intercourse and hurt by abandonment, early in adult life, united these anxieties in a unified sexual fantasy and behavior which reproduced some aspects of a childhood beating

152

fantasy. She would convince a man that he should be tied to the bed with silk scarves. She reported that no one had ever turned her down. When in the course of the analysis her fantasies turned to me tying her down to the couch, she allowed a lover to tie her down to his couch. The behavior was to repair object-loss and prevent it. To have herself tied down was to prevent herself, symbolically, from escaping the analysis which was becoming too hot to handle. Her sadism toward others and to herself was now out in the open. Revenge against an abandoning father became evident despite earlier denials.

b.   A male patient, abandoned by his mother in childhood, had an overpowering need to trust a *willing* lover. Finding this a difficult achievement, he became a self-contained unit self and object. He would truss himself and ejaculate with the fantasy that the woman-in-him was prevented from escaping. When he attempted the procedure homosexually, he was terrified that he would be murdered; this fantasy was linked to the idea that his mother wanted to abort him in utero. He was depicting his mother's hatred toward him plus his attachment to her.

THE BEATING FANTASY TURNED ON THE SELF—THE REVENGE OF THE VICTIM-SIBLING UPON THE PATIENT'S OWN SELF

As mentioned before, the fantasy "a child is being beaten" has been a consistent clinical finding in many patients with masochistic characterological symptoms. An elaboration of rivalries, jealousies and wishes for incestuous sexual gratification had early been presented by Freud as an aspect of his attempt to analyze his daughter Anna. She subsequently attempted analysis with Lou Andreas-Salome and wrote a superb paper on her own beating fantasies presented in disguised form.

In the more commonplace beating fantasy as seen in certain women, the father is depicted as beating the rival and thus serving as the model of sexual intercourse viewed as a sadistic act. A certain number of male patients have presented fantasies of the mother beating a child by spanking and have often found prostitutes to act this out, sometimes accompanied by intercourse and sometimes by masturbation. In these scenarios, the masochistic wish is linked with a moral imperative: the need for punishment in order to achieve orgasm.

This behavior can sometimes be carried out playfully so that no one is hurt.

However, sometimes it can be carried out dangerously in which serious pain can be inflicted or sustained. Piercings, penetrations, burning with lighted cigarettes or candle-wax have been described to me.

Clinical vignette:

A man seriously enraged over the birth of a brother during the patient's puberty wished to see him beaten by the mother. A profound sense of guilt turned this wish back upon himself, and he contrived subsequently to be beaten and humiliated by both men and women as punishment for his vengeful fantasies earlier in life. All these factors were renewed in the analysis. (It should be understood that, as with many of the patients, these fantasies were not central to the complex psychopathology but were found, as it were, on the edges, lived out in the transference.)

CONCLUSION

Vengeful fantasy and a need for revenge against rivals and those who have induced a sense of narcissistic mortification are universal fantasies. Sometimes they are merely evanescent and sometimes they claim the entirety of the patient's inner life. For some reason, usually object-sparing out of persistent object-need, these fantasies can be exerted against the self. The fantasies are difficult to analyze and difficult for the patient to give up, since they represent a cherished object-tie and their loss would give rise to deep loneliness. They represent the best clinical evidence of the concept: resistance of the id—the tie to the original objects and to the original modes of gratification. Hypochondriasis is a variant form of vengeful self-torture. Bondage fantasies are concrete representations of holding on to the object and exerting control. In the end, the deepest aspect of human attachment is to retain the tie, no matter what the cost.

Moral masochism and erotic masochism are at heart linked since they are connected to only different aspects of the same object-ties.

REFERENCES

Arlow, J. A. (1980) .The Revenge Motive in the Primal Scene. *Journal of the American Psychoanalytic Association* 28:519–541.

Catullus (84 BC–54 BC). *The Poems of Catullus,* transl. Guy Lee, Oxford: Oxford World's Classics, 2009.

Forster, E.M. (1910). *Howard's End*. Garden City: Dover Thrift Editions, 2018.

Freud, S. (1919) 'A Child is Being Beaten' A Contribution to the Study of the Origin of Sexual Perversions. *Standard Edition* 17:175–204.

Goethe, J.W. (1795–96). *Wilhelm Meister's: Apprenticeship and Travels,* transl. Thomas Carlyle, 2016.

Loewenstein, R. M. (1957). A Contribution to the Psychoanalytic Theory of Masochism. Journal of the American Psychoanalytic Association 5:197–234.

Novick, K. K. & Novick, J. (1987). The Essence of Masochism. Psychoanalytic Study of the Child 42:353–384.

Sappho (300 BC). *A New Translation of the Complete Works* ed. and transl. Diane J. Rayor & André Lardinois. Cambridge: Cambridge University Press, 2023.

Shakespeare, W. (1590–1605). *Shakespeare's Sonnets & Poems.* Washington, DC: Folger Shakespeare Library, 2006.

Shakespeare, W. (1603). *Othello.* Washington, DC: Folger Shakespeare Library, 2003.

Solomon (971 and 931 BC.). *The Wisdom of King Solomon: A Volume Containing: Proverbs Ecclesiastes, The Wisdom of Solomon, The Song of Solomon, The Psalms of Solomon, and The Odes of Solomon* ed. Dennis Logan, transl. J R. Harris, transl. Jerome, transl. King James, cont. Joseph B Lumpkin, Spring Run: Rolled Scroll Publishing 2020.

Sophocles (430–420 bc). *Oedipus The King or Oedipus Tyrannus.* Independently published, 2021.

Spenser, E. (1590–1596). *The Faerie Queene,* ed. Thomas P. Roche. London: Penguin Classics, 1979.

CHAPTER 10

For the Psychoanalytic Forum:
The Fear of Intimacy

I

In a remarkably perceptive commentary upon *Jane Austen's Heroines* (subtitled *Intimacy in Human Relationships*) the Australian critic John Hardy speaks of Jane Austen not as a clever delineator of comedies of manners but as someone who painstakingly depicts the intimacy between her heroines and the men they marry. This intimacy "involves a mutual recognition of the other person and leads to a shared privacy... something has caught between two people [and] there is above all the need to acknowledge and respond to the other person.'" Hardy's comment touches upon an increasingly common problem both in society in general and the practice of psychoanalysis in particular. Here I speak of the *fear of intimacy.*

Let me begin with a concrete clinical example reported to me by a colleague whose work I was supervising. (The clinical data have been disguised for purposes of confidentiality.) A young woman sought consultation with a view toward some treatment because of a persistent discontent tinged by low-level depression and mild anxiety. Within the first few consultative hours it appeared that the predominant affect was actually *loneliness* which was identified and named *by the analyst*. (This constituted the first important intervention-interpretation.) The patient's reaction was of both surprise and acknowledgement. She had never been able to sustain any long-range relationship either of love or friendship and despite numerous acquaintances and many short-term sexual connections she always ended up alone.

The colleague wisely suggested that an extended once-weekly consultation was in order in that he became aware that the patient was afraid of closeness. The patient had her own ideas of an appropriate psychological treatment for her—it was to be short-term, limited to focusing on her "current problems," and moreover she was disdainful about what she termed "Freudian preoccupation with the past." In brief, she wanted the treatment to reproduce the circumstances of her failed relations to other people throughout her life. Now it turns out that this is not a rare phenomenon— that all of you have seen such patients, I am sure.

Very large numbers of people are wary, if not fearful, of close human connections. They cannot commit themselves to marry, to stay married, to endure close friendships, or institutional loyalties. They panic at the thought of commitment, abandon spouses and children, indiscriminately shift geographic location, and quite strikingly cannot sustain the intimacy of the psychoanalytic situation. The fear of intimacy is one of the most formidable resistances to analysis. Currently, despite many rationalizations offered by patients it is one of the major determinants for wanting to avoid analysis altogether.

However, you may ask, "Don't many of these patients yearn for intimacy?" Here, the answer is clearly "yes" and we may attempt to clarify this paradox by a review of our clinical and technical experience.

II

Let me begin by giving you my own idiosyncratic view of the psychoanalytic endeavor. With Siegfried Bernfeld I think psychoanalysis is a sort of conversation, albeit strangely structured. It is a situation of shared privacy with somewhat different contributions made by the two participants. By and large the analyst usually maintains the private and confidential nature of the interchange except for a rare consultation with another colleague. The patient who values the intimacy and the shared privacy tends not to talk about the analysis with others it is a genuinely private matter. Certain patients, especially those who cannot sustain intimate connections, tend to talk about the analysis indiscriminately, a process which vitiates transference intensity through dilution. Those analysts who themselves have trouble with intimacy seem to have a tendency to gossip about their patients. If the two participants constantly take the work of the analysis out of the consulting room and spread it about to others, the necessary emotional intensity for analytic work dissipates.

The so-called ritual of the analytic work: the quiet room, the recumbent posture upon the couch, the analyst seated out of the patient's sight—all facilitate the controlled regression which we hope to achieve, a regression in Kris' felicitous phrase "in the service of the ego." We are aiming through the patient's attempt at free association and our concomitant attempt at the "freely hovering attention" to create a circumstance in which the patient's pathogenic conflicts are *re-lived*, not merely *retold*. All of this proceeds in the atmosphere of a helpful protectiveness offered by the analyst and facilitated by the analyst's interventions, especially those directed toward the awareness of unconscious resistances (and their intrapsychic counterparts in defense).

In the psychoanalytic endeavor, my experience has led me to believe that the greatest predictor of good analytic result is to be found in the history of the patient's object relations, not merely in diagnosis. Those patients unable to maintain love and friendship begin with a severe handicap because it is just that capacity which allows the patient to enter into the "conversation of analysis."

One of the earliest comments upon this problem mentioned in the psychoanalytic literature was Abraham's 1919 paper on the auto-analyst. There he describes a certain kind of envious narcissistic person who cannot sustain a "shared" work and must make *all* of his *own* interpretations. Now intimacy in all its forms involves sharing. Since as analysts we often misunderstand our patients, sometimes come to appallingly .dumb conclusions and gay egregiously wrong things, we need the constant shared input from our patients to keep things specifically relevant to *them* and not to some generically determined agenda of psychoanalytic preconception. The most frequent of these analytic preconceptions are about our etiological fantasies about early childhood development and theories of pathogenesis. We must be very cautious about holding onto reductionistic theories of pathogenesis relying on preconceptions of universal early mother-child interaction and basing our therapeutic efforts on such speculations. We and our patients are better served by the slow derivation of our data from the transference situation, understanding that the same clinical phenomenon (in this instance we speak of "intimacy") can have in different patients different origins. A shared outcome does not bespeak a shared origin.

III

I will now attempt to draw your attention to some of the many different origins of the "fear of intimacy.". Let me begin by looking at a commonplace conscious view of the problem offered by *some* patients. *They consciously* fear closeness as a trap which will lead them to feel tortured. Such a fantasy may have many differing origins. I will illustrate some by brief clinical vignettes drawn both from my own practice and from that of colleagues.

A young woman viewed intimacy as a road to torture because of a long-held beating fantasy accompanying her masturbation. In the analysis she feared a passive sexual surrender in which she would feel enslaved to a man who could rouse her to orgasm. In the analysis she wanted to do everything herself—a counterpart to masturbation.

B. Another woman with a conscious fear of being trapped and tortured was very frightened of the upsurge of her own sadism whenever she was close to anyone. This was most marked in a sexual situation when she had the impulse to strike or beat the man she was with. Her avoidances were object-sparing. She was identified with her mother who frequently vilified her father.

Here is another variation on this theme:

C. An older man who had experienced a failed analysis was afraid of being entrapped in another failed analysis. He experienced only a bland disappointment in the previous analyst—a much older woman. A lifelong fear of closeness—he never married until late in life—was related to the following sequence of fantasy: intimacy would lead to aggression, desperate guilt and the aggression turned on himself in the form of self-reproaches and self-torture. All of this was experienced as "depression." This eventuated in a low-keyed blandness and withdrawal. The fear of intimacy was a defense against the emergence of aggression toward the disappointing object: in this instance the mother who betrayed him by having other babies. The prior woman analyst had a busy practice of many celebrities.

Here again is a related theme:

D. *Jealousy as an interference with intimacy*: A man, the eldest of three children, wanted to be the only patient of the analyst. Always fearful of being intimate with anyone, he was afraid of being displaced. He was afraid to get close because he saw it as the first step to abandonment. Closeness led to the torture of loneliness and isolation.

The conscious fear of "dependency" is offered frequently as a rationalization for avoiding commitment to other people. It is a commonplace fantasy about what is viewed as a danger of analysis. This anxiety that proximity will bring "dependency" and evoke "needs" in the patient often has a profound component of disordered conscience as its backdrop.

This too can have many different origins:

E. A woman expressed a fear of "dependency" at the outset. Anxious about intimacy she longed for someone to offer reassurance and comfort for her guilty sado-masochistic fantasy life. She had the conscious fear that up close she would be found ugly and repulsive, that is that unconscious vicissitudes of the sense of guilt would be translated into "bad" and "ugly.'" She grew up in a family where self-reliance was an ideal toward which she should strive. To ask for closeness, comfort of reassurance was testimony to weakness. (Her fears of criticism stemmed from projections of her own super-ego and unconscious need for punishment.)

F. A man with a severe moral masochistic character structure spent all of his life with a sense of pride that no woman had "trapped" him. Both he and his father had been constantly criticized by his mother. He was intolerant of criticism either from others or from himself. His conscience was based upon identification with his mother.

However, he projected those criticisms *upon others* recognizing nothing of their internal origins in his own superego. He projected upon the analyst that the analyst did not tolerate intimacy, love, aggression, anxiety, depression, failure, or success. Interpretations, however tactfully offered, were viewed as criticisms . The problem of unconscious guilt is that it is unconscious, as are its origins in relation to the original objects. He was trying to make the analysis Into a replica of his past and his aim was to quit the analysis and thus run away from home.

The fantasied danger of "dependency" took another form in a case reported to me:

G. An older somewhat isolated woman came to a young female colleague after a failed analysis with a man the patient viewed as "too empathic." Very drawn to this man from the beginning she became increasingly anxious over her burgeoning sexual wishes in the transference which she could not bring herself to report. She longed to be in her sessions but was frightened of the analyst's sympathy, empathic responses and occasional self-revelations. She felt him to be "invasive" and "seductive" and trying to get things out of her, reminiscent of being given enemas by her mother. She fled to someone she felt was "cooler" and more "professional "

IV

Let me now return to a question raised earlier: What of those patients fearful of intimacy but who yearn for it? I would like to focus on this issue by some other clinical examples gathered over the years.

H., a bisexual man unable to sustain love or friendships beyond a few months at best had had a number of evanescent brief psychotherapies. The men and women in is life, his friends, his psychotherapists were all disappointments of the deepest sort. In essence, everything was a "one-night stand.": He could not abide intimacy with someone he considered "unworthy." He was searching for a mirror-image narcissistically congruent person. He could not understand, at first, that intimacy depends upon the recognition of the separateness and differences between the two people involved. Both his yearning and his disappointment were linked to intolerance of difference. Behind this facade was the wish to be like his mother and be appreciated by her. In his sexual life he was always blurring distinctions between masculine and feminine.

Now let me turn to certain other people frightened of intimacy who search out others where they might achieve a sample or modicum of intimacy. Without concrete clinical illustration because of complex issues of confidentiality, I will begin with those men, *and* women, who seek out prostitutes. I will also refer to certain patients who view, in fantasy, the analyst as a prostitute who is paid to offer a substitute for love, to accept abuse or mete out punishment. Here the search is for a time-limited "pseudo-intimacy." It is interesting that certain people will pour their hearts out to prostitutes, telling them things they could never bear to tell those toward whom they might be supposed, by the world, to be close. Shameful confessions can be made to degraded objects because they too are imagined to be performing a shameful task. For the moment there is a shared but evanescent " intimacy. The essence of the experience is that it is time-limited and often takes place in a slightly (or grossly) altered state of consciousness, isolated from the rest of life.   Now some analytic patients tell us that they experience the analytic session in an analogous fashion: separated from the rest of their lives. This helps us to understand how certain socially-isolated persons can be in various treatments, thought successful by their analysts, and never seem to improve their relations to other people. The "pseudo-intimacy" is taken as if it were real, not merely a sequestered foreign body of experience. Contrary to the opinions of many, the analytic situation is not one in which recovery from isolation can take place without concomitant object-related experience in the outside world.   In my view, analysis is *not* like practicing for life, it is about understanding how one leads one's life and why we got that way. The glimmer of change may begin in the transference situation but it requires an interchange with *others*, a 24-hour-a-day interchange, to see real results. Moreover the analyst has to be seen genuinely as a real person with a real life outside the analytic work.

V

Next, let me turn our attention to a problem best exemplified by attempts at the analysis of certain persons of narcissistic character structure, Here I refer to those whose negativism and withdrawal from intimate relationships is based upon the fear of passivity (especially sexual passivity) in relation to others and those who fear that closeness will impel them into headlong regression in the direction of psychosis (Anna Freud) . These patients treat closeness not simply as a danger but as a *terror.*

I. A woman read and re-read *The Story of O* with mounting excitement, horror and panic.She realized that sexual enslavement and mistreatment was something she deeply desired and feared.She imagined herself in such a situation with her young woman analyst, leaped from the couch and felt she would "go crazy" on the spot. The patient had been frightened that *any* closeness would be an invitation to torture and regressive psychosis that would reduce her to an infantile state.

This should put us in reminder of a caution offered by Paul Federn more than 50 years ago, In discussing the attempt at the analysis or psychotherapy of certain schizophrenic patients he warned that misguided attempts of forcing such persons into socialization carried hazards of precipitous regression, In particular, he pointed out the danger to certain very sick patients in falling in love. Where the healthier person experiences the blurring of ego-boundaries as the pleasurable state of "being one" the sicker patient sees such boundary shift as the danger of being enveloped and devoured.

VI

Finally, let me tell you of a problem I have seen, but about which I cannot give any concrete data, again for reasons of confidentiality. Analysts are not immune from the problems of our patients. When we think about problems about, and fear of, intimacy we quickly see that *certain* analysts are immersed in this difficulty. The shapes the problem takes are not only about the analyst's personal life and the analyst's own analysis. The problem characteristically invades technique and one's everyday relationship to the patients. Some fearful analysts hide behind the *relative* neutrality of the analytic work to get that stance to serve as *anonymity* or *disguise* or *mask*. Fearful of real emotional closeness for the purpose of the therapeutic effort they become sticklers for rules of analytic correctness almost always in the direction of stiffness and distance. For certain patients this exaggerated distance is seen as a protection, and such patients complain if they think the analyst friendly or concerned; the very patients we are speaking of—that is, those fearful of intimacy—might view the distant defended analyst as an *ideal*.

Another variation on this problem is the analyst whose personal life is distant and chaotic and who attempts to achieve a pseudo-intimacy by excessive warmth often to the point of falling in love with one or more of the patients. Here too the problem is to be understood in its usually *time-limited* nature. To those who think that this kind of emotional response is a replacement or substitute for what was missing in the infant's life with the mother, I would remind them of a comment made by Clifford Yorke in a recent paper: "...What kind of mother, given a choice, would see her child for just fifty minutes on five out of seven days in the week?":

VII

In conclusion, I would like to alert you to the fact that an increasing number of patients have very great fears of intimacy, and are afraid of commitment and the needed constancy of that commitment. They see attachment as a danger and want to avoid it. Such patients are often specifically terrified of the commitment of a psychoanalysis and this has to be confronted and addressed when considering an appropriate form of treatment. Analysis is *not always* the appropriate treatment, without considerable preparatory work. My own failures in this effort have been to be insufficiently respectful of the desperate profundity of resistance offered by the "fear of intimacy." For some patients it is insuperable.

SECTION 2

I. CLINICAL REALITIES OF TREATING PATIENTS AFRAID OF INTIMACY

In this portion of today's discussion, I would like to take up some practical aspects of helping those who are afraid of closeness. Moreover, I will try while thinking of the potential amelioration of the problem to venture some speculations upon some concepts of etiology,

First, let me give you my views of analytic technique in general. No two analyses are the same any more than any two people are the same. (Having treated a number of twins I assure you that my own experience is that not even twins are similar, no less the same.)

The history of psychoanalysis begins with Freud's trying to find a unitary theory of neurosogenesis based upon the premier medical scientific model of this era: Koch's postulates for tuberculosis. Prove an etiology and prove a diagnosis. Treatment follows: Find the noxious agent and attempt to get rid of it. The view presented in the 19th century Neuropsychoses of Defense papers was like Hoyle's 20th century hypotheses of the origin of the universe: a big bang event. Through sexual overstimulation, now repressed along with its strangulated affect, the original trauma found its distorted expression in symptoms. The treatment then would consist of another big-bang release. Through the recovery of the amnesia for the traumatic event, a massive release of the strangulated affect (i.e. cathartic abreaction) would take place and the symptoms which had served as symbolic partial-discharge would be removed. With the awareness that neurosogenesis was infinitely more complicated, with many maturational and developmental vicissitudes, with complex issues of object-relations and subsequent object choices and the new awareness of the röle of aggression and of complex ego-functions, the unitary theories were clearly seen to be inadequate and indeed erroneous. With the end of a unitary theory of etiology there followed an end of unitary theories of treatment. Again, no two analyses are the same. Moreover, there is no "standard technique" of analysis. To echo Kris, there is only a standard against which the necessary variations can be measured The clinical process of the concept of the fear of intimacy does not tell us of etiology nor how to treat it. That amounts to clinical exploration.

I would also like to give you my own view of concept of fantasy, which is central to our discussion today, Fantasies are not total inventions; they are imaginative elaborations upon experience with real events as the nidus upon which the fantasy is constructed. They are powerfully related to the developmental phase in which real events took place, how they were perceived at the time, and how they may have been elaborated at perhaps another time, They are charged by feelings of sexuality, jealousy, envy, aggression and wishes for revenge, for love, sympathy and the need for punishment . Fantasies are our syntheses of memory and imagination.

II. THE INITIAL INTERVIEWS

Very few patients fearful of intimacy offer that fear as a presenting complaint. Rather, they tell you of failed object-relations of the past, almost always placing the major responsibility of any such failure on the other person. Parents, lovers, wives, husbands, children, teachers, friends,

168

doctors, psychiatrists, and analysts have all been weighed in the balances and found wanting. Now these complaints may be extremely varied, but the major issue is that the *predominant* responsibility for failures in closeness is located by the patient in the outside world. That is not to say that the patient does not accept that *some* of the problem is an internal one. In practical terms, think of the number of patients you have seen with such an initial presentation. Now think of the number of times you may have thought: But I can help this patient. A history of unhappy difficulties in closeness, as told to a psychotherapist/analyst, sometimes serves as a seductive beginning of another failure in intimacy. Whatever your hopeful expectations, it is the structuralization of the neurosis, that is, its motivated patterned repetitiveness, which tends to determine transference behavior. Your personality enters the picture by giving shape and intensity to the transference, but those afraid of intimacy with others in the past are likely to be afraid with you. Those whose fantasies of closeness were those of entrapment and torture are likely (sooner or later) to see the treatment as a trap and you as the torturer. Transference is not an illusion, it is the triumph of memory over perception transference fantasies do not seem real to the patient, they are real. If the work is well-conducted and the pathogenic conflicts and events are relived (not merely retold), the etiological factors will be *alive,* not archeological artefacts.

What we do with these factors and how the patients respond to our interventions is *not* predictable. We must be prepared for a certain number of fearful patients to flee the treatment declaring us to be the re-incarnation of all their previous evils, their ears shut to interpretation and the trajectory of their lives continuing on the course of self-fulfilling prophecy, We are talking of a psychological disturbance of a discouraging, sometimes malignant coloration. The fantasy of being rescued by love that some such patients evince is severely tested by their often being unable to sustain ordinary kindness and concern. So much for the gravity of the task This gravity is hard to believe when one is young, inexperienced and enthusiastic, Long experience may allow you to remain enthusiastic, but also wary of your ability to alter poignant desperately-held defensive patterns. *All these factors are at work in the first interview.*

The first principle of initial interviews is that we take a good history in psychoanalytic terms. That is, not by the question and answer method but by allowing the patient to tell the story without too many interferences from us. We are not only listening to the history but how it is told to us. Among other things we want to know if the patient is open or guarded. Remember that a substantial aspect of resistance, especially around issues stirring the affect of shame, is that patients consciously withhold much that they think puts them in a bad light. Not all resistance is unconscious, and not all patients showing a seeming open countenance are "open" to inquiry.

What we, and the great poets and novelists of the past, know about character is that it is relatively continuous. In fact, what has been so striking about the longitudinal studies (beginning in childhood) conducted by John McDevitt and by the Yale Child Study Center (Ritvo, Solnit, et al.) are the *continuities* throughout a lifetime of characterological issues.

From the beginning of our contact with the patient we want to know the history of their object-ties, their capacities for love, friendship, loyalty and truthfulness in their dealings with those around them. We want to know, in some detail, about their rôle in, and reactions to, failure in object-connectedness. All of us have experienced disappointments in love, no life is without failures and we want to know what responses there were to those painful events This aspect of history may provide us with some short-term tentative predictions of the patient's capacity to tolerate psychotherapeutic treatment in general and psychoanalysis in particular.

One should not be afraid to conduct an extended evaluation of patients who show the fear of intimacy or who suggest it by a history of repeated inability to sustain object-ties or to sustain prior treatment, It is not infrequently an error to prematurely start an analysis with a patient for whom such closeness is analogous to a phobic situation.   One should proceed cautiously. A number of the patients I have seen with this problem had been in prior psychotherapies or analyses, sometimes with help with other problems but with the major object-avoidance and the inability to love essentially being untouched Find out what happened in the previous treatments. You are likely to find that those treatments are dismissed in a few words often with the same complaint level led against the analyst that was level led against the parents. Don't assume that the prior analyst was an incompetent, and you are going to do it better. The prior doctor may have missed things, made mistakes and showed insensitivities. You will too; none of us are perfect. *The issue is what did the patient and doctor do about things that inevitably went wrong* as they do in all human experiences. Was there mutual understanding of the imperfections of everyday life? Those who are most afraid of intimacy tend to be the least forgiving of events experienced as wounds, especially wounds to narcissism. This holds true for some analysts as well as some patients.

The patient afraid of intimacy, often laboring under the strictures of narcissistic character disorder, sometimes shows a strange grandiosity. This is easily projected onto the new doctor. You are told how special you are, how brilliant, how unlike Dr. X or the parents. Be cautious, do not be seduced into thinking you will be perceived as being so much better when the work gets under way.

On occasion, patients afraid of intimacy need a preparatory psychotherapy if they are to tolerate an analysis. During this psychotherapeutic introduction to a potential analysis, one must pay particular attention to what has transpired in a process-fashion in a failed prior treatment or in a failed love-affair. There are usually attempts to rationalize or explain these failures. Then too, there are "pseudo-insights," derived from previous psychotherapies or even from family and friends; these "pseudo-insights" tend to be formulaic attempts at explanation of behavior and are usually psychological clichés. With some regularity, "pseudo-insights" are not fully owned by the patient; they take such shape as: "Dr. So-and-so told me that my depression is only anger turned on myself. " These are not derived from self-observation and consequent exploration with another person; they are foreign bodies which are incorporated without being digested. They actually represent distance from the ideas and affects and distance from the person quoted. They are partial identifications, not the consequence of intimacy, but the outcome of defenses against the potential intimacy. Sometimes these "pseudo-insights" are mockeries of the analyst.

III. SPECIAL PROBLEMS OF TRANSFERENCE

Certain patients terrified of fantasies of sexual submissiveness and sexual thralldom must keep great distance from the analyst and from all others as well. Some of such submission fantasies have been part of the masturbation fantasies of adolescence, but some have earlier fantasy origins and still others originate in actual intrusive, abusive sexual behavior by trusted persons of the past: parents, teachers, doctors, clergymen and servants. Some patients' fear of closeness is connected to the idea that they will be exposed as limited, stupid, infantile, and sexually incompetent. (The fear of being found bodily defective is not uncommon in those overstimulated by repeated exposure to the parental nakedness and parental sexual activity.) Some are afraid that their ongoing sadistic fantasies will be punished by the sadism of others. It is not always easy to distinguish between those factors which are the result of childhood and adolescent masturbatory fantasy and those determined by the real behavior of adults. Nor is it easy to distinguish sadism arising from within as contrasted to a sadistic response to maltreatment.

All these factors will color and shape transference, often with the view of the analyst as a sadistic monster, a view held with utmost conviction. A potential defense, frequently used, is to denigrate the analyst and the analytic procedure as bad, if not actually useless. For some such patients the closer they seem to get, the more they decide that the object (analyst, friend, teacher, lover) is defective.

All of this becomes much more threatening to patients if they experience the analyst as a charismatic figure with whom they are tempted to identify deeply and thus to merge with that powerful image. This can lead to a fear of regression that may be experienced by the patient as a fear of psychosis. The patient, if on the couch, wants to sit up; if in the midst of sone exploration of fantasy wants to limit conversation to recent concrete reality. If coming frequently, the patient cuts down the number of sessions. Anything to avoid the "dangerous" closeness.

The patient gives us cues about technical issues. For some, we have to not only allow them but encourage them to proceed at their own pace in order to ultimately confront the "phobic-like" response. For some others we have to try to get them to confront their avoidances in order to forestall endless and fruitless treatments in which no good result can be expected. At all events, try not to be too intrusive, or seductive; do not try to "engage" the patient beyond the patient's tolerances. If they want to quit, do not restrain them beyond the boundaries of simple interpretations.

The interpretation of transference and resistance remains the center of our task; the results with such patients in our accepting atmosphere are not always felicitous no matter who the analyst is or what the analyst's theoretical orientation. For some, intimacy is a life-long terror ameliorated only by avoidance. In the end, as I said earlier, we have to be respectful of the reasons for terror, the power of memory and the pull of fantasy and not be grandiose in our therapeutic ambitions.

REFERENCES

Abraham,. K. (1919). A Particular form of Neurotic Resistance Against the Psycho-Analytic Method. In: *Selected Papers on Psychoanalysis*. Oxfordshire: Taylor and Francis, 1988.

Federn, P. (1934) The Analysis of Psychotics. *International Journal of Psychoanalysis* 15:209–214.

Hardy, P. (1984). *Jane Austen's Heroines: Intimacy in Human Relationships*. . Oxfordshire: Routledge, Kegan & Paul, 1985.

Reage, P. (1954). *Story of O: A Novel* New York: Ballantine Books, 2013.

CHAPTER 11

On The Reaction of Men to the Menopause of Women

Despite the centuries-old Greek injunction: "Know thyself," psychoanalytic experience of the past hundred years has taught us how variable is self-knowledge. Even more variable is the knowledge of the inner lives of others and among the areas of greatest ignorance and confusion is the knowledge of men about women and women about men.

All human beings consider themselves to be experts upon human nature. For the most part, this consists of relatively baseless extrapolations and projections of aspects of our own selves upon others. Frequently, men think about women as if they were other men, and women think about men as if they were other women. Most confusing is the viewpoint that children are merely small adults, with further blurring of the distinctions between boys and girls.

The topic of menopause has long been taboo. It is therefore not surprising that many analysts, women as well as men, claim to have little knowledge about the subject. More puzzling are the claims of some that the almost ubiquitous human responses to this developmental phase are pathological.

Thus, the reactions of women to menopause have often focused upon pathology such as "involutional melancholia." The reactions of men to the female menopause have tended to be ignored, though every man with a menopausal wife or friend or patient has had reactions to that extended series of events.

I will address my remarks to material drawn from the psychoanalytic situation. (Psychoanalytic data is essentially different from the data drawn from brief psychotherapies or from anecdote where the prevalent myths and denials about menopause claim the field.) I will report upon data from five analyses of men involved with menopausal women with a brief aside into the world-wide myths about witchcraft which arose out of one of the analyses.

When Leo Stone wrote his seminal paper on the "widening scope" of psychoanalysis he was referring to attempts to analyze patients with greater problems than had been considered analyzable by many practitioners up to that time. The widening scope now includes many older patients some of whom return for re-analyses, This includes many menopausal women as well as men connected to them who themselves are undergoing their own involutional biological changes. The concept of a "climacterium," or "dangerous age," is now many thousands of years old. The Latin grammarian and rhetorician Aulus Gellius (AD 123–170), in his work *Attic Nights*[3] commented on a then extant letter written by the Emperor Augustus to his grandson on the emperor's sixty-fourth birthday. Augustus writes, "It has been observed during a long period of human recollection, and found to be true, that for almost all old men the sixty-third year of their ageing attended with danger, and with some disaster involving either serious bodily illness, or loss of life, or mental suffering. Therefore, those who are engaged in the study of matters and terms of that kind call that period of life the 'climacteric.'"

The word climacteric derives from the Greek meaning the rungs of a ladder Years that were multiples of 7 (or 9) were supposed to be dangerous (7, 14, 21) the grand "climacteric" being 63. From the beginning of recorded

---

3 Book XV, V1.V11 line 1

history ideas about the "climacterium" in men and the menopause in women have been attended by superstition and magic as well as a kernel of truth.

The specific data from which these psychoanalytic observations have been drawn come from the re-analyses of three older men and from the analysis of one young man and one older man. The material has been disguised for purposes of confidentiality. The conclusions or suggestions drawn suffer from the smallness of the number of patients and the necessarily limited nature of the experiences. Nevertheless, the data may be worth some scrutiny because there is a reflection of many commonly held ideas.

Men vary very widely in their reactions to the menopause of women, The middle years of life offer to both men and women a series of developmental challenges of the deepest importance.

As with other developmental challenges, the individual's response is likely to be closely linked with the prior structure of character. In particular, it focusses attention on the problem of *narcissism* as one approaches the prospects of physical decline and its inevitable concomitant—the shadow of death. But, before the end there are many years that are viewed as a relief of certain biological, familial, and social tensions. Interspersed with all are irruptions of disappointments, the mourning for declining or lost functions and the endocrine and cardiovascular disturbances which tend to be experienced with depressive emotions of greatly varying intensity and duration.

Just as in earlier phases of development, the great testing grounds of these forces are in the fields of work and love.

In actual clinical experience the issue of aging in the spheres of work and love cannot often be separated. Declining abilities, beginning alterations of memory (beginning with names) and changes in judgment vary quite widely. On one side is the sagacity of age, on the other side is the folk-wisdom of "no fool like an old fool," especially in matters of love.

The older men I am speaking about did not have reactions to the overall concept of "menopause" as such; they showed specific reactions to specific experience. They reacted to the woman's depression, irritability, vasomotor instability and "hot flashes," and to the loss of her fertility. They also reacted to the woman's distress at fertility loss, the attack upon her narcissism of certain bodily changes and to one who could not take estrogen replacements to certain masculinizing effects.

As the late politician Tip O'Neil had said "all politics is local," so too, all human reactions are specific, not generic, or global. Menopause, though sharing some common biological roots in all, is experienced differently by each woman. The reactions of the men connected to them are equally specific.

Case A: An older man, very successful in the material things of this world, returned to analysis after a gap of many years. When younger he had gone to a now-deceased famous colleague and experienced some considerable relief of a potency disturbance. He married a somewhat younger woman and seemed contented with his wife and children. Shortly before entering the re-analysis, he had experienced a return of his potency disturbance. This varied from erectile impotence to premature ejaculation to retarded ejaculation. He blamed his menopausal wife for her deteriorated physical state, her depression, and her irritability. Her loss of youthful complexion and figure brought forth a hail of scorn.

He was oblivious of his own physical decline but was preoccupied by the fear of death. His erotic life had been dominated by narcissistic object-choice. Envious of his beautiful mother's hold upon his father, he had had frequent conscious fantasies in adolescence of being a beautiful woman who could entrance a man. Unconscious to him, even through the prior analysis, was his choice of those whom he wanted to be like, women who could entrance him. He chose his wife on that basis. When she became menopausal, she "lost her magic." He soon became interested in a young worshipful woman with whom he had restored potency, identifying with her seeming excitement. Despite realizing that the young woman was more interested in his money than in his person, he divorced his wife, and settled into a life of a different sort of misery. His judgment in erotic life was impaired and his judgment in his business suffered a similar decline.

The essential reaction to his wife's aging and menopause was that she was no longer suitable for identification along narcissistic lines. In the shadowy background was the wish to be his mother controlling his father.

Case B: An older man returned to analysis after some setbacks in his professional career and some decline in self-esteem with vague depressive symptoms. He mourned the partial loss of opportunities in life and saw himself as having declining powers. He too was fearful of death. His wife, in the midst of menopause and some depression, had been galvanized into action and had returned to graduate school which was proving very difficult for her. He saw himself as having a purpose in helping her. This repeated a circumstance of early childhood in which he helped care for his chronically ill mother who viewed him as a rescuing angel. His wife viewed him similarly.

This man's adaptation to his wife's menopause repeated his rescue fantasies and subsequent behavior directed to his mother. This is another example of a pre-existing character structure repeated in middle-life, but here with beneficial results.

Case C: Another older man reacted to his wife's menopausal depression with fury and subsequent withdrawal from her. He saw her as cold and "barren" and eventually related his response to her inability to any longer be pregnant. Long buried was a pre-adolescent fantasy of wanting to be a powerful woman with large breasts who could be repeatedly pregnant. His wife's fecundity had helped to satisfy vicariously this old wish, now driven into unconsciousness. The analytic exploration of a series of pre-adolescent and adolescent fantasies permitted him to react to his wife's current needs.

Rather than being cold, she was actually more sexually responsive, a not uncommon finding in menopausal women.

Case D: A younger man in analysis became romantically involved with an older, very attractive woman who was post-menopausal. The mother of a chance acquaintance, this woman, now divorced and very successful in business, played a röle in the patient's life similar to that of the Marschallin in Strauss' opera *Der Rosenkavalier*. The patient, always terrified of making a woman pregnant, was delighted that he and his older lover did not have to use birth control. An only child, he was always concerned that his mother would have another child. In this example, the disappearance of fertility was seen as an advantage.

Without being able to provide more specific detail, there is one other experience I would like to report which presents another facet of the range of response to menopause. This concerns a wife's jealousy and paranoid jealous complaints which my patient was unable to tolerate and for which there was no behavioral basis. I was reminded of Montaigne's comment on jealousy in women: "It worms itself into them under the cloak of affection but when it once possesses them, the same causes which served as the foundation of kindness, serve as the foundation of deadly hatred." (Montaigne had other things to say about jealousy in men and false concepts of revenge.) Though I could not be sure of all the circumstances, the wife's jealousy appeared in the despair of her rapidly deteriorating physical attractiveness and her insistence that he *must* want a younger woman.

Here the patient's reaction was not to the usual depressive menopausal symptoms but to a pathological formation which seemed bewildering and out-of-character.

THE POST-MENOPAUSAL WOMAN AND THE MYTHOLOGY OF WITCHES

Some years ago, a middle-aged male patient complained that his post-menopausal wife was beginning to look like a witch. I asked what he meant. She had become quite wrinkled and thin and moreover had developed some facial hair. Now short-tempered and irritable her voice had become high-pitched and screechy. As an afterthought, he added: "That witch is making me impotent. " In a flash, we were looking at material that seemed to leap from the pages of the *Malleus Maleficarium* (1489), the Inquisitor's Manual. In medieval Europe, especially in Italy and Southern France, witches were seen to be the cause of what was termed the "ligature" the production of impotence by a magic or evil eye exerted only by women. "Impotent ia ex maleficio" became a cause for accusations of witchcraft and figured prominently in the deliberations of theologians and church jurists in considerations of annulment of marriage or of divorce.

In the mythologies of every European society the witch figures prominently with heightened importance being given to the concept following a papal bull of Innocent VIII 1484: <u>summis desiderantes affectibus</u> (*Encyclopedia Britannica*, 11th Edition). "Witches" were primarily old and poor women though rarely young women or men were accused. In England, the county of Essex alone sent 90 women to the scaffold between 1566 and 1645. In that latter year the witch-finder Matthew Hopkins executed 19 women in a single day. Cambridge, Essex, Norfolk, and Suffolk were known as witch country. In the 14 months that Matthew Hopkins continued his search for witches, he put 400 mostly old women to death. Hopkins had a theory that these old women nursed imps at a supernumerary nipple which might be represented by any number of skin blemishes. Sure badges of the witch were a crone-like appearance, a snaggle-tooth, sunken cheeks and a hairy lip (Folklore, Myths and Legends of Britain, 1973, *London Reader's*

Digest). The recognition marks of the witch were exaggerated views of the bodily changes of very old and poor women of the time.

One facet of the supposed life of witches was their imagined sexual appetites and their participation in bizarre sexual rites with the Devil, Satan, sometimes depicted as having a bifid penis, could enter his partner vaginally and rectally simultaneously. Where did these bizarre ideas arise about the sexual powers of old women to make men impotent and to have unquenchable sexual desires to be serviced by the Devil?

My patient gave me an awareness of his own fantasy life which partly illuminated these wide social myths which resulted in the deaths of as many as a hundred thousand women in Europe over a period of centuries. The fantasies centered upon two factors: first, that his wife's aging and her somewhat masculinized changing appearance reminded him of his grandmother and mother both of whom disgusted him; and second, that his wife's increased sexual appetites in the post-menopausal period also roused disgust and loathing in him. He could not accept responsibility for his impotence, blamed his wife and he too turned his sexual attention to a much younger woman.

As mentioned before, many older women in analysis have reported that during menopause and post-menopausally they have felt increased sexual interest and increased capacity for sexual pleasure. All of this takes place at a time when many older men feel their sexual powers to be waning. The patient, unable to own responsibility for his own distressing symptom, had to blame his wife. He had a lifelong tendency to avoid responsibility for his behavior and held onto a personal theory of pathogenesis that everything in his life was the fault of someone else.

SUMMARY

I have tried to demonstrate from psychoanalytic data that the reaction of older men to menopause is a combination of pre-existing fantasy life coupled with their *own* physical decline as a prominent factor. An example is also given of the response of a younger man to menopause.

DISCUSSION

I have deliberately presented my contribution in two sections, the first dealing with clinical observations from the psychoanalytic situation, disguised only to protect confidentiality. The second section will deal with some *speculations* on the topic. I have been somewhat dismayed in recent years at psychoanalytic meetings in local psychoanalytic societies and in the American Psychoanalytic's deliberations that much of the material presented has been anecdotal, material from brief psychotherapies, vague impressions and extended comments on the works of other authors, living and dead. I have come to believe even more strongly that good clinical observations are durable and that explanatory hypotheses are evanescent. This despite the fact that theory tends to "color" observation but may not totally dominate it.

I have a distinct preference for case reports. I think that the case material presented today will hold up to further scrutiny. My discussion, however, consists of my opinions about that data and is instantly open to revision,

Dr. Phyllis Greenacre, in a case discussion, once remarked that increasing age tends to accentuate pre-existing structures of character. (That is a paraphrase of my memory of what she said, not an exact quote.) I would add my own observations mixed with the opinion that, by and large, we become caricatures of what we were as the years progress. Not only are traits of character exaggerated, but the conditions of object-choice and the requirements of ongoing object ties become accentuated. In brief, most people of equable personalities become mellow, and the cranky tend toward being curmudgeonly. Those that made their object choices on a predominantly narcissistic basis tend toward a heightened narcissism with its concomitant disappointments in the objects (spouse, children); and those that made more anaclitic choices (that is based on the model of the childhood caretakers) tend to be more responsive to the needs of a spouse, children, and grandchildren. (Parenthetically, this is often reflected in the work of older analysts in relation to their patients. Where unresolved narcissism was an important part of career-choice, increasing age often makes such analysts increasingly disappointed, sometimes bored with their work. Sometimes they give the work up claiming what they call burn-out, seeking instead to replace the painstaking work of analysis with the magic of authoritarian psychotherapy or an unreasonable and unscientific reliance on prescribing drugs whose efficacy and long-term consequences are still not known.

On the other hand, certain analysts whose career-choice was based on identifications with a caring parent or sometimes a caring teacher or analyst become mellower in the work, more sagacious and more skillful. Along with the concept "no fool like an old fool," is the concept "the wisdom of age." Where I use the term "wisdom" I mean the uncertainty of knowledge and the assumption of human fallibility. Narcissism goes with certainty and authoritarianism.

Let me offer some speculations about the maintenance of object-relations with increasing age, The 18th century ballad about Darby and Joan, written by Henry Woodfall, presented us with a picture of an old-fashioned loving, virtuous couple based upon real people. Woodfall had been John Darby's apprentice. Here is a "mythologized" picture of an old and loving couple who care for each other, for better, for worse in the terms of the marriage vows. Such couples did *and do* exist despite a current societal tendency to go in an opposite direction. What is it that seems to make it possible for people to share in each other's age, physiological changes and decreasing powers? What makes some couples wise and other couples foolish? Why do some couples remain loyal to each other, and their children and others abandon those for whom they had promised fidelity? By and large my clinical experience tends to look in the direction of the vicissitudes of narcissism. Freud's concepts of narcissism began with the exploration of the psychology of the psychoses and by an intuitive leap began the exploration of object-choice. By narcissistic object-choice for love, Freud meant looking for someone who represented what one was like in the past, is like in the present, what one would like to be or someone who was once part of oneself. Recent psychoanalytic interest, ideas and publications about narcissism have tended toward the manner in which these ideas illuminate the unfolding of *transference fantasies* in some of our more troubled patients. Many analysts have come to realize that these issues are qualitatively ubiquitous but there is a very wide range of the question "how much" narcissism in each individual's capacities for love that represents caring for someone else. Here the questions become intertwined with the complexities of super-ego function and towards problems of morality.

Let me now turn my attention to menopause and the reactions of both men and women to the psychological and physiological changes of advancing age. A cult of perpetual youth has become part of many societies with varying rationalizations about participation in that cult.

The concept of growing old gracefully has receded in many Western and Latin-American societies. Manias for "working-out, " thinning, plastic surgery, hair dyes, skin treatments, youthful clothes are a major growth industry and television is its evangelist. Its poignant caricature is in "anorexia nervosa" and the body-image fantasies which are part of that disorder. Both men and women are bombarded by these ideas of the desirability of perpetual youth. They provide a cultural pathway for the expression of

185

personal concerns along the lines of Hartmann's comment that culture provides a pathway for the discharge of the drives.

Almost all aging and all infirmities concomitant with age tend to lead in the direction of at least partial and temporary regressions. Here the question clinically is *not* whether regression takes place but how much and with what reversibility. The regression can take place in the narcissistic mode or in the anaclitic mode. As for the latter, often one sees regression in the increased need to be cared for by both men and women along infantile lines. However, I would like to keep our focus upon the narcissistic issues, and narcissistic object-choice.

An older person, undergoing narcissistic regression, tends to be cranky, irritable, unsatisfied, and critical of spouse and children. This is only partly a function of depression. It is more related to anger over disappointment in the way in which a real person is compared with some fantasied person; here we are speaking of narcissistic issues. Furthermore, one's own weaknesses and failures may be attributed to the disappointing person. Where narcissism tends to hold the patient blameless and the object blameworthy, the usual solution is to look for a new object closer to the narcissistic fantasy. This often means someone actually youthful/or *more frequently* turning to a child. Men tend to look for a younger woman, a few women look for a younger man: either in fantasy or reality for *both* men and women. For many the younger target is a child in whom hope is placed and who is then viewed as a disappointment: "How sharper than a serpent's tooth it is to have a thankless child" is a complaint of the climacterium. To paraphrase Freud, the last pitiful remnant of our narcissism is in the overestimation of our children.

CONCLUSION

The reaction to aging in oneself or in a spouse is frequently related to the titer of narcissism. The irritability so often seen in this epoch is usually related to anger and disappointed narcissistic wishes and is only partly related to the depression common in this age, A final technical comment: the patient and the analyst should look within rather than place all emphasis on the object and the external world. Intrapsychic conflict and its exploration are more likely to have therapeutic yield than other attempts at magical alteration of the external reality. In any event, we are good at the examination of the intrapsychic and as likely to be unrealistic about the outside world as the next person.

REFERENCES

(1910–1911), *Encyclopedia Britannica, 11ᵗʰ Edition.* Chicago: Miriam Webster.

Gellius, A. (177). *Attic Nights, Volume III, Books 14–20.* Cambridge: Harvard University Press, 1927.

Kramer, H. & Springer, J. (1489). *Ma Ileus Maleficarum (The Inquisitor's Manual),* Transl. Montague Summers. San Diego, CA: Book Tree, 2000.

Various Authors (1973). *Folklore, Myths, and Legends of Britain.* New York: Reader's Digest Association, 2nd edition, 1977.

CHAPTER 12

Object Loss, Fetishism, and Creativity

This communication attempts to explore the relation between some aspects of literary creativity, fetishism, and object loss. The central thesis is that early object loss and certain rage-charged infantile experiences predispose to a more than ordinary severe castration anxiety in the phallic phase development. Certain defensive maneuvers and actions may alleviate this anxiety. An attempt will be made to demonstrate this fetishistic sexual behavior and literary creativity in gifted individuals may serve a linked defensive and restitutive purpose. The paper derives from the extended analysis of a talented author. Though details of his neurosis can be reported (leaving out identifiable data) problems of tact and discretion prevent reporting connections between his personality and his work. This will give the narrative an uneven quality. However, the writings of Count Leo Tolstoy have a texture which will allow comparison.

Tolstoy lost both parents early in his life. His mother died when he was less than three years old, and his father died when he was nine. Throughout his creative life Tolstoy tried to restore not only the world that was, but also the wishful world that never existed. In his writings he made not only his dead parents come alive, he made them greater than life: immortal.

No one would remember the pathetic Princess Marya Volkonsky who was Tolstoy's mother, but Princess Marya Bolkonsky in *War and Peace* is known to us all. The profligate Count Ilich Tolstoy is more real in the character of Nicholas Rostov. They were restored in an idealized life in which they were desexualized and sanctified, though simultaneously given the trappings of flesh and blood. In his novella, *Boyhood*, Tolstoy describes a scene in which he (as a child) is locked in a dark room, awaiting his tutor. He has a series of fantasies culminating in the fact that he too will die.

> After forty days my soul will fly to heaven; there I shall see something wonderfully beautiful, white, transparent, tall, and feel that it is my mother. That something white surrounds and caresses me, but I feel disquiet, and don't seem to recognize her." "'If this is really you,' I say, 'show yourself to me better so that I can embrace you!' And her voice answers me: 'We are all this here; I cannot embrace you better. Don't you feel happy so?'
>
> 'Yes, I feel very happy, but you cannot tickle me and cannot kiss your hands.' 'That is unnecessary, here it is beautiful without that,' she says, and I feel that it really is beautiful, another together we fly higher and higher. At that point seemed to awake and find myself again on the trunk in the dark box-room, with wet cheeks, and repeating without any idea the words, *'We fly higher and higher'*. For a long time I make every possible effort to clear up to myself my position, but my mental vision presented in the present only a dreadfully gloomy and impenetrable distance I return to those comforting, happy fancies which the consciousness of reality had interrupted, but to my astonishment, as soon as fell into the rut of my former fancies, I found it was Impossible to continue them, and—most astonishing—of all that they no longer afforded me any pleasure.

However, the idea that in heaven one could have a beautiful life without tickling and kissing could not be sustained on earth. Tolstoy was under constant strain to control his sexual impulses. He feared their uncontrollable power and became phobic. V.I. Alexeev, who was the tutor for Tolstoy's children tells the following story of 1860 in hie memoirs,

> Tolstoy came to up to me in agitation and asked me to help him. I looked up and saw that he was out of countenance, and wondered how I could help him. He said in an agitated voice: 'Save me, I am falling.' I saw that something had gone wrong with him, and I was frightened.

'What is the matter with Leo Nikolavich?' I asked.

"I am overcome by sensual temptation and feel quite powerless. I fear I may yield to temptation. Help me!'

'I, myself am a weak man. How can I help you?' I said."

'You can help me. Please don't refuse.'

'But what can I do to help?"

'This: Don't refuse to accompany me when I go for my walks. We will walk together and talk, and the temptation won't come to my mind." Tolstoy would pray to his mother. She was always real, always present. Henri Troyat in his biography of Tolstoy quotes from Tolstoy's diary in 1908 (written a few years before his death: I walk in the garden, and I think of my mother, of Maman; I do not remember her but she I-as always been an ideal of saintliness for me." In 1906 he had written:

'Felt dull and sad all day. Toward evening the mood changed into a desire for caresses, for tenderness. wanted, as when I was a child, to nestle against some tender and compassionate being and weep with love and be consoled, become a tiny boy, close to my mother, the way imagine her. Yes, yes, my Maman, when I was never able to Il that because I did not how to talk when she died. She is my highest image of love—not cold, divine love but warm, earthly love, maternal Maman, hold me baby me! All that is madness, but it is all true.' These notes were written when he was almost 80!

The patient under discussion came for analysis after being plagued by guilt over a variety of perverse sexual practices. In his early thirties, married and with several young children he was fearful that his repeated homosexual adventures would destroy his family. He was devoted to his children whom he described with maternal doting. Filled with anxiety during the first interview, he leaped from his chair, paced the consultation room, and confessed a life-long secret, The name he bore was not his own. His own father had died when the patient was two and the mother had changed his name to hide what she considered the father's social inferiority. However, the dead father, though hidden, was sanctified and revered by the patient, his sister three years his senior. and his mother. He recalled regular Sunday trips, via subway train, to the cemetery where his father was buried. At his grave, inscribed with the words "Till We Meet Again" the bereaved family would have a picnic lunch. the mother tending the grass or arranging flowers. Even after remarrying, the mother continued to take these dutiful pilgrimages, though the children were under the strictest injunction against revealing the father's name.

Immediately after the father's death, the mother had attempted suicide with the children. Closeting herself and the children in the kitchen, she sealed off windows and doors and turned on the gas oven jets. She and the children huddled on the floor for a few moments, and she leaped up in panic and opened the windows.

The patient had been sickly since birth and during his first year developed a severe and unremitting eczema. He remembered himself as always itching and covered with scabs. His bed-sheets were often bloody and to prevent excoriation, he regularly had his hands tied and bandaged. He was always ashamed of his eczema and his mother viewed it as a consequence of his father's inferior social and racial stock. When the analysis began, he was under the impression that his father died of hemophilia, but subsequent analysis and investigation demonstrated that he actually died of a septicemia following a dental extraction. The myth of the hemophilia, created by the mother, had two roots: in the one the father was biologically inferior, but in the other connected to the Royal Households of Europe. The patient searched the house in early childhood for relics of his father. He found his father's World War I puttees and wrapped them around his legs. He had a fantasy that the father's body was stuffed (like a doll) and hidden in a kitchen cabinet. There had also been some photographs of the father, but they disappeared.

Some short time after the father's death, the patient developed a severe asthma. He was often terrified of choking and dying, especially when his mother was away. He would anxiously await her return when she would give him an injection of adrenalin. During these moments of terror, he would appeal to his sister for help, but she would make fun of his anxiety. The mother insisted that the children do everything together and they were endlessly in each other's company. They rarely played with other children, but played together, bathed together, went to school and church together. The patient was intensely sexually curious about his sister but was very inhibited. He admired her clear white skin which he contrasted with his scarred, scabrous, excoriated eczema. When he was six he had a large abscess in his groin which was incised and evacuated by the surgeon who had cared for his father in the latter's final illness. Following this procedure, the patient became even more fearful. He became even more increasingly identified with his sister. She would tell him what she remembered of their father and the patient interpreted these stories as meaning that the father loved her best. He became intrigued with her breast she entered puberty and envied her prettiness. When boys became interested in her, he became violently jealous.

If she west out upon a date he would have fantasies that she might be, and he would become agitated until she returned.

His pubescent masturbation was accounting of being a virile strong man with dark hair. However, he was fascinated by girls with what he termed very clear white "flesh." By "flesh" he meant not only the skin but the entire texture of the body surface. These two trends remained in his sexual life: homosexual interest a strong man, coupled with interest in the woman with special "flesh" who also possessed large breasts. Sexual potency with a woman as only possible he had a homosexual fantasy at the same time that *he touched and stroked the special* "flesh," i.e., the object had to fulfill what Freud called a fetishistic condition. A woman with blemished could rouse disgust and he would be impotent even if he liked her for other reasons. His mother's varicose veins brought him to a high pitch of loathing. Another requirement was that the woman had to a certain smell. A specific perfume worn by a woman he had lost intrigued him. He would buy it and give it as gifts to other women so that they might remind him of the one lost. It was quickly discernible in the analysis that the homosexual fantasy and the special helped "contain" an enormous castration anxiety and to repair the image he had of his damaged body. There was a specific narcissistic character to his object choice. The women possessed the clear skin he lacked, the homosexual fantasy provided him with the phallic power he missed and smell of the perfume allowed of respiratory introjection of that which he had lost.

As described by Greenacre as related to fetishism, he had a pseudo-addiction to drugs. He was plagued by recurrent sleeplessness and had to have a supply of barbiturates on hand. He would dole them out to himself in response to the promptings of anxiety and not necessarily because of the actual sleeplessness. He carried with him, at all times, various medications for his asthma. The need for these drugs and for an inhalation apparatus was real but tended to view these drugs as necessary attachments to his body.

During the analytic sessions there were frequent interruptions to use the inhaler whenever material related to object loss would appear. On the rare occasions when he left home without the inhaler he would be panicky with the thought ae he might have an asthmatic attack. Sexual excitement, particularly if related to homosexual fantasy or experience, served as a guarantee against asthmatic attack. He was preoccupied with death and was particularly fearful of dying in an asthmatic attack, choking and helpless. The drugs served as a magic talisman against the feared smothering. Behind the fear was the image of his mother; on the one hand, she envelope and smothered him; on the other hand, she rescued and breathed life into him. His first manifest homosexual experience occurred in late adolescence when his mother followed him to his college town and wanted to live with him giving him the feeling of being strangled.

Certain aspects of his appearance were striking. His posture was particularly Interesting. He stood quite erect, with his shoulders back—the auxiliary muscles of' respiration quite taut in his neck. However, his head was bent, and he looked at the ground as he walked. His gait was particularly bouncy. He spoke of the posture and gait of woman and men with special interest in long-legged women who "strutted" as they walked This was later understood as having meaning in the context of a body-phallus equation, while he depicted himself as broken.

When the analysis began, despite financial success he owned almost no personal possessions. He often borrowed clothes and particularly borrowed shirts. Rarely did he wear a suit jacket, preferring soft sweaters. The "touch" of clothes seemed as important as the touch of 'flesh." He would run his long fingers along the soft nap of the sweater. There was a special need to be touched by some repugnance at being touched.

His homosexual escapades were set off by experiences of feeling lost, abandoned, or impotent. The smallest reproach from a woman was experienced as a deep humiliation. He would wander about in foul-smelling subway toilets looking for a homosexual connection which would be fleeting and evanescent. The man involved was of little importance and was rapidly discarded. The memory of the experience however, served to fortify the patient's potency in future encounters with women. Numerous dreams he helped us to understand that he was constantly searching for underground for his lost father. The potency problem with women had two major aspects. His fear of seeing a naked woman (i.e., her lack of a penis) led to difficulties in penetration. The second aspect was anxiety about the inside of the vagina. He reported at the outset, with a thrill of horror, a fantasy of the inside of a woman's vagina having a pair of razor blades which would shred his penis. When with a woman, he would the last homosexual episode re-animated and embellished, and could thus sustain his erection.

The fear of castration had a counterpart wish to be castrated. In a vivid masochistic fantasy, he imagined him beaten by a sadistic policeman who then cut off the patient's genitals and then raped the wound as a bloody genital opening. His own masochism horrified him when its full extent was revealed.

The demonstration that "perfect flesh" gave the woman a phallic quality was quickly forthcoming in the analytic work. The analysis of an often repeated childhood fantasy confirmed the displacement from the penis to the skin:

The Lone Ranger and Tonto are inseparable companions. The Lone Ranger had a treasure map tattooed to the of his chest. Tonto is lured away. The Lone Ranger is drugged, bound, or asleep and bad men cut the treasure map from his chest.

This was also associated to Michelangelo's self portrait as the flayed skin of St. Bartholomew (in the Sistine Chapel Last Judgment). Damaged skin being equivalent to castration, the woman with perfect flesh was "intact."

The eczema provided a regressive pathway for the definition of castration as a skin disorder. In the analysis his writing was always closely guarded and protected. He was afraid to tell me of any in work in progress. He feared that I would make fun of it and view it as inconsequential.

This was a transference manifestation whose source was in his mother's disparaging attitude toward his early attempts at writing. This was specially painful since his capacity for storytelling was a piece of identification with his mother.

Intense periods of work, however, would lead to an intensification of his sleep disorder often leading to a reversal pattern. He would be in a state of constant excitement, masturbating frequently. As the analytic work progressed it could be seen that the masturbatory and his dreams would be worked into the fabric of the writing. Selma Fraiberg had reported some years ago, upon the way in which Kafka had translated the imagery of his dreams into the imagery of his writing and this patient amply demonstrated this phenomenon, though without the same *conscious* method employed by Kafka.

As commented upon earlier, problems of discretion prevent comparison of his fantasies to his work. The work performed the same functions as the sexual fetishistic behavior disordered body image was restored, and repaired. The lost father was endlessly revived and revered. An early denial of his father's death had allowed for a defensive split in the ego. At one level he knew his father was dead, at another level he searched for him everywhere. An interesting transference representation of this problem appeared a symptom of repeatedly thinking he saw me on the street. I was omnipresent; no separation was possible.

Tolstoy describes the denial of death succinctly in *Anna Karenina*. Anna' s son, Serezha, sits thinking before lesson from his father: Among his favorite occupations was keeping a lookout for his mother when he went out walking. He did not believe in death in general, and especially not in *her* death, despite what Lydia Ivanovna had told him and his father had confirmed, and therefore even after he had been told she was dead, he went on looking for her. Then on his walks. He imagined that every well-developed and graceful woman with dark hair was his mother. At the sight of any such woman a feeling of such tenderness awoke in his heart that he grew breathless and tears came to his eyes. He expected that at any moment she would approach and lift her veil. Then he would see her whole face, she would smile, embrace him, and he would smell her peculiar scent, feel the tenderness of her touch, and cry with joy as he had done one evening when he lay at her feet and she tickled him while he shook with laughter and bit her white hand with the rings on the fingers Though in fictional setting, the feelings are clearly autobiographical. Mourning, in the usual sense, was never accomplished. The work of mourning is described by Freud in *Mourning and Melancholi*a:

> The testing of reality, having shown that the loved object no longer exists, requires forthwith that all the libido shall be withdrawn from its attachments to this object. Against this demand a struggle of course arises—it may be universally observed that man never willingly abandons a libido-position.... The normal outcome is that deference for reality gains the day. Nevertheless its behest cannot be at once obeyed.

The task is now carried through bit by bit Anna Freud in her discussion of Bowlby's 1960 paper on "Grief and Mourning in Children" comments:

> The process of mourning taken in its analytic sense means to us the individual's effort to accept a fact in the external world (the loss the cathected object) and to effect corresponding changes in the inner world (withdrawal of libido from the lost object, identification with

the lost object). At least the former half of this task presupposes certain capacities of the mental apparatus such as reality testing, the acceptance of the reality principle, partial control of id tendencies by the ego, etc. i.e., capacities which are still undeveloped in the infant according to al other evidence. We have hesitated therefore to apply the term mourning in its technical sense to the bereavement reactions of the infant. Before the mental apparatus has matured and before, on the libidinal side the stage of object constancy has been reached, the child's reactions to loss seem to us to be governed by the more primitive and direct dictates of the pleasure-pain principle.

Tolstoy never fully accepted his mother's death, nor was his father's death fully and realistically appreciated. He was left with nagging and persistent questions about "what really happened in the past?" In his masterpiece, *War and Peace*, he not only makes the past come alive, and not only does he revive his dead parents, but in his celebrated theory of history he attempts to give a philosophical basis to the issue of "What really happened in the past " Professional historians have tended to dismiss Tolstoy's historical views as naive and amateurish. Turgenev viewed these ideas with contempt and Flaubert viewed them with chagrin. However, the historical theory of *War and Peace* is not merely an addendum to a vivid narrative about the lives, feelings, motives of real people; rather, it is an attempt at stating that official histories are collections of mythological nonsense; and, that men's actions are not free but that they are swept up in inexorable streams. One does not know the *causes," one can only know what happens in the lives of individuals. Isaiah Berlin essay "The Hedgehog and the Fox" views Tolstoy's historical theories in the context of the history of ideas, and correctly credits Joseph de Maistre as providing Tolstoy some of the inspiration for the content of the theories. However, there may be some value to recognizing that Tolstoy beyond contributing to the philosophy of history, was also attempting what we term the "reconstruction" in the process of analysis.

More than that, it is suggested in the text of *War and Peace* that he was striving to accomplish something that would actively please his dead father. On the pages just preceding the Second Epilogue containing the central portion of the historical ideas, he represents the young, orphaned Nicholas Bolkonski:

Meanwhile, downstairs in young Nicolas Bolkonis bedroom, a little lamp was burning as usual. (The boy was afraid of the dark and they could not cure him of it.) Dessalles slept propped up on four pillows, and his Roman nose emitted sounds of rhythmic snoring. Little Nicholas, who had just woken up in a cold perspiration, sat up in bed and gazed before him with wide open eyes. He had awoken from a terrible dream. He had dreamt that he and Uncle Pierre, wearing helmets such as were depicted in his Plutarch, were leading a huge array. The army was made up of white slanting lines that filled the air like the cobwebs that float about in autumn, and which Dessalles called le fil de la Vierge, in front was Glory, which was similar to those threads but rather thicker. He and Pierre were borne along lightly and joyously, nearer and nearer to their goal. Suddenly the threads that moved them began to slacken and become entangled and it became difficult to move. "And Uncle Nicholas stood before them in a stern and threatening attitude 'Have you done this?" he said, pointing to some broken sealing wax and pens. "I loved you, but I have orders from Arakcheev and will kill the first of you who moves forward." Little Nicholas turned to look at Pierre, but Pierre was no longer there. in his place was his father—Prince Andrew— and his father had neither shape nor form, but he existed, and when little Nicholas perceived him he grew faint with love; he felt himself powerless, limp and formless. His father caressed and pitied him. But Uncle Nicholas came nearer and nearer to them. Terror seized young Nicholas and he awoke. "My father," he thought, (Though there were two good portraits of Prince Andrew in the house, Nicholas never imagined him in human form.) Father has been with me and caressed me. He approved of me and of Uncle Pierre, whatever lie may tell me, I will do it. "Mucius Scaevola burnt his hand. Why should not the same sort of thing 'happen to me? I know they want me to learn. And I will learn. But some day I shall have finished learning, and then I will do something, I only pray God something may happen to me such as happened to Plutarch's men and I will act as they did. I will do better. Everyone shall know me, love me, and be delighted with me... And my father? Oh, Father Father! Yes, I will do something with even he would be satisfied..."

But pride in his work was not his only attitude. He also had to despise it and feel ashamed of it. He had to rid himself of his cherished creations. Fetishists often describe a feeling of disgust which follows the sexual experience.

The fetish is thrust away only to be searched for in a time of renewed sexual need. The disgust is only a seeming disavowal of the fetish which remains invested with narcissistic magic. The patient and Tolstoy both reacted in this way to women following sexual intercourse and similarly reacted to their completed literary works. The patient would not even proof-read his galleys. He noted that he was finished he "really finished," a reaction akin to disgust. Tolstoy reacted in a similar way, late in his life, refusing to be interested in new editions of his works income the work, etc., and he assigned all those tasks to his wife.

There are not clearly convincing' indications of specific fetishistic interest in Tolstoy' s life. However, there are innumerable references to feet and boots. He made many statements about women's feet, bare feet, disgust at dirty feet of wandering of religious pilgrims and extolling boots and shoes. Late in life he avidly took to book-making and repairing old-tattered boots. He was inordinately and childishly proud of the boots he made. However, toward his novels he had striking ambivalence, dismissing them as frivolities. Of the boots he made, Aylmer Maude (his official English translator) says asked a man he her given a pair and who had worn them, whether they were well made. "Couldn't be worse" was his reply. His seeming bad judgment about the value of his creations was striking. But this was more seeming than real.

AN HISTORICAL REVIEW

The study of fetishism occupies a special röle in the psychoanalytic theory of the perversions. It may illuminate this presentation to briefly review its pertinent history. In Freud's *Three Contributions to the Theory of Sexuality* the sexual perversions are viewed as the persistence the infantile sexuality into adult life. In this persistence we detect a fixation to specific component sexual instincts.

However, in discussing fetishism, Freud says:

There are some cases which are quite specially remarkable—those in which the normal sexual object Is replaced by another which bears some relation to it but entirely unsuited to serve the normal sexual aim. What is substituted for the sexual object is some part of the body (such as foot or hair)... or some inanimate object which bears an assignable relation to the person whom it replaces.... A transition to those cases of fetishism in which the sexuality whether normal or perverse, is entirely abandoned is afforded by other ones in which the sexual object is replaced to fulfill a fetishistic condition such as the possession of some particular hair-coloring or clothing or even some bodily defect if the sexual aim is to be attained. No other variation of the sexual instinct that borders upon the pathological can lay so much claim to our interest as this one, such is the peculiarity. of the phenomena to which it gave rise.... The point of contact with the normal is provided by the psychologically essential over-estimation of the special object, which inevitably extends to everything associated with it. A certain degree of fetishism is thus habitually present in normal love especially in those stages of in which the normal sexual aim seems unattainable or its fulfilment prevented....

The subject was next explored by Abraham. in "Remarks on the Psychoanalysis of a Case of Foot and Corset Fetishism"(1910). There he pointed out that fetishism and neurosis were often present in the same individual and he emphasized the partial repression which Freud had held to be typical of this disorder. Also emphasized was the coprophilia which entered into the choice of the fetish. Abraham also noted that "side by side with a sexual overestimation of the fetish a pronounced tendency toward. emotional rejection of it." In 1920 Freud added a footnote to the *Three Contributions*: "Behind the first recollection of the fetish appearance there lies a submerged and forgotten phase of sexual development. The fetish, like a screen memory, represents this phase...."

The concept of sexual perversion-as-fixation was not tenable in the light of the clinical evidence of beating fantasies and in "A Child is Being Beaten," (1919) Freud demonstrated masochism to be related to defenses against the Oedipal situation. This view was elaborated upon by Hanns Sachs (1923) in a paper "On the Origin of Perversions," Sachs depicted perversions as having a compromise structure in which certain phenomena undergo repression, but one aspect of the infantile sexual organization is allowed expression and gratification. In fetishism, the major content of the Oedipus complex is repressed and one aspect of it—represented in the fetishistic behavior—remains like a screen memory. Glover (1929) was to comment upon the screening function of traumatic memories. In fetishism, however, it would seem that a benign screen covers the traumatic memories which in turn cover the repressed Oedipal conflict with its castration threat.

Glover, following Sachs's lead, explored the relationship between drug-addiction and fetishism (1932) He viewed the drugs and the fetish as having value as "repair-activity" such as is found in the restitution products of psychosis. In another paper of 1932, he viewed perversions as helping to patch flaws in the developing reality sense. In these works, he also saw. obsessional fears of "contamination" as negative aspects of the fetishism. Having conducted an increasing number of analyses of fetishists, Freud in 1927 carne to the conclusion that cases the "meaning and purpose" of the fetish was the same:

> The fetish is a substitute for the woman's (mother's) phallus which the little boy once believed in and does not wish to forego. In sone cases, the actual choice of the fetish, was related to chance observations of "the last moment the woman could still be regarded as phallic.

But Freud commented that fetishism also interested him because he found exceptions to his Idea

> that in neurosis the ego suppresses part of the id out of allegiance to reality, whereas in psychosis it lets itself be carried away by the id and detached a part of reality.... In the analyses of two young men that each of them—one in his second and the other in his tenth year—had refused to acknowledge the death of very important piece of reality had thus been denied by the ego, in the same way

as the fetishist denied the unwelcome fact of the woman's castrated condition.

However, "the two young men had no more scotomized the death if their fathers than the fetishist scotomizes the castration of women." In *one* current of mental life the facts were acknowledged, in *another wishful* current the facts were denied.

These latter ideas were to form the nucleus of Freud's 1933 fragment of a paper: "The Splitting of the Ego in the Defensive Process." In that unfinished work Freud saw the castration threat is handled in certain children, a split course of action. On one hand "he rejects reality and refuses to accept any prohibition of masturbation;" on other hand "he recognizes the danger of reality, takes over the fear of that danger as a symptom and tries subsequently to devest himself of the fear." The fetishist continues his masturbation "and protects his penis by creating a substitute for the penis he missed in women i.e., the fetish. He does not "hallucinate a penis where there is none to be seen; he effected no more than a displacement of value he transferred the importance of the penis to another part of the body...."

Fenichel's study of transvestitism (1930) continues the line of reasoning in Sachs paper. He said "the homosexual has no regard for any human being who lacks the penis, denies that such beings exist... while the exhibitionist, the scoptophilic and the transvestite try incessantly to refute the fact. Thus, we see that these perverts are endeavoring to master their anxiety by denying its cause." In transvestitism and in fetishism the essential unconscious fantasy is that the woman is phallic. In his study of *Respiratory Introjection* (1931) Fenichel beautifully documents the rôle of such introjection in the analysis of a transvestite, the object relation of all pregenitality respiratory pathway is closely Inked with *oral* eroticism, through certain analytic observations have connected the desire to anal eroticism.

Kronengold and Sterba in 1936 reported two cases of fetishism in order to suggest hat Fenichel's transvestitism (i.e., that the transvestitism-identified with the phallic woman wears feminine clothing in order to *reduplicate* the phallic nature of women) might also be applied to certain fetishists. This reduplication serves the purpose of a vigorous denial of a deficiency. In both cases the fetish had to be placed next to the genitals, in one case, there was a repeated history of object separations and object loss. In the other case the patient is said to have identified himself with his mother against the threat of losing her when his brother was born. In both patients there was an avoidance of sexual intercourse, and the fetishistic activity was entirely masturbatory.

In Sylvia Payne's paper "Some Development the Ego Development of the Fetishist" (1939). emphasis was placed on the defense against destruction of the object. The rôle of aggression against the object was investigated as a point to the rôle of the fetish as defense against castration anxiety. Also emphasized in her case report were the patient's experience of being tied down in infancy. This also true of Abraham's patient with foot fetishism and Fenichel's transvestite patient. The interference with normal muscular activity was seen to cause disruption of normal development by focus in aggressive discharge upon the excretory functions and heightening the sadistic element of pregenital activities. "The ego which cannot increase its strength by proving its capacity actively is driven to reinforce itself by reliance on objects..." Furthermore she, with Ella Sharpe, sees unconscious connections between artistic products and the fetish; and she links both phenomena to the "introjected imagoes of the early phases of ego development" (Payne's paper gave wider evidence to James Glover's (1927) assertion of the sadism of the fetishist.)

W.H. Gillespie in 1940 stated what he thought to be the crux of the problem of fetishism:

"Is fetishism primarily a product of castration anxiety, to be related almost exclusively to the phallic phase, and concerned to maintain the existence of a female penis; or the main dynamic force really come from more primitive levels, which undeniably contribute to give its ultimate form to the fetish?" He then demonstrates determinants of the fetish coming from each pregenital phase. He emphasized that if anything was established with certainty.... It was that the fetish saves the object from the dangers inherent in the fetishist's sadistic love with its annihilating tendency. He suggests that fetishism is the result of castration anxiety, but of a specific form produced by a strong admixture of oral and anal trends.

Wulff in 1946 investigated what he termed "Fetishism and Object Choice in Early Childhood." In this paper he notes that there are two forms sexual aberration in regard to object choice homosexuality and fetishism. He asked if fetishistic activity occurs in young children and describes phenomena similar to those to be later described by Winnicott his study of "Transitional Objects" (1953). He reports upon the use of inanimate things used by children to reduce tension and in sleep preparation. He noted the relationship of the "fetishes" to sucking, noted that they appeared following weaning, and that they induced sleep. He concluded that the "fetish" substituted for the mother's body and breast. The blanket, bib, etc., used in this process gave rise to pleasurable tactile sensations. When he attempts to relate these observations to Freud's view of fetishism as a solution to castration threat he concludes that the earlier experiences of "loss" and replacement are given meaning in retrospective fashion after the traumatic observation of the anatomical difference between the sexes.

Robert Bak in 1952 reemphasized fetishism as a special solution to castration threat. Surveying the development of fetishism he emphasized:

1. "Weakness of the ego structure that may be inherent or may come about secondarily through disturbances in the mother-child relationship that threaten survival."

This may account for the inordinate separation anxiety that results in clinging to the mother totally or to a substitute part of her as a *pars pro toto*, leaving behind erotization of the hands and predilection for touching.

2. "Fixation in pregenital phases, especially anal erotism and smelling in the service of maintaining mother-child unity, wherein respiratory introjection plays an important rôle besides scopophilia."

3. "The symbolic significance of the fetish corresponds to pregenital phases and thus may represent separately or in condensation: breast-skin, buttocks-feces and female phallus."

4. "Simultaneous and alternating identification with the phallic and penis less mother, corresponding to the resolution of the ego."

5. "Identification with the penis less mother leads to the wish for giving the penis up...both phases of danger i.e., of separation and castration are defended by the fetishistic compromise."

D.W. Winnicott's study of "Transitional Objects and Transitional Phenomena" centered about the first not-me possession. Using some of the same kinds of observations reported by Wulff, he notes that infants soon after birth use fingers and hand to stimulate the oral erotogenic zone and that after a few months they take up some doll, teddy-bear or blanket and their mothers expect them to become...addicted to such objects." There is a relationship between these two sets of phenomena that are separated by a tine interval. The terms transitional object and transitional phenomena designate the intermediate area of experience, between the thumb and the teddy bear, between oral erotism and true object-relationship.

He relates these phenomena to the issue of illusion. "The transitional objects. belong to the realm of illusion which is at the basis of initiation of experience. This early stage of development is made possible by the mother's special capacity for making adaptation to the needs of her infant, thus allowing. the infant the illusion that what the infant creates really exists,"

He notes also that under ordinary circumstances the transitional object becomes gradually decathected.

However, in psychopathology:

"*Addiction* can be stated in terms of regression to the early stage at which the transitional phenomena are unchallenged.

"*Fetish* can be described in terms of a persistence of a specific object or type of object dating from infantile experience in the transitional field, linked with the delusion of the maternal phallus."

The papers most relevant to this study are three contributions which deal with fetishism and faulty development of the body image, published in 1953, 1955 and 1956. Greenacre aptly pointed out that fetishism in well developed form does not often come under analytic scrutiny. She reviews the literature of published cases and notes the history of papers on the subject reflects the development of psychoanalytic theory in general. The objects used by fetishists are closely related to the skin and particularly to odoriferous skin, sometimes to the odor Itself. But thongs, laces and straps are noteworthy. She describes a case of marginal fetishism in which the fetish was women's underwear and corsets, and comments that mild forms of fetishism are probably quite common and do not appear as particularly strange. It is a condition almost limited to males although she reports a female case and Hug-Hellmuth had reported another female fetishist in 1915.

She comments that fetishism usually becomes manifest early sometimes being able to be traced into childhood. It is almost always associated with other manifestations of perversity especially with voyeurism, sadistic practices, homosexuality, and transvestitism.[4]

There is also an impression of severe narcissistic well as sexual disturbances Compulsive masturbation and diffuse castration hypochondria are usually seen. A tendency to genitalization of the body and a peculiar predilection for the mechanism of displacement in body terms.

She sees the problem of fetishism from tile standpoint of faulty development of the body image. She raises questions similar to Gillespie's and concludes the fetishist enters the phallic phase with rifts in early ego development which sharpens the castration problem and draws primitive denial into its service. She then goes on to document early body image disturbances during two periods of early childhood during the first 18 months and then in the period 2 to 4 years.

During the first 18 months disturbances in the mother-child relationship are most noteworthy. Deficient holding or cuddling gives inadequate body-surface stimulation and the body surface may not be well-defined in the central image. Other occurrences producing specific disturbances body Image may be actual changes in body nutrition with rapid alterations of size; physical conditions producing sensations of size alteration (fevers, anesthesia, rage states, sone skin conditions); certain activities applied to the child (massages, tossing, tickling).

She also comments upon the persistence of an unusual degree of primary identification. This is often connected in the boy who becomes a fetishist with persistent close visual contact with a female (either mother or sister).

---

4 (Though Freud had commented upon fetishism as protection again homosexuality, the reported cases and a review of cases at Discussion Group at a recent meeting of the American Psychoanalytic Association demonstrated the presence of manifest homosexuality or open homosexual found in many of the cases in analysis.)

During the era 2–4 years she considers traumatic the witnessing of a bloody mutilating event as the special sensitivity to castration anxiety evidenced by children having gross pre-genital disturbances.

Discussing the choice of the fetish, Greenacre emphasizes the rôle of the fetish in stabilizing the sense of the body, counter-acting the anxiety of the sensations of changing of size and shape of phallus and body.

In these ideas, she elaborates and expands upon Glover's view of "repair-work" similar to the restitution-products of psychosis.

In her 1955 continuation if the study she deals with the interrelation between different types of perversion; on problems of body reality; and the general sense of reality; and aggression and acting-out in relation to the reality sense. Her clinical experience demonstrates that the patients range of perverse activities and that overt homosexuality always breaks forth.

Traumatic disturbances of the phallic period are those which are compulsively repetitive and acted out by the fetishist. The whole body is treated as a phallus and every part of it may be genitalized. She views the fantasy life of the fetishist to be limited and stereotyped, repetitive and ritualized. Acting-out is implicit in their character structure. Childhood traumatic experiences suffuse the entire body with aggressive stimulation. This results in frozen immobility with a susceptibility to active irritability when the crisis is past.

In her 1960 contribution Greenacre reports on the connection between fetishism and the pseudo addiction to drugs which protects against anxiety in a manner similar to the fetish. This use of pills "contains, and defends against, strong infantile dependence on the mother and wish for the breast, similarly may Interfere with adequate mature sexual functioning."

A paper by Werner Muensterberger (1961) "The Creative Process: Its Relation to Object Loss and Fetishism" approaches the topic of my contribution from a somewhat different viewpoint. Reviewing both anthropological and psychoanalytic materials he studies fetishism and creativity as related but somewhat contrasting solutions in the restitutions of loss. The fetishist and creative personality struggle with a similar dilemma but their different libidinal directions may be caused by the conditions for identifications, their sensitivity, and flexibility in sublimating aggression their use of the mechanism of denial. He says: "The propensity of the fetishist for restoration versus the tendency for representation with greater alloplastic syntonicity in the creative personality can be mentioned as one important distinction"

Katan's 1964 paper "Fetishism, Splitting of the Ego and Denial" is an interesting dissent from the concept of the splitting of the ego. Katan, discussing Freud's contribution emphasizes the rôle of the fetish in maintaining a denial of the traumatic observation of the woman's lack of a penis. The fetish is chosen from organs or objects observed before the trauma struck i.e., |at the last moment that the woman could be considered phallic.". The fetish does not have to symbolize the female phallus, the cathexis originally attached to the expected female phallus, being displaced on to the fetish. Katan does not think that it is feasible to maintain the denial; rather that through the denial the ego is enabled to establish the fetish by focusing on pretraumatic experiences. However, once the fetish is established its greater cathexis helps to maintain the denial, and there is a fixation to the pretraumatic ego state of sexual excitement. Katan does not think it feasible to maintain the concept of split of the ego despite its descriptive value. The two "spilt" ideas are not formed simultaneously: one comes from the ego's state of excitement the other from a calmer state. He pays tribute to Greenacre, asserting that Freud's statement that the fetish protects against homosexuality is valid only for conscious thinking. For the fetishist intercourse takes place with a phallic woman. The fetish gives support to the first phase of intercourse, i.e., penetration. In the second phase within the vagina, the castration threat may be nullified by a variety of fantasies.

The review of the literature offers many points of relevance to the case described by me in this paper and it would be redundant to go over them all.

I will concentrate my remarks upon four major issues:

1. the defect in the body image, especially in the body surface with a propensity for touching.
2. the problem of respiratory introjection and the issue of literary inspiration.
3. the manner in which the sexual life on the one hand and the literary creativity on the other hand served as alternative, yet complementary methods of restitutive to loss experiences.
4. the manner in which the earlier pregenital experiences are crystallized in the phallic phase and take form under the impact of castration anxiety.

The peculiar structure of the Oedipal constellation in my patient (the omnipresent ghostly father) accentuates the meaning of the Oedipal conflict as nuclear in the final form of the illness.

1. Defects in the Body Image

The patient's severe eczema was not only excruciatingly painful but there were often raw, bleeding, itching areas all over his body. His hands were often swollen and practically useless. He remembers scratching himself with a mixture of relief and violent pain. His mother would bandage his hands with rolled gauze and tie him down to prevent further excoriation. Some of this could be reconstructed in the analysis through his anxiety about the forced immobility upon the couch (which also reproduced the doctor's examining table upon which his groin abscess was incised). Being led to a suffusion of the body with rage and a sensation of' flying to pieces.

Strikingly Tolstoy writes in his *Reminiscences* what Is obviously a screen memory which he attributes to the era before his mother's death: "I am all bound up; I try to stretch out my hands and I cannot. I scream and cry and hate my own screaming, but I cannot stop. People are leaning over me. I can't remember who—and everything is shrouded in semi-darkness. There are two of them. My screaming affects them; they are anxious; but they do not release me as I want them. to and I scream still louder." (Russian infants were usually bound.)

Another "memory" is ascribed to a somewhat later period— about three, He was being bathed in a wooden tub, surrounded by a sourish smell, scrubbed with bran by a servant woman. "For the first time, I became aware of and liked my little body with the ribs sticking out on my chest, and the steaming agitated water and its lapping noise *and most of all the polished feel of the wet rim of the tub when I ran my little hands along i*t."

The propensity for touching, described in mv patient was also very much part of Tolstoy's life. Maxim Gorky in his *Literary Portraits* was fascinated by Tolstoy's fingers which always seemed to be modeling something in air.

Gorky also remarks upon Tolstoy's habit of touching visitors. He recalls Tolstoy's putting his arm around Chekhov's shoulders, with an affectionate smile, much to the embarrassment of Chekhov.

Touching allows not only for contact with the object but allows for the cathexis of the body-surface so that the body boundaries can be appreciated. The sense of where the self ends, and the non-self begins can be studied in a wide variety of clinical entities and is particularly observable in schizophrenic children. *The need to painfully cathect the body surface* is seen in certain masochists and was observable by me in a case of. trichotillornania and in a case of head banging persisting into adult life. These experiences allowed for hypercathexis of the body boundary, allowing for the control of rage and preventing the feeling of' dissolution.

In the patient described the analytic work demonstrated that the skin was also used as an introjective pathway and that an important function of touching the special "flesh" was to make it part of himself, to increase his intactness. The eczematous skin was seen as a bleeding wound genitalized and "anal-ized" it left him open to invasion, vulnerable to attack and these fantasies predisposed him to special vulnerability to castration-anxiety.

2. Respiratory Introjection and Literary Inspiration.

The patient viewed his life as a struggle for breath. Plagued by persistent asthma and having had several episodes of status asthmaticus he was pre-occupied with choking and smothering.. When talking of his mother giving him the necessary adrenalin injections in childhood, he viewed her as "breathing life" into him.

As reported, sexual excitement and intense period of creativity dispelled some of these fears. Life was breathed into him under these circumstances. Using the breath to "draw in life" could be accomplished by having the woman wear a special perfume. Smelly subway toilets accomplished the same aim in the homosexual encounters. If in the transference situation, he felt deprived and he supplied his own breath with the inhaler, He had a vivid memory for smells, it will be recalled how Proust (also an asthmatic) talked of the of memories which filled his masterpiece *La Recherche du Temps Perdu*. Memories were brought back by the taste and smell of a madeleine (a small cake).

Inspiration—to be filled with the divine creative breath—formed an important part of the patient's work. His inspiration was based upon stored memories. He had an uncanny ear for dialogue and remembered conversations heard years ago.

However, in the analysis this memory was seen to be selective and special. He regularly distorted my comments to the most primitive wishful masochistic lines so that he could feel misunderstood and abused by me. People all around him were incorporated by him to be used in his work. He stored and assembled his literary characters in a manner characterized by "sucking the life out of them." This was also conspicuous in his homosexuality. However, spared from. representation in his work were any open depictions of his mother, his sister, or his incestuous fantasies about them. The writing served an aggressive, destructive purpose as a well a restitutive purpose. Those closest to him were spared his destructiveness and were cherished and stored within..

The secret of his true name also served this purpose, similar to descriptions of the "secret" offered by Greenacre. Narcissistically shielded, the most important objects were secret within him.

3. The Alternative Methods of Restitutive Solution

It is important to recognize that the perverse sexual organization and the creativity seem to stem the same matrix and utilize the same conflicts. However, it would be erroneous to assume with the patient that his creativity stemmed from his sexual perversions. The two phenomena, like a variorum edition of a classic, could be seen as alternate readings of the same text.

Hunan beings do not easily tolerate object loss on any level of development. After grief, the most commonplace reactions to object loss in adult life actually involve replacement of the object. Sometimes this is symbolic oral incorporation, e.g., of drinking at an Irish wake, the lavish feasts at Chinese funerals. However, often the replacements take place after searching for a real object, A mother who loses a child often becomes pregnant without delay. Loss of a parent often leads to a love affair with an object unconsciously viewed as an Oedipal figure.

Tolstoy demonstrated a remarkable connection between object loss in adult life and immediate replacement via creative work. This is also convincingly confirmed in his diaries and letters. Two examples will illustrate this trend.

His brother Nicholas died on September 20, 1860. For a few days, Tolstoy was in despair. He could not work.. "Nikolenka's death has hit me harder than anything I have ever experienced.' But on October 29, 1860, he notes:

"For the last three days I have been by a host of images and idees such as I have not had for ten years. In 1875 Tolstoy's infant son Nicholas (named after Tolstoy's father and brother) was dying of hydrocephalus. He wrote a letter to Strakhov four days before the child actually died..

"In the last four months he has gone through every phase of this incurable disease. My wife is feeding him. Part of the time she is in despair at the thought that he is going to die, and part of the time she is in terror lest he live and remain an idiot. As for myself, it is curious, but I have never wanted to write as intensely, as joyfully as I do now".

It should be remembered that writing a novel is the creation of an illusion in Winnicott's sense.

(A few comments upon the use of books as transitional objects in adults may be in order at this point. In the period after giving up thumb-suckling and the teddy-bear, children often require a bed-time story as the *central obligatory* aspect of the sleep ritual. The emotional cathexis of the more-complex, more-sensual ritual sleep procedure (mild thumb, teddy, *and* story-lullaby) becomes focused upon the book. This frequently continues into adult life and people cannot fall asleep without reading.

It is also remarkable how often bedside table books are viewed as having lesser literary value than other books. Their content is referred to as 'trashy" or 'light" reading. Detective murder mysteries rank high as bedside literature. There is often a faint tinge of shame about reading them, and the actual books are viewed as worthless and degraded.

Similar to the way fetishes are often treated, they are often thrown away, to be immediately replaced. They are often in bought batches and stored for future needs.

A specific ego/super-ego intersystemic functional relationship may be attached to such reading. The analysis of this phenomenon in a detective-story "addict" demonstrated a marked relief of Oedipal guilt in the act of bed-time reading. Put in succinct terms, the patient was saying, of the characters in murder mysteries "They have committed murder, have not." With the relief of guilt sleep could ensue, the book still clutched in his hand. Its masturbatory equivalence is also clearly demonstrable. The spoken word of the earlier bed-time story becomes the written word of the detective novel. It is interesting to note how often favorite fairy-tales are compromise formations between cautionary tales, on one hand, and direct infantile wish-fulfillment on the other. Repetition of these tales allows for mastery of associated anxiety in a process analogous to working-through. The rôle of auditory incorporation in super-ego formation has been explored by Isakower. Further study will be needed to determine what the pre-sleep auditory experiences have some special rôle in this process.)

4. The Phallic Phase and Castration Anxiety

Though the early material of the analysis gave, greater emphasis to the pre-genital experiences and the special rôle of the father's death, a fuller understanding of the organization of his personality was screened behind the groin operation. This became accessible to analysis by reference to a painting by John Singleton Copley called Watson and the Shark. It depicts a naked man hauled into a boat having been bitten by an enormous open-mouthed shark who is being harpooned by a sailor. Originally described as a picture of a man being devoured, not being saved, the patient harangued me about misunderstanding and mistreating him. The transference picture revealed me as the doctor holding him down to the examining table, lancing his abscess and castrating him. This was the punishment for his childhood masturbation and incestuous fantasies. Though the father had been dead, the Oedipal conflict existed in full force. In one aspect of his ego, the father was not dead at all, His spirit was always present as after all the mother would talk to him in his grave. His vengeful "spirit" was around everywhere—to be breathed in from the very air to give life but also to destroy life. Identified also with the harpooned shark, he felt enormous guilt for his oral sadism and the fantasy of destroying his father.

The earlier trauma of object loss took on full meaning only in the context of the castration throat and the experience of the groin operation. However, masturbation and open incestuous fantasy were not abandoned. They took on a split life of their own. The persistent contact with his sister had predisposed him to identification with her. There existed a simultaneous wish to be castrated and therefore similar to his sister. Thia would later appear in his masochistic fantasies of being beaten and humiliated but therefore loved as a woman. The earlier experiences were given heightened poignant meaning in the context of the Oedipal configuration. The rift in the ego stemming from the reaction of denial of the father's death could be utilized as prepared pathway for the denial following full awareness of his sister's castration. Her perfection (i.e., her phallic state) could be displaced to her perfect skin. Behind his representation of the sister was the image of the phallic mother. The splitting of the ego and consequent disruption of its integrative and reality-testing functions may be one method by which early object loss predisposes to a more intense castration anxiety. In the fetishist, it also sets the model for the restitutive behavior.

A case is presented of a talented author, fetish and homosexual in his erotic life, who demonstrated actual at restitution of experiences of loss in his creative life as well as in his sexual life. Furthermore, he used the restitutive pathways to deny castration anxiety and to patch up a disordered body-image. Discretion having prevented using examples from his work, fragments from Tolstoy's life and work were presented as a comparable, if not precisely similar, experience.

REFERENCES

Abraham, Karl.(1910). Remarks on the Psycho-Analysis of a case of foot and corset fetishism. *Selected Papers on Psycho-Analysis.* London: The Hogarth Press, 1942.

Bak, R.C. (1953) .Fetishism. *Journal of the American Psychoanalytic Association* 1:285–298.

Berlin, I. (1951). *The Hedgehog and the Fox: An Essay on Tolstoy's View of History.* Princeton: Princeton University Press, 2013.

Fenichel, O. (1930) The Psychology of Transvestitism. *International Journal of Psychoanalysis* 11:211–226.

——— (1931) Über respiratorische Introjektion. *Internationale Zeitschrift für Psychoanalyse* 17:234–255.

Freud, A. (1960). Discussion of Dr. John Bowlby's Paper. *Psychoanalytic Study of the Child* 15:53–62.

Freud, S. (1905). Three Essays on the Theory of Sexuality. *Standard Edition* 7:123–246.

——— (1917). Mourning and Melancholia. *Standard Edition:* 14:237–258.

——— (1919). 'A Child is Being Beaten' A Contribution to the Study of the Origin of Sexual Perversions. *Standard Edition* 17:175–204.

———— (1938). Splitting of the Ego in the Process of Defence. *Standard Edition* 23:271–278.

Gillespie, W.H. (1940). A Contribution to the Study of Fetishism. *International Journal of Psychoanalysis* 21:401–415.

Glover, J. (1927). Notes on an Unusual Form of Perversion. International Journal of Psychoanalysis 8:10–24.

Gorky, M. (1919). *Reminiscences of Leo Nicolayevitch Tolstoi.* London: Forgotten Books, 2018.

Greenacre, P. (1960). Further Notes on Fetishism. *Psychoanalytic Study of the Child* 15:191–207.

Hug-Hellmuth, H. (1915). A Case of Female Foot or More Properly Boot Fetishism. In *Int. Zeit. Artlkhe Psychoanal.* (vol. 3).

Katan, M. (1964). Fetishism, Splitting of the Ego, and Denial. *International Journal of Psychoanalysis* 45:237–245.

Kronengold, E. & Sterba, R. (1936). Two Cases of Fetishism. *Psychoanalytic Quarterly* 5:63–70.

Muensterberger, W. (1963). The creative process: Its relation to object loss and fetishism. *Psychoanalytic Study of Society* 1:162–185.

Payne, S. M. (1939). Some Observations on the Ego Development of the Fetishist. International Journal of Psychoanalysis 20:161–170.

Sachs, H. (1986). On the Genesis of Perversions. *Psychoanalytic Quarterly* 55:477–488.

Tolstoy, L. (1852-1856). *Childhood; Boyhood; Youth,* ed. & transl. Judson Rosengrant. London: Penguin Classics, 2012.

———— (1869). *War and Peace,* transl. Rosemary Edmonds. London: Penguin Classics, 1982.

———— (1928). *Diaries,* ed., Transl. F. Christian & transl. Raimonda Kavaliauskienė. New York: Harper.

———— (1931). *Tolstoy Literary Fragments, Letters and Reminiscence.* New York: Ams Pr Inc..

Troyat, H. (1967). *Tolstoy,* transl. Nancy Amphoux. New York: Grove Press, 2001. Collins, 1994.

Winnicott, D.W. (1953). Transitional Objects and Transitional Phenomena—A Study of the First Not-Me Possession. *International Journal of Psychoanalysis 34*:89–97.

Wulff, M. (1946) Fetishism and Object Choice in Early Childhood. *Psychoanalytic Quarterly* 15:450–471.

CHAPTER 13

The 1994 Freud Lecture: Adolescent Daydream and Creative Impulse

PREFACE

Humans are story-telling animals adept at the making of images and the expression of music and dance. All this begins in childhood, but the adolescent daydream is the prototype of works of art. The daydream and the creative impulse are pieces of the same process.

Since analysts are creatures of habit, the reading of this paper will take fifty minutes.

All of us are dreamers but few of us are poets. Yet in adolescence the daydream is a theater of the mind, starring oneself and often rich in plot and characterizations.

Consciously wished-for or sometimes seemingly unbidden, the daydream achieves a structural architecture and heads toward a goal. Attended by powerful sexual and ambitious aims, daydreams serve purposes of gratification, control, consolation, reward, revenge and re-invention of oneself and the world. Though the life of fantasy persists as long as we live, the adolescent daydream seems specific to that period. We enter adolescence with all the remnants of the unfinished business of childhood, now inhabiting a newly bulky, changed body with violently intensified sexual and aggressive needs and wishes. With bewildering rapidity, we enter a new world with upheavals in family relationships, new inner demands, heights and depths of passions and intensifications of excitement, joy, anxiety, depression, guilt, and shame. New choices of friends. imagined sexual partners, new interests in learning, music, literature, movies, television, art, sport, power, and money crowd in upon the adolescent.

Adolescent daydreaming, now the counterpart of childhood play, gives shape and form to this panoply of desire. Moreover, the daydream often has its immediate translation into creative acts: love letters, love poetry, diaries and journals filled with hope, longing and despair, music, sport, and challenging deeds of prowess. Mountains are climbed, inventions are constructed, skills developed, and business schemes hatched. The daydream is often the preparation for a life of work and love but as frequently it is the repository of old hopes and lost hopes, paralyzed intentions, and the psychology of regret.

Psychoanalysis, with its roots in the biology of human development and its methodology based upon the disciplines of history and literature, shifted its philosophical ground from the experimental methods of natural science to the observational methods of the poets, novelists and historians. Sigmund Freud, trained as a neuropathologist, was himself taken aback as he realized his case-histories read like novels. But we should not be surprised by this trajectory of Freud's career, and we have the most striking remnant of his adolescence to guide us. Ernest Jones in his biography of Freud tells us of an experience which Freud shared with Jones. I will quote the episode in its entirety:

In 1906, on the occasion of his fiftieth birthday, the little group of adherents in Vienna presented him with a medallion, designed by a well-known sculptor, Karl Maria Schwerdtner, having on the obverse his side-portrait in bas-relief and on the reverse a Greek design of

Oedipus answering the Sphinx. Around it is a line from Sophocles' Oedipus Tyrannus.

ςτά κλέίν άιήίγματ ήσξι κάί κράτίςτος ην άήνρ

("Who divined the famed riddle and was a man most mighty.)

When he showed it to me a few years later I asked him to translate the passage, my Greek having rusted considerably, but he modestly said I must ask someone else to do it. Thanks to Dr. Hitschmann's kindness I am happy to possess a duplicate of this medallion.

At the presentation of the medallion there was a curious incident. When Freud read the inscription he became pale and agitated and in a strangled voice demanded to know who had thought of it. He behaved as if he had encountered a revenant, and so he had. After Federn told him it was he who had chosen the inscription, Freud disclosed that as a young student at the University of Vienna he used to stroll around the great arcaded court inspecting the busts of former famous professors of the institution. He then had the phantasy, not merely of seeing his own bust there in the future, which would not have been anything remarkable in an ambitious student, but of it actually being inscribed with the identical words he now saw on the medallion.

Not long ago I was able to fulfill his youthful wish by presenting to the University of Vienna, for erection in the court, the bust of Freud made by the sculptor Königsberger in 1921, and the line from Sophocles was added. It was unveiled at a ceremony on February 4, 1955. It is a very rare example of such a daydream of adolescence coming true in every detail, even if it took eighty years to do so.

Freud's daydream and its ambitious goal was a commonplace, grandiose in outlook and almost poignant for a member of a despised minority born in provincial Moravia. Identified with the tragic hero-king, Freud set about his own solution to the riddle of the Sphinx: how to understand the stages of human life by observation and inquiry. Despite endless individual variations, Freud saw that the developmental tasks bore some remarkable similarities in individuals, despite the gaps of culture and circumstance.

In a set of creative works, beginning with the observations that all human infants are helpless, and must mature and develop only with the help of others, he and a few colleagues created psychoanalysis. The childhood need for nurture and help is the basis for what was called transference. Viewing human behavior through its conflictual vicissitudes, psychoanalysis became an observational method, a therapeutic modality, and a set of explanatory hypotheses about the operation of the mind throughout the life cycle. A mixture of scientist and poet, Freud created something new which has proved durable despite endless attacks and frequent premature notices of its demise.

It has been my very great privilege over many years of psychoanalytic practice to have known and treated many creative artists, people who have often been more intelligent and more capable than I was. Creative artists authors, poets, playwrights, painters, composers, and scientists seek analysis for the same reasons as others less talented. Troubled in love or work, beset by anxiety and depression, they seek relief of pain. They agonize over the ubiquitous inhibitions in their creativity. Initially, none have ever presented issues of their adolescent daydreams and fantasies as having any special importance. Yet in almost every instance, those fantasies were crucial in understanding their subsequent careers. Was the content of those fantasies remarkably different from those of other adolescents? What seemed so striking to me was that the content was commonplace. So, what made all of us dreamers but only some of us poets? Here I think that much of what has been written psychoanalytically about art has foundered because of focusing on the "content" of fantasies. Most artists I have known do not recognize themselves in conventional psychoanalytic formulations which seem to them to be far-fetched and speculative. What seems recognizable to them is that they had to find shapes or forms for the expression of their artistic choices. The day-to-day work of the artist is often in the making of a choice even when the ideas seem to come unbidden, even when the procedure seems either arbitrary or aleatory, whether the work proceeds from spontaneous gesture or planned measured event. The work may document the creative process as well as present content representing a variety of sources: of wishes, of needs, of observations of man or nature, of terrors and horrors, rhythms and sounds, words, music, color and light.

Of talent, we can say little other than about special sensitivities which began in early childhood, and that is *very* little. Of craft, we can say much and of inhibition we can say even more. Central to all creative work are identifications with parents, admired figures from present or past, other artists and the higher concept of "art" itself. It is those identifications which both fuel the works and give rise to the ubiquitous fears of plagiarism which have haunted every artist I have known.

The need for confidentiality has restrained me, and almost every other analyst, from reporting upon the only specific information that would convey to an audience any sense of conviction that we have something to say about creativity.. The method I have chosen is to try to convey some of my observations through a series of disguises, a masked-ball of the Beaux-Arts. This was a method used by Phyllis Greenacre in her paper on "The Family Romance of the Artist," but will be put to some different uses here.

I will try to present material from the writings and the biographies of Anthony Trollope, Leo Tolstoy, St. Augustine, Jean-Jacques Rousseau, Nicolas-Edmé Restif de la Bretonne, Napoleon Bonaparte, Elizabeth Gaskell, Charlotte Brontë and Virginia Woolf. I have chosen examples from these authors because I have in them pieces of documented information which are close to observations that my patients have shared with me. Each of the authors is a mask for issues encountered in real patients. Though the content used was derived from public sources, the psychoanalytic experiences are real and vivid and private. The patients' experiences are theirs alone and though your conviction may be incomplete, we may approach the task knowing that the crucial issues are real and only the method of exposition contrived Anthony Trollope, one of the most readable of Victorian novelists, had his literary career undergo an eclipse with his posthumously published autobiography. In it, Trollope had described a method of writing his forty-seven novels, five volumes of short stories, biographies and travel books as well as a translation from the Latin. Trollope assaulted the sensibilities of those with pre-formed notions of the travail of creativity by reporting that he had assigned himself the task of writing a certain number of words, instantly *ready for publication,* every morning. His mother Frances had been a much-published writer who had abandoned him for a crucial period of his childhood, leaving him with his half-mad father. The pinnacle of Trollope's success was in his two sequences of multiple novels: the Barsetshire novels and the Palliser political novels. Here is a remarkable excerpt from the Autobiography (please understand that this book was not written for publication; it was given as a memoir to his son Henry in 1876 and was published by him seven years later, only after Trollope was dead):

I will mention here another habit which had grown upon me from still earlier years I myself often regarded with dismay when I thought of the hours devoted to it, but which, I suppose, must have tended to make me what I have been. As a boy, even as a child, I was thrown much upon myself. I have explained, when speaking of my school-days, how it came to pass that other boys would not play with me. I was therefore alone and had to form my plays within myself. Play of some kind was necessary to me then, as it has always been. Study was not my bent, and I could not please myself by being all idle.

Thus, it came to pass that I was always going about with some castle in the air firmly built within my mind. Nor were these efforts in architecture spasmodic, or subject to constant change from day to day. For weeks, for months, if I remember rightly, from year to year,

I would carry on the same tale, binding myself down to certain laws, to certain proportions, and proprieties, and unities. Nothing impossible was ever introduced, nor even anything which, from outward circumstances, would seem to be violently improbable. I, myself, was of course my own hero. Such is a necessity of castle-building. But I never became a king, or a duke much less when my height and personal appearance were fixed could I be an Antinous, or six feet high. I never was a learned man, nor even a philosopher. But I was a very clever person, and beautiful young women used to be fond of me. And I strove to be kind of heart, and open of hand, and noble in thought, despising mean things; and altogether I was a very much better fellow than I have ever succeeded in being since. This had been the occupation of my life for six or seven years before I went to the Post Office, and was by no means abandoned when I commenced my work. There can, I imagine, hardly be a more dangerous mental practice; but I have often doubted whether, had it not been my practice, I should ever have written a novel. I learned in this way to maintain an interest in a fictitious story, to dwell on a work created by my own imagination, and to live in a world altogether outside the world of my own material life. In after years I have done the game, with this difference, that I have discarded the hero of my early dreams, and have been able to lay my own identity aside.

Here, Trollope touches upon a theme repeated in the memoirs of many artists, his tendency to give an extended, ongoing, and continuous shape to his thought-productions. This shaping helped him achieve what some composers refer to as his "own voice," the unique signature of sound and style. Trollope described his trajectory into being an artist.

It is important in understanding creative experience that we not try to interpolate our own biases and expectations. Much psychoanalytic writing about art has the flavor of "what the artist must have thought, what the artist might have referred to, what childhood experience should have contributed" and so on. We should always keep in mind an aphorism of Ludwig Wittgenstein: "Of that which nothing is known, nothing can be said."

Virginia Woolf provides us with yet another example of achieving form in relation to memory as well as daydream. In a "Sketch of the Past" Woolf says: "I find that scene-making is my natural way of marking the past." For Woolf, memory and fantasy could be woven into scenes providing much of her writing with a gorgeous visual vividness; she invites us to "see" along with her.

Adolescence heightens the ability to create such "scene-like" imagery and to attach it to a narrative which offers vividness, excitement, and continuity. It is an ability described by playwrights and directors of film and stage.

For some the "scene" is not just visual but a mix of sight, sound, and word, not just a theater of the mind but the mind as a recording device that mixes perception, memory, and invention. Old events are recalled in entirety to give vividness to the new work. Saul Bellow reminded us recently that a writer's productions were not autobiographical jottings but were the product of imaginative invention. He noted that the words uttered by a character in a novel did not necessarily reflect the mind of the artist but of a personality *invented* by the writer. Woolf was adept at such imaginative invention in the creation of characters derived from memories. However, Woolf's invitation to the reader to join her in the "scenes" is not so specific as to limit the audience's participation. A genius for ambiguity as demonstrated in "Orlando" allows time to be kaleidoscoped and sexual identity to be transformed. Here too is a commonplace of adolescent daydream: ambiguity of time and sexual identity. Peter Blos, many years ago, alerted us to the frequency with which pre-adolescent and adolescent boys consciously fantasy themselves as women imagined to be powerful, and Robert Bak, Otto Fenichel and Bertram Lewin all described patients' fantasies of a woman with a penis, anatomically ambiguous. Ambiguity can also mask hidden precision (Kris).

Now one of the contrasts between my actual clinical experience and the written memoirs of artists is that written memoirs tend to be sanitized, that is, they tend to be either totally or partially stripped of their sexual and aggressive intensities. Many, if not most, adolescent fantasies and daydreams have some connection to masturbation and sexual excitement. (We might pause for a moment for some thought about the terms "fantasy" and "daydream." I do not think that there is always a clear distinction.)

Psychoanalysis has tended to view fantasy as having unconscious roots reaching up into consciousness in a derivative form, much like the distinction we make in studying dreams between a "manifest content" and latent dream thoughts. In the psychology of dream formation, as distinct from the physiology of dream formation, we have been much concerned with the manner in which dream images arise through the entrepreneurial use of remnants of perceptions while awake, the so-called "day-residue." So too we recognize that the conscious daydream has latent thoughts derived from old memory, unconscious wishes (i.e., fantasy), and a day-residue that gives it form. In common English usage, the daydream as described in the *Oxford English Dictionary* is "a dream indulged in while awake, especially one of happiness or gratified hope or ambition, a reverie, a castle in air. Its first quoted use, by Dryden in 1685 (Lucretius): "…and when awake, thy soul but nods at best, Day-dreams and sickly thoughts revolving in thy breast." In Steele's 1711 Spectator essay #167: …the gay Phantoms that dance before ray waking Eyes and compose my Day-Dreams" place the spectator in a passive position observing the dancing Phantoms.

Accompanied by a mild alteration in consciousness, the daydream is experienced sometimes passively as if unbidden and sometimes as an active conjuring-up of a created event. The daydream is a triumph of the synthetic, integrating, and organizing functions of the ego.)

To return to the edited and sanitized versions as depicted in memoirs, as contrasted to excited masturbatory adolescent memories frequently described by patients, we must remember that this editorial process may not have been merely for purposes of "respectable" publication. Anna Freud had noted that in a manner analogous to the amnesia for events experienced by patients trying to recall early childhood, there is a related amnesia of adolescence. This is usually not about events but about the emotional *intensities* of that period. Many of us have forgotten the emotional roller-coaster of our adolescent years. Racked with love, with rage, with shame and despair, high on joy, thrilled by love, oscillating between fickleness and promises of endless fidelity, adolescence usually gives way to a calmer period. The driven intensity of sexual feeling and aggressive impulse is partially replaced by something less driven. There have been endless speculations about the endocrine basis for these intensities and concomitant speculations of Darwinian "survival-of-the-species" forces at this period of erupting sexuality. I do not believe these speculations add much to our understanding except to provide an image of *impetus*. What is later sanitized for the press is also seen in this amnesia for adolescent peaks of emotionality as observed in older patients. However, the direct connection of daydream and intense sexuality may be seen in the work of Nicolas Edmé Restif de la Bretonne. Restif was born in 1735 and wrote many novels of blatant sexuality. In *Monsieur Nicolas*, an autobiography subtitled *The Human Heart Unveiled*, Restif reports numerous daydreams and conscious fantasies. Restif, who kept diaries and journals throughout his life, recorded all his sexual adventures in a manner comparable to the memoirs of Casanova. Whether real or invented, these lists bid fair to rival Don Giovanni's "1003" in Spain. Restif was known in French literary circles as "Le Rousseau du ruisseau," the "Rousseau of the Gutter" and Restif viewed the two great confessions of St. Augustine and Rousseau simply as apologias. Restif records the following daydream of 1748, age 13:

> I thought of Jeannette and imagined that I was ten years older, and had worked and won a position, and become an advantageous match for her, and that I presented myself to ask for her in marriage. I won her. But my fantasies about her were never such as I sometimes wove about other girls—for in my frequent lapses into despair of ever obtaining Jeannette, I used to fall back on others such as Marianne Taboué, the pink-cheeked Nolin, a certain Adine, young Bourdlllat; and I even imagined Mme. Chevrier a widow and I her husband. All these fantasies ended in marriage; but although they were not without a certain sweetness, they left a trail of lassitude, disgust and remorse; whereas, when Jeannette was the heroine they only grew more exquisite after marriage.

He then goes on to spin a narrative into old age, with children married, the daughters-in-law chosen from "the children of those who most attracted me after Jeannette." The "pure" Jeannette and the others who gave rise to guilty disgust describe a splitting of the images of women analogous to his own splitting of himself into a saint of truthfulness and a confessed sinner. Restif was a shoe-fetishist of whom Grand-Carteret said, "If Restif was a fetishist, the whole eighteenth century was fetishist with him." Restif's autobiographical confessions and novels had great influence. They are said to have "modelled the soul" of the writer Gérard de Nerval. Furthermore, Schiller called Goethe's attention to Monsieur Nicolas as of incalculable value. The daydream and the sexually-explicit confessions of Rousseau and Restif leaped into the romanticism of the nineteenth century. Schiller's *The Robbers* and its extolling of revenge, Goethe's *Werther* and its picture of hopeless love and romanticized suicide, Berlioz's Symphonie Fantastique, and the explosion of "Wagnerism" were the high-water marks of this trend, and psychoanalysis with its emphasis on emotion was an important romantic spin-off into the twentieth century. Young love, young revenge, young poetry leaped on the stage. Shelley, Keats, Byron, Coleridge, Wordsworth what a cast, extolling youth and passion. The Gothic novel (Shelley wrote two) sent shivers up young spines; Mrs. Radcliffe's *Mysteries of Udolpho* was a best-seller, Walpole's *Castle of Otranto* titillated numerous English readers and Jane Austen and Thomas Love Peacock laughed at them all with mockeries of overblown horror.

Now everyone has *some* masturbatory fantasies, everyone has had frightening dreams, but only artists give them specific ongoing form and give them a quality related to what has been styled the secondary revision of dreams. The ideas and sensations must be placed in communicable extended forms, a process I have chosen to call *thematic elaboration*. The essence of romanticism was *thematic elaboration*. Thematic variations add "richness" to the tapestry of creative work in which inner conflicts could be represented in many forms, and repeated patterns; multiple meanings served as a further invitation to the audience to participate. This too helps us to understand the difference between the private thought of many adolescents which tends to be repetitively stereotyped and limited, and the richness of elaboration and the need for communication which characterizes the future artist even where that artist has *some* elements of stereotypy in the daydream. The daydream is close to the wish for immediate gratification, but the construction of a work of art usually (though not always) is a form of delayed gratification (Kris).

For a few moments I would like to turn your attention to the man about whom more has been written than about anyone who ever lived, not excepting Jesus Christ. That man was Napoleon Bonaparte. Napoleon wrote fiction, though that is a surprise to many, and though he aped Rousseau in the attempt to write romances, he was a failed artist. Napoleon could not elaborate. He wrote in a condensed manner some rather puerile and soupy attempts at explications of love when he was an adolescent cadet and young officer. In 1802 in a conversation with Claire de Remussat he said: "...I often let myself dream in order that I might afterwards measure my dreams by the compass of my reason." He told her how he contrived his youthful novels, using, without credit, Rousseau's description of how *La Nouvelle Héloïse* was written. Napoleon's *Clisson et Eugenie, a* caricature of Rousseau, is a bare-bones outline of a romance without any meat on its flesh. Napoleon had a passion for condensation and summary. The late eighteenth century was no time for minimalist art. When reading works of history, he crossed out ruthlessly what he considered excess verbiage in his attempt to distil essences. Finally, on the voyage to conquer Egypt, having carried a library aboard, he upbraided his secretary Bourrienne for reading *Paul et Virginie* and Berthier for reading Goethe's *Werther*. He commented: "Books for lady's maids; only give them history books. Men should read nothing else." He had turned from his attempts at being a man of sensibilities, a replica of Rousseau, and was now wholly a man of action, identified with Paoli, the hero of Corsican resistance against the French. Having confided in Bourrienne, his military schoolmate since age eight, he revealed his wishes and daydreams: "I will do these French all the mischief I can...but you do not ridicule me, you like me." He reported daydreams of the liberation of Corsica, the heroism of Paoli and a glorification of his own father as Paoli's adjutant. His daydreams became less personal and more political; he wrote about the overthrow of kings *before* the Revolution *and* ideas of revenge in the *New Corsica*. The theme of revenge thereafter occupied his life. Its consequence was fateful for the world. His most profound creation was himself, a re-invention of a four-foot eleven-inch outcast into the Emperor

235

Napoleon, now identified with Caesar. His revenge on the French was complete on June 18, 1815 at Waterloo. Napoleon destroyed himself and France in a disastrous and helpless campaign.

Daydreams of revenge are commonplace in adolescence and though few become Napoleons many become sado-masochists, and many become criminals. A few creative artists express their needs for revenge in creative work; rarely is revenge the actual theme of the work; more often revenge fuels ambition. They desire to "get back" at someone or something, to "show" someone. It is in these circumstances that one can witness the re-invention of the self as an act of creation. Changing one's name, immersion in family romances, grandiose new identifications—sometimes with another artist—spring forth and fuel the re-invention. I have seen this more in performers than in creators. A recent biography of the singer Josephine Baker documents such a re-invention: a poor and despised black child who transformed herself into a heroine of the French resistance as well as a renowned sexual figure, sought after by both men and women, successful and a failure in rapid cycles.

The acts of vengeance for the hurts of the past have some resemblance to a commonplace childhood fantasy: "When I am big, and you are little, I will spank you, where a wished-for reversal of positions is the modality of revenge.

Loneliness has often been central to the young lives of many artists, sometimes persisting throughout the life cycle. In a scientific era when a tendency of psychiatric diagnosis is to pare the wide range of human affects down to only two—anxiety and depression—loneliness seems to get short shrift by professionals. But loneliness is one of the most painful of emotions and an important aspect of the life of most adolescents. It is the spur to daydreams, and the invention of stories. Nowhere in the history of art is this more poignant than in the history of the Brontë sisters, especially Charlotte. What a piece of good fortune it was for the world of literature that Charlotte Brontë s biography was written by her friend, the skilled novelist Elizabeth Gaskill. In my view it remains one of the best biographies ever written, though little read now. Mrs. Gaskell, an acute observer of the psychology of women and an early champion of women's rights, especially the rights of poor women, had the deepest sympathetic response to the plight of the Brontë sisters as lonely children. And she deeply understood the relationship of loneliness to daydreaming. This from the biography:

> Life in an isolated village, or a lonely country house, presents many little occurrences which sink into the mind of childhood, there to be brooded over. No other event may have happened, or be likely to happen, for days, to push one of these aside before it has assumed a vague and mysterious importance. Thus, children leading a secluded life are often thoughtful and dreamy: the impressions made upon them by the world without—the unusual sights of earth and sky—the accidental meetings with strange faces and figures (rare occurrences in those out-of-the-way places)—are sometimes magnified by them into things so deeply significant as to be almost supernatural.

This view is repeatedly confirmed in Charlotte Brontë's novels, especially in the masterpiece, *Jane Eyre*. Loneliness led to daydreaming, to invention, to story-telling and the playing of röles. It was not only true that women had enormous difficulty gaining access to publishers, leading them to frequently adopt men's names: Currer Bell, George Eliot, George Sand, but that the weakness of the girls, compared to what Charlotte termed her "august Father," led her to extolling hero men and identifying with them in adolescence. Central to this attitude was the extolling of the Duke of Wellington; almost all Charlotte's juvenilia were said by her to have been written by a "Lord Charles Wellesley" (the Duke's family name). The manuscript for Jane Eyre was submitted with the author's name *Currer Bell* and it probably would not have been published if sent by *Charlotte* Brontë. But realistic and practical matters were not all that was involved. Charlotte wrestled with issues of masculinity and femininity for much of her early life, she saw literature as a path with which to express this conflict and the poetic gift as a mode of compromise resolution. She writes to C. H. Lewes on January 18, 1848: "It is *poetry* as I comprehend the word, which elevates that masculine George Sand, and makes out of something coarse, something Godlike. " The letter is signed Currer Bell. When she finally met Lewes in 1850 she again knit together masculine and feminine. In a letter to a friend, she says:

> I have seen Lewes too … I could not feel otherwise to him than half-sadly, half-tenderly—a queer word that last, but I use it because the aspect of Lewes's face almost moves me to tears; it is so wonderfully like Emily—her eyes, the features, the very nose … even at moments the expression."

(Lewes was later George Eliot's husband.)

All hopes in the Brontë family had been centered by the father upon his ne'er-do-well son, Patrick, who died of alcoholism, Charlotte commented, "My poor father naturally thought more of his only son than of his daughters," She married late to her father's curate, an event which had been her father's wish, and died following childbirth. She had spent a lonely childhood, beset by losses, always trying to please her over-idealized father and his glorious, imagined counterpart: the Duke of Wellington. Her lonely daydreams and her adolescent writings, especially her poetry, culminated in the masterpiece Jane Eyre. She had combined her conflicting adolescent masculine/feminine images and emerged one of the greater writers of the last century.

The multiple deaths and losses in Charlotte Brontë's life are not uncommon in the life of artists. In fact, there is considerable evidence in my own psychoanalytic experience that loss and the need to replace that loss in an act of new creation is a powerful motive for some artists. This seems especially intense when the losses occur in early childhood. I will introduce in my masked-ball of artists the figure of Leo Tolstoy. Tolstoy was remarkable in his need for truthfulness and in his recording of his childhood and adolescent daydreams in very slight fictional disguise in his short novellas, *Childhood, Boyhood and Youth.* His letters, now translated into English, reinforce our awareness of commitment to historical truth much colored by his deep and his moral needs. Tolstoy's mother died when he was two, his father. when he was eight. He was raised by someone styled as his "Aunt Tatyana." He records the following in *Youth:*

I am convinced that there is no human being and no age devoid of this benign, consoling capacity to dream. But except for a general characteristic of impossibility and fairy-likeness, the dreams of each man and each period of life have their own distinctive characteristics. At that period, which I regard as the end of boyhood and the beginning of youth, my feeling: love of *her,* I always dreamt in one expected at any moment as the end of boyhood and dreams were based on four the imaginary woman of whom I always dreamt in one and the same way and whom I expected to meet somewhere. She was a little of Sónya, a little of Mäsha, Vasili's wife, when washing linen in the wash-tub, and a little of a woman with pearls round her white neck whom I had seen long ago at the theatre in the box next to ours. The second feeling was the love of being loved. I wanted everybody to know me and love me. I wanted to tell my name—and for everybody to be struck by this information, to surround me, and thank me for something. The third feeling was hope of some

239

unusual, vain-glorious good fortune, and was so strong and firm that it verged on insanity. I was so convinced that I should very soon by some extraordinary occurrence suddenly become the richest and most distinguished person in the world, that I was continually in a perturbed state of expectation of some magic happiness. I kept expecting that it would now begin, and I should attain all that man can desire, and I was always in a hurry, imagining that it was already beginning somewhere where I was not. The fourth and chief feeling was self-disgust and repentance, but repentance so mingled with hope of happiness that it had nothing sad about it. It seemed to me so easy and natural to tear oneself away from all the past, to alter and forget all that had been, and to begin one's life with all its relations completely anew, in such a way that the past would not oppress or bind me. I even reveled in my reputation for the past, and tried to see it blacker than it really was. The blacker the circle of my recollections of the past, the clearer and brighter stood out the clear, bright point of the present, and the fairer streamed the rainbow colors of the future. That voice of repentance and passionate desire for perfection was the main new sensation of my soul at this period of my development, and it was this that laid a new foundation for my views of myself, of mankind, and of God's universe.

Tolstoy daydreamed throughout his life, always full of wishes, always full of guilt. He recognized that the content of daydreams shifted with the developmental epochs, and he recorded his daydreams as he documented his memories. The act of remembering, fused with acts of invention, were his working methods. They were attempts at the mastery of loss.

A letter, in French, to his "aunt" Tatyana tells a daydream when he was 24. He is on his way to the Caucasus and writes:

This is how I picture it to myself... I am at Yasnaya... you still live at Yasnaya too. You have aged a little, but are still fresh and in good health... I work in the morning, but we see each other almost the whole day; we have dinner; in the evening I read you something that doesn't bore you; then we talk... you talk to me of your memories of my father and mother. We recall the people who were dear to us and who are no more; you will weep, I will do the same; but these tears will be sweet... You know that perhaps my only good quality is my sensibility.

War and Peace with its depiction of Tolstoy's family, member by member, set against the then antique backdrop of the Napoleonic wars, is the artistic outcome of this daydream and the culmination of this sensibility. Tolstoy recreated his own lost world in a glorious novel and its stunning essays on how little one can know about history even if one is an eye-witness observer. But the deepest poignancy is in the last line before the second epilogue when the little Prince Nicholas, after the death of his father Prince Andrew, daydreams of doing "something with which even *he* would be satisfied." *War and Peace* was that "something." The wish to have someone proud of you is one of the great motivating factors of adolescence and a momentous union of self, parents, and conscience. It has been one of the important factors in the life of every artist I have known, even if unconscious at the outset of the analysis. The one who is to be proud is the unseen audience whose love is needed.

Now just a few words about conscience, guilt, shame, and exhibitionism in the creative. The two great confessions dominated by guilt, shame and explosive exhibitionism were those of St. Augustine and Rousseau. Both writers were seeking to exculpate themselves from sins of which they felt horribly guilty—sins of the flesh, rejection of God and morality, excesses leading to shame, but all *continuing* while the breast was being beaten.

Augustine says of his youth, addressing God: "Give me chastity and continence, but not just now" (VI Il, 7). His memory of himself as a whoring, thieving pagan adolescent was linked to his pagan father and distant from his saintly Christian mother.

It is one of the characteristics of adolescent remorse over masturbation that however many times it is abjured, it is repeated. Religious and moral daydreams, and their promissory counterparts—religious and moral vows—are there to be broken and repudiated, only to be renewed again. Confessional literature, novels, and poetry of sin and expiation seem to bear a special relationship to exhibitionism traceable to specific experiences of adolescence. Religious and quasi-religious political conversions are often presented with great fanfare. The need for punishment *and* forgiveness is so great at that period of stormy and imperious sexual need that it must be trumpeted as an aspect of those needs and a derivative of them. It is a forerunner of the exhibitionistic need to declare oneself a good and kind person a variety of reaction formation. But to cast one's ideas as a confession has an enormous appeal and a ready audience. Everyone likes to hear about the crimes of others. Millions of people read murder mysteries in order to find the bad culprit and hold themselves blameless of wishes to murder. So too there is a ready audience for sexual confessions. At the same time, they are stimulating and also offer distance from the described events. The observer may be titillated but free of guilt, as with the murder mystery. The shape and form of the Confessions of Augustine and of Rousseau are not only derived from the periods in which they were written but also reflect the emotional position of their authors: Augustine, now a disciplined churchman, identified with his mother, Santa Monica, and with St. Ambrose; Rousseau, feeling freed of restraints, patterned himself upon the fictional Robinson Crusoe. The model of the confession has as its backdrop the need for an audience to participate, be excited, and be forgiving. It is the model derived from both wishing that one's incestuous and murderous masturbatory wishes be fulfilled and simultaneously being relieved of guilt. Its motto is: "Give me expiation, but not yet." (What awaits my further study are those confessions about one's family which lead to greater guilt and to inhibition about telling more.)

I have presented to you a variety of experiences derived from the analyses of creative people in which their adolescent daydreams and the special shapes and forms which mediated their talents seem to have had some influence upon later works. To do this I have taken you to a masked ball populated by the famous and the dead where you may have access to their published works, and no one's privacy has been compromised.

THE PLACE OF ADOLESCENCE IN PSYCHOANALYTIC THEORY AND PRACTICE

Creative artists are not a race apart. The content of their fantasies from childhood onward are no different from the content of similar fantasies of almost all people. It has been speculated by some that there is a higher incidence of depressive illness among artists; that has not been my experience in the analytic treatment of artists and the many more that I have seen in consultation. It was once speculated that there was a higher incidence of family romance fantasies in artists. Some artists have family romance fantasies but so does one-third of the population at large. In their personality structure, artists are much more similar to the general population than they are different. They come to consult analysts for the same reasons others seek our help. They suffer. They experience anxiety, depression, guilt, shame, phobias, sexual problems, love problems but for them work problems, especially inhibition, seem to loom larger than to others. The work of the artist, the making of art, seems to occupy a greater rôle in the picture of oneself and the regulation of self-esteem than is common. That is not to say that work is not central to the identity of most of our patients. It is that the artist's products are always under scrutiny and judgment: his or her own, the opinions of other artists, the rôle of critics, the opinions of publishers, gallery owners, museums, collectors, producers, directors, and ticket-buyers. In fact, everyone is a critic, everyone has what is considered "taste" and all have a judgment. They may not know much about art, but they know what they like. (Most critics and some psychoanalysts are failed artists; oscillating between awed admiration and bloody-minded envy they can write much that is puzzling. We expect insight in psychoanalysts and are astonished to find that insight in the critic.) Few of us are under constant scrutiny with such diverse possibilities of success or failure. Though there are some differences between the "popular" arts such as theater and film requiring instant audience approval and other art forms as the novel, poetry, painting and sculpture, criticism is ubiquitous. (For example, a book might sit on a shelf for later appreciation, but a closed play or musical has no audience.)

And of course, it is the emphasis on product which has occupied us in our masked ball. How one became an artist is in my view the special consequence of whatever constitutes innate talent and intelligence *and* the special circumstances of adolescence which gels and coalesces the identity of the adult. Now adolescence serves that same function in everyone. What has been there in earlier development now either comes together or falls apart. Adolescence is a time both of burgeoning development and rapid regression, sometimes in cycles. I have given particular emphasis to daydreams because they are so accessible in the analysis of adults. I have often been impressed by the relative absence of information about adolescence in psychoanalytic case reports and in the psychoanalytic literature in general. I have rarely seen a candidate in supervision who had a clear picture of the patient's adolescence, information that was almost immediately accessible. Rather, endless speculations are offered about "what must have happened" in the earliest childhood where no memory is available, and the only evidence is in questionable interpretations of actions observed in the transference situation. This tendency to bypass the accessible and seek to search out earlier and earlier etiologic formulas now seems endless. Anna Freud once attempted an explanation of this trend. She said that once her father was able to trace the origins of adult sexuality back to the earliest infancy, the issues of adolescence seemed to recede into the background. Those analysts whose roots were in education never relegated adolescence to a secondary position: Miss Freud, Mrs. Bornstein, Peter Blos, Erik Homburger Erikson, and August Aichhorn. When Siegfried Bernfeld demonstrated to us in 1938 that adolescence offered a glimpse of recapitulation of all the earlier phases of development we should have been alerted more intensely. But even the wheel needs to be rediscovered periodically. The exploration of adolescence is the potential gold-mine of every adult analysis. Evidences of all the earliest object relations re-emerge, all the old impulses, all the old desires, and all the old fears. And, some new ones, defenses change and consolidate; conscience, standards, and moral issues shift and structuralize as never before; object-choice and gender identity emerge in new form and both work and love take on new meaning. Central to this study is the rôle of conflict which achieves new importance, both in its intensity and in the methods of conflict resolution. It is the exploration of a remembered adolescence that then allows us a better chance of understanding a forgotten childhood and infancy. It is certainly, in my experience, not the other way round. There was some wisdom in an old analytic idea that we should analyze from the surface to the depth.

Some few adolescents will grow into future artists, some potential future artists will have their talents wither if not encouraged either from within or without. (Gray's country churchyard: where "…some mute inglorious Milton here may rest…") But all of us emerge into adulthood with a somewhat new personality, a new identity; few Tolstoys or Napoleons, but many of us with new self-inventions, to be known not by our products but by our personalities.

245

AFTER THE BALL

I attended my first Freud Lecture in 1952 and I reacted to it with a sense of wonder and astonishment. It was given by Ernst Kris and was titled *Psychoanalysis and the Study of Creative Imagination.* I had just applied for admission to the Institute and what I knew about psychoanalysis was very, very little and that was linked to issues of psychiatric pathology. Kris' lecture was a revelation. I was suddenly aware that psychoanalysis was about the life of humankind, about its long history, the capacity to create art as the one really durable product of human endeavor, and that traces of creativity were within each of us though few of us were artists. All were dreamers, all daydreamers, all living in various levels of conflict. The creative imagination was at work in all, tending toward problem-solving and the emergence from conflict. Most importantly for me, I could envision the "creative imagination" as essential to psychoanalytic work, part of the art of psychoanalysis, a link to the poets, albeit a tenuous link.

For those that have read *Winnie-the-Pooh*, I knew then what Tigger likes best. I wanted to learn from artists: what went into their work, and I could do that by offering help with their suffering. I knew I would have to be knowledgeable about development. Eventually I became in charge of the adolescent service at Bellevue, an experience for which I am forever grateful. I also discovered that I learned more about the inner workings of adolescence from my adult patients than from my adolescent patients, much as I tried. Real adolescence is full of emergencies that require instant attention, and exploration of inner life is so difficult that it was clear to me that adult memories of adolescence were actually a much richer mine. How order is created out of chaos seemed to me a worthy study, how art emerges from conflict, how a good interpretation arises out of a welter of associations, how insight develops out of pain all impressed me in conceptualizing psychoanalysis as an art.

Psychoanalysis is not a lonely endeavor, but the making of great art is. Psychoanalysis is a *joint* collaboration. I am always with the patient and psychoanalysis is a conversation, though peculiar in its structure. Moreover, the long apprenticeship aspect of analytic education with exposure to many teachers and supervisors, students and colleagues makes for an awesome richness of identifications and new learning. Sometimes it seems like work done by a committee.

That richness of background is an ever-present part of the work supporting the imaginative equipment of the analyst. Many of our identifications, beginning with our link to Freud himself, have developed in our adolescent and early adult life, whatever the earlier models were. All contribute to how we work, sometimes styled the "technique of analysis." I soon found that in each analysis, there were two techniques of working, my "technique" and the patient's "technique," each based on myriad antecedents and each subtly containing complex—often unconscious— identifications with persons of the past. All hinged upon the capacity for creative imagination in both participants, both undergoing various levels of access to that imagination, some of it depending upon a capacity for a kind of self-observant irony.

REFERENCES

Bernfeld, S. (1938). Types of Adolescence. *Psychoanalytic Quarterly* 1938,7: 243–253.

Bonaparte, N. (1795). *Clisson and Eugénie.* London: Gallic Books, 2013.

de la Bretonne, R. (1794–1797). *Monsieur Nicolas or The Human Heart Unveiled.* Five [of six] volumes, eds. Paul Binding Nash & Havelock Ellis. London: John Rodker, 1931.

de Saint-Pierre, B. (1788). *Paul et Virginie.* Kindle Edition, 2012.

Dryden, J. (1685). Lucretius' On the Nature of Things. In Sylvae: r, the Second Part of Poetical Miscellanies. London: Jacob Tonson, 1685.

Gaskill, E. (1857).The *Life of Charlotte Bronte*, London: Penguin Classics, 1998,

Jones, E. (1953–1961). *The Life and Work of Sigmund Freud* (Three Volume Set). New York: Basic Books, 1960.

Kris, E. (1953). Psychoanalysis and the Study of Creative Imagination *Bulletin of the NY Academy of Medicine* 29(4): 334–351.

Milne, A.A. (1925). *Winnie the Pooh: The Classic Edition.* New York: Sky Pony, 2022.

Radcliffe, A. (1794). *The Mysteries of Udolpho.* In *Mrs. Radcliffe's Novels. The Italian, the Romance of the Forest, The Mysteries of Udolpho.* Charleston, SC: Nabu Press, 2010.

Rousseau. J.-J. (1761). *La Nouvelle Héloïse: Julie, or the New Eloise : Letters of Two Lovers, Inhabitants of a Small Town at the Foot of the Alps.* transl. Judith H. McDowell. University Park, PA The Pennsylvania State University Press; abridged edition, 1986.

——— (1765–1770). *Confessions,* eds. Angela Scholar & Patrick Coleman. Oxford: Oxford World's Classics.

Schiller, F. (1781), *The Robbers.* In T*he Robbers and Wallenstein,* transl F.J. Lamport. Penguin Classics, 1980.

Shelly, M. (1818) *Frankenstein.* CreateSpace Independent Publishing Platform, 2020.

——— (1819–1820) *Matilda.* Yuma, AZ: Bandanna Books, 2013

Sophocles (430–420 bc). *Oedipus The King or Oedipus Tyrannus.* Independently published, 2021.

Saint Augustine (397 & 400). *Confessions,* transl. R.S. Pine-Coffin. London: Penguin Classics, 1961.

Tolstoy, L. (1852–1856). *Childhood; Boyhood; Youth,* ed. & transl. Judson Rosengrant. London: Penguin Classics, 2012.

———— (1869). *War and Peace*, transl. Rosemary Edmonds. London: Penguin Classics, 1982.

Trollope, A. (1876). *An Autobiography of Anthony Trollope,* eds Michael Sadleir, Frederick Page. Oxford: Oxford World's Classics, 1999.

von Goethe, J. W. *The Sufferings of Young Werther,* Ed Stanley Corngold. New York: W. W. Norton & Company, 2012.

Walpole, H. (1764). *The Castle of Otranto,* eds Randy H. Sooknanan & Denise K. McTighe. Independently published, 2022.

Woolf, V. (1928). *Orlando: A Biography.* Boston: Mariner Books, 1973.

———— (1939). A Sketch of the Past. In: *Moments of Being.* Boston: Mariner Books Classics, 1985.

CHAPTER 14

Self-Observation, Self-Analysis and Re-Analysis

INTRODUCTION

It may be that the most profound and enduring biological fact governing the lives of each of us is that we are born helpless and must depend upon others for many years of childhood. Much of our development is in an attempt to achieve some sort of mastery over helplessness. Sometimes this mastery is achieved without the help of others but more often than not mastery is not simply the outcome of one's own effort but the amalgam of that effort with the input from others.

Previous successes do not guarantee against the never-ending human capacity to feel frightened and helpless, a testimony offered by the dreams of the healthy as well as the sick. Psychoanalysis has taught us that danger lurks within as well as coming from the outer world. The danger from within can arise from the importunity of our wishes, both loving and destructive, expressed in the continuous flow of unconscious fantasy. How to understand these fantasies, and the resistances against their expression, is the analytic work whether done by oneself or with the help of someone else. In adulthood, as well as in childhood, the easiest path to dealing with the pain and unpleased is through magic and wishfulness, and not through adaptation to reality.

As analysts we tend to equate self-enquiry and self-knowledge with high moral value. Acknowledgement of the past is not always so viewed either by individuals or societies. Most human beings want to forget the past or re-invent it to suit their own purposes. In a now famous speech to the West German Bundestag some years ago, Richard von Weiszäcker, the president of Germany, upbraided the nation that wanted to forget the past, quoting the sage the Baal Shem Tov: "Repentance comes through remembrance." We may expand that to the idea that understanding comes through remembrance of the imperfections and limitations of our parents, our analysts and ourselves. No matter how we strive, no one is perfect nor ever can be.

Almost a century ago, in the summer of 1897, Freud began what he termed a self-analysis and the history of the psychoanalytic endeavor of the 20th century was catapulted away from the constricted scope of the *Studies in Hysteria*. Freud's self-analytic work seems to have started as a response to his work with hysterical patients, most particularly in the study of their dreams and the attempt to study his own dreams. He noted that he worked at this form of self-knowledge as if he were an "outsider," trying to be "objective" about his own "subjective" experiences. Within a very short time he recognized that the hazard in self-analysis was self-criticism or censorship, or resistance as the obstacles were variously termed. The value of this new form of self-observation was rapidly demonstrated in the widening of his field of observation in his patients and in a marked shift in his theoretical explanations of the observed phenomena.

The technique of free-association, the recognition of infantile sexuality, the rôle played by unconscious drive impulses, the rôle of fantasy, the structure of Oedipal phase conflict, the operation of repression in the distortion of memory, and the screening function of certain "memories" led to an astonishing conclusion: Freud, in studying himself in relation to his patients, recognized that he was opening a new horizon to the study of all of the whole range of normal human beings, not just those suffering from psychological disturbance. With his awareness that fantasy can have the force of real experience, he could put to one side his oversimplified view of the exclusively traumatic origin of neurosis to one which was much more complex and was rooted in a developmental schema. Throughout his scientific life he was aware of the limitations of self-analysis because of the unconscious resistance to uncovering resistances; as late as 1935 he cautioned against the incompleteness of self-analytic work and the tendency to abandon the effort and be too-easily satisfied. He even questioned whether genuine self-analysis were possible. He suggested writing down one's associations was an aid in putting aside self-criticism which would lead to abandoning a direction of thought. (It is in fact this attention to resistance which partially differentiates Freud's self-observation from the "introspective" techniques of the philosophers and the predominantly English introspective psychologies of the prior century.)

In his letters to Fliess, Freud's self-observations were laced with self-reproaches for having failed to understand adequately his patients' symptoms and complaints. Self-analysis and Freud's method of self-observation were always connected to a set of moral issues and imperatives about responsibility and truthfulness. The initial advice to prospective analysts to conduct such self-inquiry gave way to the desirability for "training analysis" as first exemplified in the work of the Zurich school, though the two forms of personal analytic experience were always seen as complementary. The moral imperative of self-analysis has been both an encouragement and a burden for several generations of psychoanalysts. Self-analysis, as many of us have discovered, is easier said than done, and the central problem remains the unconscious nature of resistances. Freud's subsequent recommendation to analysts that they return periodically to analysis has not achieved universal acceptance. Many analysts have been disappointed in their own analyses and have great conflict about returning to a situation which did not lead to adequate therapeutic result.

SELF-OBSERVATION AND SELF-ANALYSIS

In 1966, Martin Stein raised a series of interesting questions about the relationship of self-observation to the ego-function of reality-testing as well as the relationship of self-observation to self-evaluation. These issues bore directly upon Freud's linking of self-observation and moral issues, and some of Hartmann's views of the "self" and the adaptive ego functions which during development modify the "superego" and its moral imperatives. One major element of reality-testing in the course of development is distinguishing between "inner" and "outer" and ultimately understanding what is part of oneself and what are characteristics of other people. This differentiation is crucial to the understanding of transference and to the recognition of the mechanisms of projection and identification. Furthermore, the early development of self-observation and of reality-testing are closely linked to the approval of early objects. Here we also touch upon the rôle of companion or "witness' in early development as well as in subsequent fantasy, The "superego" may, in fact, be viewed as a psychic precipitate of experiences with important people in early life as well as having roots in the drives themselves. Both loving and competitive relations to later "objects" can lead to modifications of the superego, and to enhancement or inhibition of self-observation. *Adolescence* is the fertile ground for these changes in relation to new ideals or to the rejection of old ideals. In order to investigate that which is hidden or forbidden there has to be some sanction from conscience. Masochistic characters in attempting self-analysis often turn it into punishing self-criticism. (Self-analysis, unaccompanied by a protective person, is not always a harmless undertaking.)

254

The function of self-observation almost always contains some trace of the presence of important people from early life. Self-analysis often is done in front of a hidden and secret audience of these early objects or their later transference representatives. A patient, describing a piece of self-analytic work, remembered wanting to be admired for her courage in confronting a forbidden sexual impulse. "Look how brave I am" was something she wanted to show her father as part of a desire to be loved. As opposed to this libidinal wish is the competitive fantasy of another patient in a re-analysis, He remembered "analyzing" a symptom after an unsuccessful analysis and silently reproaching his analyst: "I can do it better than you." This fantasy fed a resistance which both hampered the first analysis and made starting a new analysis difficult. It was the resistance first described by Abraham at the turn of the century in a brief paper on the "auto-analyst" and contributed to both Joan Riviere's and Horney's views on negative therapeutic reaction. Defiance and competition may be part of self-analysis, (something of this sort may have been at work when E. Pickworth Farrow wrote his *Self-analysis* to which Freud attached a preface.)

Another variant on the fantasied relationship of the parent or to the analyst is demonstrated by the report of another patient. When in a re-analysis he remembered a feeling of elation in the fantasy of being linked to an analyst of the past; this occurred when remembering a piece of old analytic work leading to a diminution in a current anxiety situation. Here, there could be discerned a pleasurable fusion with the old object leading to the elated affect.

Yet another patient remembered the wish to "analyze" himself rather than returning to analysis did so out of the fear of regression and dependency upon a new analyst. In this patient the need for mastery over the *temptation* toward regression was very great. For this patient, his concept of self-analysis was one of self-accusation. It served a masochistic need to be a self-contained unit playing both victim and torturer. Following such an episode of self-attack he was very self-congratulatory and felt some degree of smugness and superiority.

With the previous brief clinical examples, I hoped to show that the very issues related to the individual structure of neurosis are issues which color the attempt at self-analysis, That is to say, it is not only the problem of "resistances" which may hamper self-analysis, it is the very nature of the tendencies to conflict which characterize neurosis that may place limitations on self-analytic work. There is not only the problem of "incompleteness" (Freud, 1935) but predilections to choose only certain topics or materials for the self-analytic work. Often this material is a repetitious re-working of things examined in a prior analysis without an advance in understanding. There may be a stereotypy of response.

Gardner in his volume on *Self-inquiry*, by contrast, describes an unending innovative re-working of some themes raised by his interaction with a patient leading to an advance in understanding both himself and the patient. My own experience and the experience of my analyst patients is that one cannot always depend on such felicitous results of self-inquiry. The ability to achieve such self-knowledge may depend upon specific talents and the individual capacity for the heightening and recession of some specific ego functions. For example, analysts vary greatly in their ability to "visualize" that which their patients describe, and even those who possess a talent in "seeing" what is described to them may have this capacity fluctuate with different patients. In this regard, we should keep in mind a comment made by Kurt Eissler in discussing Isakower's concept of the analyzing instrument that it may be the capacity to achieve a "mental picture" which characterizes analytic talent. This capacity is closely related to what Kris termed "regression in the service of the ego."

SELF-OBSERVATION AND SELF-ANALYSIS IN THE ANALYTIC SITUATION

Freud's self-analysis led to his view of universal human tendencies and developments as well as unique differences. His patients did not seem different from him and his friends. He developed a therapeutic and research method based upon conversation and intimacy albeit a special and structured form of conversation and a special form of intimacy. When Freud suggested that it was the patient who chose the topics of the conversation and that the analyst must use his own unconscious as an "instrument" in the analysis, both participants were placed on an equal footing with comparable tasks; the patient was to attempt "free-association," the analyst to attempt "freely-hovering attention," it presumed that both attempts would give rise to some conflict, i.e., that both participants would have to confront resistances. The hope was that the analyst would have better awareness of his own defenses and resistances. Moreover, it became clear that both participants possessed the ubiquitous capacity for transference, i.e., the coloration of current perception by past experience. It was the responsibility of the analyst to keep as clear a picture of his own transferences and counter-transferences as compatible with the persistent awareness of the patient's therapeutic needs.

This demanded of the analyst a continuous self-observation in the analytic situation as the backdrop of all ideas of technique. In this situation, the analyst's self-observation was limited in an interesting way. We discovered that an important affective discharge aspect of the patient's work was achieved through verbalization which also forwarded the free-associative process. The analyst, on the other hand, was more-or-less limited in his verbalizations to that which was relevant to the patient. The attention to the patient could not be preempted by private reverie or by irrelevant intrusions into the patient's mental space. When the clinical situation might demand a piece of rapid self-analytic work, we might have to content ourselves with a self-observation, the self-analytic work to follow at another time. Emergency self-analysis is not always available, nor is an immediate understanding of transference to a patient, or to the patient's objects (parents, spouse, etc.) always possible on the spot. This delay, or refractory time, offers varying technical challenges. It is this challenge which often pushes analysts toward re-analysis and is a pathway we revisit with Freud 's sense of guilt in an early letter to Fliess that he was not offering the patients the best treatment because of his own limitations.

Our own limitations touch upon our narcissism in two conflicting directions; in one sense we want to offer something better, in another sense we may be afraid to confront our own deficiencies. This was best said by Virginia Woolf in 1920; afraid to confront her own feelings of inferiority by writing them in her journal she said, "Why then don't I write it down oftener? Well, one's vanity forbids. I want to appear a success even to myself."

RE-ANALYSIS

There comes a point with many of us that our own efforts at self-analysis have been inadequate to the task of mastering the continuing overstimulation of old pathogenic conflict by doing analytic work. The time has come for renewed analytic work with another person. As I mentioned before, another person has often been there in the mental shadows of the attempts at self-analysis. There is for many of us a fantasy of an intrepid rugged pioneer standing alone to face the onslaughts of life, an ego-ideal especially for many Americans which would be thought very strange by many people of other cultural expectations. In reality, independence is only relative. We all need all the help we can get in the endless attempts at adaptation and mastery as we go through the life cycle. We constantly need to be aware of our own limitations and of the limitations of psychoanalysis itself. We as analysts often need to return to analysis for a refresher either to one's original analyst or a new analyst for a longer or a shorter time, with the clear awareness that no analyst, as parent, is entirely satisfactory for all purposes.

I will give a brief list of what I consider indications for re-analysis for analysts:

1. An upsurge of old neurotic symptoms or a development of new symptoms; here, shame about one's work is of particular importance.
2. A deterioration of object-ties including very unstable marriages and lack of human gratifications outside the office.
3. Excessive pre-occupation with and attachment to patients.
4. Excessive hostility toward patients.
5. Inability to terminate cases; the interminable case may be related to a hopelessness of achieving results, a circumstance sometimes seen in analysts who never achieved relief of their own difficulties.
6. Inability to adequately help patients to stay in analysis.
7. Boredom with work.
8. 8. Deterioration and regression of insight leading to disillusionment.
9. Marked intolerance of regression in oneself or in others .

Re-analysis presents the analyst with an opportunity to achieve new and more durable insight in relation to new experience with another person, The ancient dictum: Physician, heal thyself applies to us with special force, but sometimes we need to call for help.

Experience of re-analysis assists us to evaluate earlier analytic experience and earlier self-analytic experience. In recent years, my practice has essentially consisted of re-analyses of colleagues. Their re-analyses have continuously stimulated new analytic experience in me which for many years had been reinforced by periods of exploration with my own

259

analyst as well as by enlightenment by case discussion with colleagues. Insight, self-observation, and self-analysis all require *continuous* revision throughout life.

Re-analysis gives fresh perspective to self-analysis Self-interpretations, just as interpretations in analysis, are merely temporary explanatory hypotheses. They are only stimuli to further thought, not end-points in themselves. Psycho-analysis is a never ending process, not a time-limited event.

As I once commented elsewhere, the work of re-analysis is a continuing study of both the psychology of disappointment and the inner workings of hope. It is a reminder of the limitations imposed on us by life not only by the limitations of analysis.

REFERENCES

Breuer, J. & Freud, S. (1893). Studies on Hysteria. *Standard Edition* 2:1–305.

Farrow, E. P. (1941*). Psychoanalyze Yourself : A Practical Method of Self-Analysis Enabling a Person to Remove Unreasonable Fears and Depression from This Mind* Madison, CT: International Universities Press, 1948.

Freud, S. (1887) *Letter from Freud to Fliess,* November 24, 1887. The Complete Letters of Sigmund Freud to Wilhelm Fliess, 1887–1904, 42.

——— (1935) Inhibitions, Symptoms and Anxiety. *Psychoanalytic Quarterly* 4:616–625

Gardner, M.R. (1989). *Self Inquiry.* London: Routledge.

Horney, K. (1936) The Problem of the Negative Therapeutic Reaction. *Psychoanalytic Quarterly* 5:29–44

Riviere, J. (1936) A Contribution to the Analysis of the Negative Therapeutic Reaction. *International Journal of Psychoanalysis* 17:304–320

Stein, M. H. (1966). *Self Observation, Reality and the Superego.* *Psychoanalysis–A General Psychology: Essays in Honor of Heinz Hartmann*, ed. R. M. Loewenstein, L. M. Newman, M. Schur, & A. J. Solnit. New York: Int. Univ. Press.

CHAPTER 15

On Beginning a Reanalysis

The work of reanalysis is a continuing study of both the psychology of disappointment and the inner workings of hope.

It is difficult to attempt any systematic evaluation of reanalyses. Generalizations are difficult and the sufferings of individuals are rarely comparable. The experiences of different analysts are also difficult of comparison. I have loosely assembled some personal impressions gathered over many years. These notes are based upon seventeen reanalyses. In three of the cases I worked with patients I had seen earlier in my career where the analyses had seemed to have terminated in an adequate way. Two more cases were patients seen by me where the work had been interrupted. The other twelve had worked with other analysts, in analysis not in psychotherapy. About half the patients initially viewed the first analysis as successful and the other half considered the earlier work to have failed. In addition, I had the opportunity of comparing notes with three analysts who had reanalyzed patients seen by me in the past, two where my work had been a failure.

Kris (1951) noted that: "no truly experimental conditions can be achieved in which the effects of alternative interpretations can be studied" (p. 21). He then commented that reanalysis provides a possible opportunity for such study. We may now add that reanalysis provides an opportunity for the reevaluation of the entire analytic endeavor: diagnosis, indications for analysis, technique, and the theories of therapeutic results and therapeutic failure. Analysts and analysands may have quite different theories of therapeutic success and failure. Such theories are rooted in the mélange of observations and old fantasy systems that are characteristic of human thought.

These notes will emphasize real clinical experience and only touch upon theoretical considerations. They will not be systematic nor complete but are aimed toward achieving an overall perspective on beginning reanalytic work.

THE INITIAL CONSULTATION

Here is a rare and dramatic interview between the author and a man in his forties, academic in outlook, seeking a third analysis.

> *Analyst:* How may I help you?
> *Patient:* This is like the myth of Sisyphus.
> *Analyst:* The myth of Sisyphus?
> *Patient:* (impatiently) You know the myth of Sisyphus!
> *Analyst:* Yes, but tell me…
> *Patient:* (with mild irritation) You know! Sisyphus had to roll a rock back up a hill; it would slip back; that's what all these analyses have been. (Pause) He was punished for treachery to the gods. (Pause) Oh my God! This is too pat! I don't believe it. (Quietly) I don't believe it.

The patient then went on to describe his feeling of responsibility in revealing to his father that his mother was having an affair with a neighbor. The father packed a suitcase and left home. The parents were divorced. These facts had been repeated throughout the two prior analyses. He insisted that he was "responsible but definitely not guilty." Until this interchange, despite repeated prior interpretation, he had denied the feeling of guilt. His life history had been replete with self-punishing failures and disastrous relationships with women; it was an unrecognized model of moral masochism. His character structure was obsessional, and isolation of affect was prominent in his presentation of himself. Interpretations of his need to punish himself for the disruption of his parents' marriage had been warded off by saying that he "didn't feel it." When, during the course of the new analysis, we reviewed the first session, he thanked me for what he called my "naivete" in making him tell the myth of Sisyphus. This unusual event illustrates an overriding principle in consultations, especially with patients seeking reanalysis. Make no assumptions that you know what the patient means, or that you "understand" the patient. The wish and the need to be understood, important as they are for all human beings, may serve as a resistance against being explicit or candid. The "empathic" response may facilitate work with some patients but hinder it with others where an illusion of being understood clouds the patient's exploratory curiosity. This patient's childhood curiosity, exploration, and explicit tattling had all led to disaster and guilt. What a set of choices! But in this interview, guilt momentarily became conscious and meaningful change in the structure of conscience could begin.

The initial consultations are to set an analytic atmosphere to establish a connection between patient and analyst which is explanatory and in which issues of transference and resistance make their appearance at the outset. During the consultative process patients often begin, unconsciously, as if the analyst knew a great deal about them. The consultation seems to be a continuation of the prior treatment. The analysand is in the midst of something and the analyst has to begin from scratch.

The initial task is to try to know the total personality and not merely to search out the psychopathology. The suffering patients are likely to present themselves with symptoms uppermost. Their positive capacities and strengths are frequently kept in the shadowy background. The panoramic view of the total personality is the guide for the entire analytic endeavor.

The concept of psychoanalytic "diagnosis" is a very broad one, embracing not only the descriptive phenomenology but much else. We want the widest assessment of object relations and the capacity for love and sexuality. We need an understanding of ego functions (memory, thinking, self-observation, identifications, defense, control of regression and affect, adaptiveness, capacity for work, for playful imagination, for humor). Moreover, we want to understand superego functions (guilt, self-criticism, self-punitive trends). Not only is the cross-sectional viewpoint necessary (how do things look at the moment), but the longitudinal viewpoint of history provides a glimpse of indications for analysis as well as some prognostic clues. Not every patient seeking reanalysis should be back in analysis. For about half of the patients I have seen in consultation, other forms of treatment seemed more appropriate. Focusing on symptom complexes alone will obscure the picture; two patients with somewhat similar symptoms may have vastly different underlying psychopathology and vastly different prognoses. Choice of treatment should hinge upon the more wide-ranging attempts at "diagnosis." Ultimately, for some patients, diagnosis will depend upon a trial of analysis.

These early interviews have to narrow the gulf between two people engaged in a rather peculiar form of conversation. The patient is also assessing the analyst and the analytic procedure. Prior analysis does not mean that the earlier treatment was appropriate then or now, or that the choice of analysis was or is appropriate. For some patients earlier analysis had been undertaken incautiously. Everything is to be the subject of inquiry.

A lonely man of forty-two had been in an extended, unsuccessful analysis for many years, concluded only by the illness of the analyst. The patient described a pan-neurosis with anxiety, phobias, depression, and obsessional symptoms. He was very successful at his work, which required little contact with other people. His only partial therapeutic relief had been in the continuous supportive link with his devoted analyst, which had been accompanied by the patient's fantasies of fusion. An extended consultation helped clarify the contained borderline schizophrenic process. Both the patient and the prior analyst had been clearly aware of the severity of the disturbance. A directly supportive psychotherapy without analytic trappings proved helpful.

FANTASIES OF THERAPEUTIC SUCCESS OR FAILURE

Very soon after beginning the evaluative process, patients tend to present their ideas about why the prior analysis did not succeed or why it did not prevent a return of suffering. With rare exceptions, the "blame" is placed upon the person of the analyst. The analyst is said to have done something noxious or not to have done something loving or caring. As with many human attitudes, there is usually a kernel of truth in the report. But with striking regularity the "theory of therapeutic failure" offered by the patient bears uncanny resemblance to the patient's fantasies of neurosogenesis.

Abend (1979) and Arlow (1981) explored the relationship between unconscious fantasy and theories of cure and of pathogenesis. The authors emphasized that both analyst and analysand might share similar fantasies and that technique and outcome may well be influenced by jointly held unconscious wishes. Each individual has a wholly idiosyncratic unconscious fantasy life which tends to become patterned through a lifetime. The transformations of these fantasies become more complex with maturation and development. New events lead to new conflicts and alterations of function into new editions.

Old fantasies can serve new functions. Fantasies about pathogenesis, however, tend to be simplified and reductionistic and generally fall into a few categories: traumatic, toxic, and deficit disorder. Arlow described these as related to the "quest for the villain." Patients' fantasies of therapeutic failure usually parallel their ideas of pathogenesis. The "quest for the villain" now falls upon the analyst, and seems to be unrelated to the analyst's school of thought or theoretical predilection. Sometimes the appearance of new symptoms brings a patient back after a successful prior treatment. When the patient tries to explain the earlier success, he often falls back upon fantasies of curative factors whose unconscious roots had been present long before the treatment started. It is one of the tasks of reanalysis to address the relative fixity of old fantasy and psychic structure. In no instance did any of the seventeen patients spontaneously connect therapeutic outcome with those resistances to exploration and change which subsequently appeared in the reanalysis. The very nature of these fantasies invites a countertransference response. The patients make an appeal to any new analyst's narcissism and competitiveness. They often want the old analyst to be castigated for imperfection of character, bad technique, insufficient empathy, too much empathy, talking too much, talking too little. There are projections of defense: a sexually inhibited man said his analyst would not let him be sexual, a masochistic woman said her analyst would not let her be angry. The new analyst is implored to be the vehicle of delivery of the fantasy of cure. If something did not work in prior analysis, the task is to search out the complexity of contributing factors, not to be in competition with the analyst whose work was not sufficiently fruitful.

TRANSFERENCE RESPONSES AT THE ONSET OF REANALYSIS

Generally, my experience has been that the many issues of transference to be explored are clouded at the beginning by a facade of idealization. In the hope that this time analysis might work, the new analyst is imbued with the characteristics of a redeemer. The analyst is asked to make all the old dreams come true. A clinical vignette follows:

A fearful, angry unmarried woman in her forties sought consultation after a failed analysis. A few sessions later, she looked at me with starry-eyed hope. I was supposed by her to have understood her remarkably. I was flabbergasted; I was in fact completely puzzled by her. After the analysis began, she told me that she had heard of a former patient who had married after an analysis; moreover, she heard that all my patients got married! This feat was to be performed for her and this action would serve as reproach to her younger sister who had declared the patient "unlovable." In the patient's fantasy, this had come to mean "unanalyzable." Her hoped-for success would then reproach the first analyst.

The wish for revenge is a powerful motive for both seeking analysis and defeating it.

A man in his fifties had been in analysis with many analysts since his twenties. It was difficult to know what first brought him to analysis or why he continued to seek it out. His complaints about the various analysts paralleled his reproaches to his parents: lack of concern and coldness. The issue of empathic lack was specially virulent toward someone he styled as a "self psychologist" who was "supposed to be a specialist in empathy." The patient had a fantasy that all his failures in life were reproaches to his parents whose crime was that they had many children. The patient's unconscious crime was in wishing the death of the whole lot. To justify his sadistic fantasies, he had to prove his victims dastardly. He was deeply ashamed of his identification with the Nazis, and pitifully apologetic to his Jewish analyst. Careful analysis of the past relationships to the other analysts demonstrated that they were not as originally depicted; instead of being lumped together in a category of defect, they took on individual character. Many of them had, in fact, been helpful.

It is the new analyst's task to facilitate the reevocation of the older therapeutic efforts and to analyze them in the present.

RESISTANCES IN REANALYSIS

When Freud at the end of his career placed the greatest emphasis on the analysis of resistance he was pointing to the necessity of reliving pathogenic conflicts *in the analytic situation*. It was not an intellectualizing process that was sought but something that touched the heart. Insight is not an intellectual process but an affect-laden triumph of integrating functions (Kris, 1956b). Insight usually follows the crumbling of resistance structures. In a recent paper on insight (1987), I had noted how frequently insights achieved in prior treatment had been reduced to cliches. These precis like statements have a structure similar to screen memories. The reductionistic formulas of Pseudoinsight serve as resistances against exploration of what actually happened with other therapists. They were often mocking, as if to say "What nonsense! A recent supervisory experience with a colleague conducting a reanalysis alerted me to a related phenomenon: the patient behaved as if only the present experience was meaningful and the past was dross, echoing Henry Ford's dictum that "history was bunk." The recent past and the distant past were hidden behind a sarcastic antihistorical stance.

WHY ANALYSES FAIL

The most frequently clinically demonstrated reason for therapeutic failure is that certain analyses should not have been attempted in the first place. Sometimes this is because of inadequate evaluation and faulty analytic diagnosis. Sometimes it seems related to a mismatch between analyst and analysand. Not every patient is analyzable by every analyst. But there are many instances where failures are only partial. Here my experience seems to point toward two major factors:

1. unanalyzed and perhaps unanalyzable transference reactions, and
2. unanalyzed and perhaps unanalyzable resistances.

These factors had been highlighted in Freud's *Analysis Terminable and Interminable* (1937) in a manner which remains powerfully useful, Freud discussed what he considered limiting factors in the work:

1. The tendency to cling to the mental representation of the early objects and the early modes of gratification.
2. The special tendency toward conflict in certain individuals, a tendency Freud related to aggression. To this we may add constitutionally determined predispositions to anxiety.
3. Conflicts about masculinity and femininity (i.e., fantasies about genital damage and the wish to be of the opposite sex).
4. Resistances determined by the unconscious need for punishment.

These limiting factors do not predict failure; rather they serve to scale down our expectations in some cases and to increase technical alertness in others. Freud's comments provide us with a framework of questions we may ask of the clinical data when starting a reanalysis. In each instance we must try to gauge the contribution to the process made by both participants: the patient and the analyst. Technique has seemed the province of the analyst. Little examined in discussions of technique is the question of how the patient worked at the analysis, in essence, the patient's technique. Analysis is a conjoint effort, not something analysts do to patients. The study of the patient's contribution to the mode of analyzing is critical to understanding clinical failure and clinical success. It ·is almost instantly directly observable but attention must be drawn to it.

Early dreams tend to alert us to powerful resistances which will appear in more explicit form later in the analysis. I will single out one issue in relation to early dreams: femininity and masculinity.

A woman dreamed after the first consultation (following a partially failed an analysis) that she and "an analyst" were on a hiking trip in the Rockies. A rest stop is made, and she urinates with a very thick penis. She awakens with the feeling that the consultations are unnecessary. Her associations were of envious memories of her brother who has a close business relationship with their father. Furthermore, she envied her first an analyst's male patients whom she took to be analytic candidates. "You will ascribe that to penis envy," she says dismissively. When I intervene and point out how lonely she feels, she cries. She hates to cry and thinks only women cry. If she were a boy she wouldn't need analysis. She claims that she didn't dream much during the first analysis.

A man dreams after the second month of the new analysis that he arrives at the waiting room to find a very beautiful woman lounging seductively. He is enraged at the idea that the analyst has given the hour to this woman. She is short and wearing very high-heeled shoes. The patient is short and used to try on his mother's shoes in early adolescence.

In both examples the dreams had their counterparts in shame-laden masturbatory fantasy. In both patients, specific fantasies linked to specific masturbatory practices presented powerful resistances to the analytic work. In effect, both patients desired an abrogation of their biological reality. The pattern of resistance had been heralded in the early dreams, but did not assume full form until considerably later in the course of the work. The connection to masturbatory practices took a very long period of time.

Early dreams often alert us to negative therapeutic reactions and the underlying unconscious need for punishment.

A woman who had a disastrous attempt at analysis with a very imperious, poorly trained woman analyst dreams that she pulls a lever and hits the jackpot at a casino slot machine. Silver dollars pour all over the floor. When she tries to pick them up she sees that her hand is cut and bleeding and she cannot gather up the money. She associates the new analysis to hitting the jackpot but conveys the fantasy that when ever anything good happens something bad follows. She believes that she chose the first analyst thinking that she wasn't a good doctor, but she charged small fees.

The dream announced a pattern of suffering and failure following each advance. This daunting resistance makes one very respectful of the power of guilty fantasy. Being alert at the beginning could do nothing to head off the full force of self-punitive ideas, but having a roadmap reduces the surprises of the journey.

THE IMPORTANCE OF FANTASY LIFE IN THE MAINTENANCE OF RESISTANCE

The relative persistence of organized fantasy in the life of individuals who have subjected themselves to analytic scrutiny is quite astonishing. I n the realm of un conscious fantasy there tends to be a remarkable sameness, with some small variations, throughout most of a lifetime. The stereotypy of conscious daydreams becomes subject to day to day variations. A phenomenon akin to the use of the day residue in the dream work would seem to account for these variations. New perceptions and new objects of desire are incorporated in t old basic patterns giving the illusion of new fantasy. Essentially one sees a new cast of characters playing out an old script.

Daydreams and masturbatory fantasies are directly available to the patient's consciousness. Often, they are kept from the analysis by a barrier of anxiety, shame, or guilt; sometimes the patient will not share the fantasies because they are greatly cherished and there is a fear that the analyst will plunder them or destroy their magic for secret pleasure. Unconscious fantasy is allowed conscious representation by a variety of deletions and other unconscious editorial practices.

In many of the patients I have seen in reanalysis there seems to have been a widespread blockage against the exploration of daydreams. Though in some instances this is a special example of clinging to the early objects and to early modes of gratification, in many patients the early model of fantasy undergoes a change of function. It becomes a template of the ego function of defense.

A clinical example follows:

A young woman who had attempted an unsuccessful analysis in her late adolescence and early adult life had a persistent secret masturbatory fantasy which she withheld. She is lying in bed in a darkened room. A very tall man enters the room, undresses slowly, and reveals a huge penis. She feels almost hypnotized and powerless. The man whispers to her that he will force her to have an orgasm. She silently vows that she will not respond. The painful intercourse seems interminable and against her will she has an explosive orgasm. After months of analysis, she reveals with shame that she has masturbated with some variations of this fantasy every day since she began to menstruate. The revelation follows an interpretation that she behaves as if she is being forced to be in analysis. The fantasy had become the model for resistance in the analytic work.

Conscious fantasy may provide important data in understanding the form of resistance. The shape of inner life determines the shape of behavior.

Conscious fantasy about the analysis itself can be sequestered and thus can hide other fantasies critical to the understanding of the total neurosis.

A man had been in an analysis which had failed to relieve his symptoms or his characterological difficulties. He was very angry with his older, illustrious analyst who had disappointed him. Throughout the first analysis the patient who had the session following his had been a very pretty woman.

He had the conscious fantasy that he was an irritant to his analyst who preferred her. He imagined that he and the analyst had to endure the frustrations of "fruitless" analysis while the woman patient and the analyst carried out an illicit romance. None of this was revealed to the first analyst on the basis of its being "foolish." Hidden in the fantasy was the patient's wish to be a woman, to be pregnant ("fruitful"), and to enthrall his father. His hypochondriacal mother seemed to have captured his father's attention through the means of endless complaints.

The reanalytic experience puts into high relief the necessity of exploring every available avenue of fantasy. I often ask patients if there is anything they didn't tell the first analyst. The answers have sometimes been quite astonishing. The experience has alerted me to the likelihood of repetition in the new analysis and should warn us about the importance of conscious withholding in any analysis.

REANALYSIS OF TRANSFERENCES TO THE PREVIOUS ANALYST

It is a frequent analytic experience that after a very brief period filled with anamnestic data, it is as if the patient lost sight of his or her own life story and focuses all attention upon the analyst's person, the analyst's functions, the setting of the analytic procedure, the other patients, and so on. The transference phenomena, many of which were latent, now become manifest; the past has kaleidoscoped into the present. In fact, resistance appears to be an exploration of the past, recollection and memory having been replaced by the need to repeat the past in transference action. In reanalysis, there is a tendency for the earlier analytic work to be effaced. The relatively recent past of the other analysis follows the infantile past into an oblivion, only to resurface in transference repetition. One of the major tasks of the new analysis, from its onset, is the exploration of the earlier transference situation. This task is resisted with the entire force of transference resistances, and after the initial idealizing honeymoon, resistances are relived with the new analyst. What is of significance is the question: "What actually happened?" with all its initial "Rashomon" implications.

A male patient had a persistent fantasy about his first analyst that she had a "countertransference" problem with him. He depicted her as "unempathic," irritated, and bored by his temper outbursts during his sessions. She had declared him "unanalyzable" and attempted to do some supportive psychotherapy. He abandoned the effort. Later, he resumed analysis with me, but soon began a repetition of temper outbursts in the new analysis. These experiences interested me because occasionally he held his breath, turned bright red, clenched his fists, and altogether resembled a small child in a tantrum. Surprised that I was interested in the similarity to childhood experiences and not at all critical of him, he developed some heightened curiosity. He had been an "impossible" child and his parents had "given up" on him. They seemed to have been "good enough" for the other siblings. Gradually, he became aware that many experiences in the first analysis belied his conviction that the analyst had been bored. In fact, there were many examples of her being in tune with him. His aroused curiosity caused him to speak to his mother about his infancy and childhood. He had been a colicky, unsatisfiable baby, severely hyperactive and aggressive, different from his siblings, and requiring her constant attention. His fantasy of being unloved had to be revised to include his early physiological disturbances and the need to externalize blame. The transference fantasies about the woman analyst could be seen as repetitions of earlier fantasies of maternal badness. He began to feel a love for his mother never before experienced; his anger with the first analyst gave way to sadness about the many missed opportunities in his life, especially with women. Here the emphasis is upon repetition in the transference of a mélange of early experience and resultant fantasy. What had been unanalyzable with someone who directly represented mother could be analyze n the slightly more neutral atmosphere presented by a male analyst. Much of this work took place within the first year of the new analysis. It is not usually so easy. Though the patient was left with a greater than usual volatility, his temper tantrums disappeared; he had developed a capacity for control that he had thought impossible. His reexamination of the prior analysis became a regular part of the analytic work, usually initiated by him. Here we see that the exploration of transferences in the reanalysis hinged upon the development of heightened ego capacities of self-observation, curiosity, and insight. The mere reliving of certain crucial affect-laden experiences had been insufficient to effect change. Even the "good-enough" mother can be discouraged by her inability to comfort a distressed infant, and even the "good- enough" ("empathic-enough") analyst may have difficulties with some patients.

All technique has to be attuned to the real needs of each patient. There cannot be a Procrustean couch. Life is not dreary repetition. It is ever new. Analysis should be no less.

REFERENCES

Abend, S. M. (1979). Unconscious Fantasy and Theories of Cure. *Journal of the American Psychoanalytic Association* 27:579–596.

Arlow, J. A. (1981). Theories of Pathogenesis. *Psychoanalytic Quarterly* 50:488–514.

Freud, S. (1937). Analysis Terminable and Interminable. *Standard Edition* 23:209–254.

Horowitz, M. H. (1987). Some Notes on Insight and its Failures. *Psychoanalytic Quarterly* 56:177–196.

Kris, E. (1951). Ego Psychology and Interpretation in Psychoanalytic Therapy. *Psychoanalytic Quarterly* 20:15–30.

——— (1956) .On Some Vicissitudes of Insight in Psycho-Analysis. *International Journal of Psychoanalysis* 37:445–455.

CHAPTER 16

Freud's Enduring Legacy: The Flexibility of Psychoanalytic Technique

Today as we commemorate the fiftieth anniversary of Freud's death, we remember his rôle in the shaping of twentieth century thought. We also commemorate the survival of a great humanistic tradition which was on the edge of destruction in 1939. Psychoanalysis, born in the German-speaking community, was forcibly expelled from that society leaving its founder to become a citizen of the world.

> Heinrich Heine in 1820 (Almansor) had said:
> "Wherever books are burned,
> men also, in the end
> are burned. "
> [Dort, wo man Bücher Verbrennt,
> verbrennt man auch
> am Ende Menschen.]

Much of Freud's universe was destroyed and millions of mankind were burned but the books survived and the ideas live.

Psychoanalysis was the product of a tradition that honored the value of life, the value of thought and emotion; it saw both the lyric and tragic poetry of existence and created a research and therapeutic tool out of conversation and intimacy. The special forms of that conversation and that intimacy are the history of psychoanalytic technique.

Much of psychoanalysis has grown, changed, and shifted in the passage of time but all of it bears the imprint of its first begetter. Freud's legacy to us has encompassed much more than concrete clinical experience.

However, it is from the clinical situation that psychoanalysis draws its strength. Like Antaeus, psychoanalytic vigor derives from having two feet on the ground—the actual conversation and the actual intimacy of shared exploration by analyst and analysand.

The "technique" of psychoanalysis has been praised and vilified, sanctified and caricatured, much of the mythology about technique having very little bearing upon its sources or actual current practice. Emphasis is often placed upon its least significant quality—the "ceremonial" of the couch. Its greater significance was the openness of exploration and the use of the creative imagination by both participants akin to a collaborative work of art.

As in many other aspects of Freud's work, it is hazardous to view his scientific contributions outside their historical context. The technique of analysis has had an interesting relationship to the explanatory hypotheses of psychoanalytic theory. As Hartmann, Paul Gray and others have shown, there has been a series of lags and discontinuities between theory and practice.

Freud 's specifically focused papers on technique were written in 1913, 1914 and 1915. These were "recommendations. " They were not prescriptive and did not constitute a " how-to" manual. These technical papers centered on the phenomena of transference and resistance. In them, the major *outlines* of the analytic situation were approached utilizing the concepts of their time. But these were merely outlines, only a hint at what was to come.

What proved of enormous significance was Freud 's advice that the analyst not "select particular elements or problems to work on, but to start with whatever" the patient presents "on the psychic surface, and to use interpretation mainly for the purpose of recognizing the resistance and making it conscious to the patient" (Hartmann, 1951) . This, the basis of standard analytic technique, was a major shift in thinking about the observational method of analysis: In the period in which Freud used hypnosis as the major investigative instrument, the symptom was the starting point, the analyst was the investigator, and the patient was a relatively passive participant. When hypnosis proved unreliable, and Freud shifted to a "concentration" technique, symptom and pathology were still the starting points. With the introduction of what became the standard *of* technique a special form of Conversation (to use Bernfeld's term) became the investigative *method*. Standard technique did not mean "invariable"; rather, it meant the standard against which variations might be compared (Kris). The patient was now a full participant and since the selection of topics was the patient's choice, the field of investigation shifted from the narrow issue of pathology to the wide range of the *total* personality. The patient, not the analyst, set the daily agenda.

Psychoanalysis, henceforward, was not limited to the understanding of symptoms but also could study what Hartmann termed the "etiology of health." Defense and resistance were no longer viewed as pathological phenomena but a vital aspect of the functioning of the total personality. Reality relationships, the ties to other people—past and present—the capacity for work—in and out of the analysis—the ability to enjoy life, the resilience to deal with "necessary losses" all became the proper subjects of shared analytic scrutiny.

Further, as more and more varieties of suffering, illness, and character disturbance came under analytic study—the widening scope (Stone)—an increasing flexibility in technique became a necessity. This is all on the patient 's side of the peculiar conversation of analysis. When Freud noted that each analyst would have to utilize his own unconscious as a tool in the analysis, a shift was required in the analyst's contribution. Technique could be as variable as its two participants. Variable, however, did not mean random. Nor it did it mean "wild." The variations themselves would become subject to the analytic scrutiny.

An endless series of individual differences could now be introduced, provided that they were examined. The *analytic* procedure *itself* became the proper study of *both* participants. Symbolic interpretation with its relatively mechanical formulations and tendency toward universal generalization gave way to the study of the individual's capacity for fantasy and to form individual "symbols." Jungian analysis was the inheritor of the search for universals. What began as a study of nosological entities became a study of individuals: individual patients and individual analysts. No two individuals had exactly the same experiences, though we might share some "final common pathways," to borrow a term from physiology.

No two analysts would have the *same* capacity for "freely hovering attention," the counterpart to the patient 's free association. Just as we learned that the "basic rule" of analysis could not simply be carried out but would give rise to conflict in self-revelation, so the analyst might experience conflict in attention. Analysis of analysts became a necessity, and ongoing self-analysis an occupational requirement. Countertransference response was to be henceforward the subject of self-scrutiny. Symptomatology became differentiated from psychopathology; two patients might have similar-appearing symptoms and have quite different underlying developmental and experiential factors leading to symptom-formation. (An interesting current tendency in psychiatry tends once again to make equivalents of manifest symptoms despite individual differences in symptom-formation.)

At the time of writing of the technical papers of 1913–15, with their emphasis on transference and resistance, Freud had hinted that no two analyses could be the same. Interestingly however, the focus remained upon symptom-formation and symptom-resolution. The nature of the "constitutional" factors of illness remained a puzzle. He had earlier hoped to find inherited characteristics and even considered the rôle of parental infection (syphilis, for example). But the method of psychoanalysis at the time was to elucidate "meaning" by making the warded-off (unconscious) mental contents accessible to conscious re-working.

Little noted in the history of analytic technique was Freud's observation that both patients and physicians tended to trivialize neurotic symptoms and neurotic suffering. Henceforth, nothing was beneath notice; moreover, premature ranking of data in terms of supposed importance was called into question. Not only was all subject matter to be scrutinized but its significance was to be studied rather than subjected to peremptory judgment by anyone. (Trivialization not only serves defense and resistance; it often has high superego value as a fantasied mark of endurance, strength, or bravery and may be designed to bring forth the admiration of others.)

On the other side of the game coin was a new task for the analyst: if importance of data could not be estimated until analytic scrutiny, then the analyst's theoretical predilections had continually to be called into question until demonstrated to be applicable to the given case. With the recognition that there were two people sharing the analytic work, "technique" was no longer the sole province of the analyst; the patient, too, has a "technique" of analyzing.

NEW CLINICAL ENTITIES

The 1913–15 technical papers of Freud clearly were not his last word on the subject; in fact, they were the beginning of what proved a complex legacy. They were suggestions about what might now be considered brief therapy designed for symptom-removal.

Some of the greatest technical advances proceeded from the study of new clinical entities. The interest of Jung and the Swiss analysts in the treatment of schizophrenia led not only to a series of therapeutic failures but also produced a theory of narcissism which has ultimately proved useful in many ways. The experiences with the traumatic neuroses of war in the 1914–18 conflict raised many interesting issues in the repetitive nature of painful experience. The study of character disturbances pointed toward the patterning of behavior as well as its repetitiveness. The röle of aggression was given new importance. The view of anxiety as a biological response to danger, real or fantasied, necessitated significant shifts in technique as well as a revision of the theory of affects.

Analytic observations and developmental studies of children focused attention on a much wider range of developmental sequences other than infantile sexual development. It is perhaps of importance that some of the early child analysts were trained as teachers because of the complex development of language development, thinking styles, flowering of transference responses *without* early interpretation. With certain patients some transference manifestations ("idealization," "mirroring") were heightened. A special emphasis was placed upon "empathic" response. Though technically handled in a different way from Greenacre who had also described such transferences, individual differences by different analysts *in response* to transference lead to differences in technique which then have to be compared. Similarly, the treatment of certain "borderline" patients has led Kernberg and others to develop technical procedures which now invite comparison with other techniques. As demonstrated by Arlow, varying theories of pathogenesis will lead to varying technical procedures. Varying theories of development will also have technical implications.

Mrs. Klein's focus upon the fantasy life of children has led to a group of technical ideas about the psychological treatment of certain depressed patients (and others). The British "object-relations" theorists placing special importance upon early interactions with others have led to still other technical innovations. Each analyst tends to pick out special areas of importance to him or her creating a mosaic of observations and methods. As Fred Pine pointed out in a series of papers, we all *clinically* utilize the ideas of others by varying selection and emphasis. The technical consequences can, however, be quite different in practice.

What is of interest is that all analytic theorists base their ideas upon Freud; all utilize the method of intimacy and conversation. What is now needed is systematic comparison of methods from the viewpoint of research into the psychological origins of behavior and therapeutic result. (Interpretations and other interventions are merely provisional explanatory hypotheses We await the patient's response—the conflicts to which interpretation gives rise. Cleverness or inventiveness are of no particular value; only the interaction of the two participants will ultimately matter.) Moreover, we are now at the point where in the biological studies of psychiatry some more bridging concepts must be attempted to define more clearly the constitutional underpinnings of psychological states. Here, too, Freud pointed the way. Like any explorer of a new world, he could not draw us an accurate map, he could only indicate a direction for further voyages.

To re-read Freud, to see the flexibility of observational and therapeutic method bequeathed to us, is to feel "like some watcher of the skies when a new planet swims into his ken," and today we look "at each other with a wild surmise—Silent, upon a peak in Darien."

REFERENCES

Bernfeld, S. (1985) The Facts of Observation in Psychoanalysis. *International Review of Psychoanalysis* 12:342–35.1

Freud, S. (1913). On Beginning the Treatment (Further Recommendations on the Technique of Psycho-Analysis I). *Standard Edition* 12:121–144.

———— (1914). Fausse Reconnaissance ('Déjà Raconteé') in Psycho-Analytic Treatment. *Standard Edition* 13:199–207.

———— (1915). Instincts and their Vicissitudes. *Standard Edition* 14:109–140.

Greenacre, P. (1954) The Röle of Transference—Practical Considerations in Relation to Psychoanalytic Therapy. *Journal of the American Psychoanalytic Association* 2:671-684.

Greenacre, P. (1959) Certain Technical Problems in the Transference Relationship. *Journal of the American Psychoanalytic Association* 7:484–502.

Hartmann, H. (1951). Technical Implications of Ego Psychology. *Psychoanalytic Quarterly* 20:31–43.

Heine, H. (1820). *Almansor: Eine Tragödie* (German Edition), Maroussim, Greece: Alpha Editions, 2022.

Keats, J. (1816). On First Looking into Chapman's Homer In: *John Keats: The Complete Poems*. New York: Penguin Classics, 1977.

Klein, M. (1935) A Contribution to the Psychogenesis of Manic-Depressive States. *International Journal of Psychoanalysis* 16:145–174.

Klein, M. (1952) The Mutual Influences in the Development of Ego and Id—Discussants. *Psychoanalytic Study of the Child* 7:51–53.

Kris, A. O. (1990) The Analyst's Stance and the Method of Free Association. *Psychoanalytic Study of the Child* 45:25–41.

Stone, L. (1954) The Widening Scope of Indications for Psychoanalysis. *Journal of the American Psychoanalytic Association* 2:567–594.

CHAPTER 17

On The Evolution of Psychoanalytic Technique

Ernst Kris, in his paper, "The Personal Myth" (1956), described a tendency—present in all of us—to view our own life story as having characteristics similar to myths. That such personal mythology serves a defensive purpose and may be expressed in formidable resistance is a commonplace of psychoanalytic practice. Thomas Kuhn (in *The Structure of Scientific Revolutions*) presents us with a striking analogy in the history of science, something which is a contribution to the *mythology* of science. Kuhn describes[5] "a persistent tendency to make the history of science look linear or cumulative, a tendency that even affects scientists looking back at their own research.[6] Although idealization and oversimplification. it is made to appear that the *current* problems faced by any particular branch of science have *always* been the problems approached by that discipline, Though Kuhn uses this concept to describe the invisibility of scientific revolutions, the mythology of linear or cumulative development also can be seen in the problem-solving workings of science in postrevolutionary non-crisis phases.

In this brief set of notes on the development of psychoanalytic techniques, we will attempt to explore such a problem. It may be observed

---

5 Page 138.

6 *Studies in Hysteria, S.E.* 2, pp.108 ff..

superficially that there has been a seeming linear development from the "hypnotic" and "cathartic" phases of Breuer and Freud's therapeutic work to the development of free association, the analysis of transference and resistance, and thus to the more meticulous analysis of defenses and other phenomena grouped together as "functions of the ego." That is to say, there seems to be a linear development from a) attempts to "translate" the contents of the unconscious and discharge their pathogenic quality, while circumventing the conscious aspects of personality, to b) attempts to enlist the aid of the patient's ego in a complex task involving a wide range of functions of the mental apparatus.

To give the problem its full mythological quality would be to say that Freud at the turn of the century, was confronting the same therapeutic and technical problems confronted by psychoanalysis today. This. is manifestly *not* the case, and not because the cases have changed (e.g., it is equally mythological to assert that hysteria has disappeared). What started as an attempt to treat hysteria became expanded into a sweeping exploration of human behavior.

Psychoanalysis, as other sciences, proceeded by fits and starts; new pathways were attempted and rejected; fruitful avenues were explored, leading to new problems; fruitful avenues were abandoned, to be picked up later or not at all. The development was chaotic but can be given mythical coherence by retrospective distortion and idealization.

I shall attempt to pick our way through the history of the development of psychoanalytic technique, hoping to demonstrate the evolution of modern technique through its many vagaries. At the end I shall attempt to discuss some of the limits of our technique at present, *without* any premature suggestion for remedy.

The early history of all things psychoanalytic is essentially the description of Freud's effort; and the history of psychoanalytic *technique* began with the hypnotic treatment of hysteria.

Breuer, in 1880–82, treated a young hysterical woman with hypnosis and conveyed the information to Freud. After studying with Charcot, Freud established practice and attempted to treat his hysterical patients with the then accepted methods of rest and hydrotherapy, with little result. He undertook hypnotic treatment with increased interest, modifying Breuer's technique of hypnotic suggestion into the technical procedure which became known as the "cathartic" method, Breuer, in his treatment of the patient designated as Anna O., had utilized hypnosis in two ways; first for direct therapeutic suggestion, and, secondly, for the recovery and reproduction of memories (and associated affects), to abolish the amnesia for pathogenic events. This aim was the essence of the cathartic method and of the phenomenon of abreaction. Freud found that it was difficult for him to produce the somnambulistic state in certain patients he attempted to hypnotize.[7] Instead of suggesting sleep, he suggested merely that the patient concentrate. The recumbent position, closed eyes and pressure of the physician's hand on the patient's forehead, all continued as remnants of the previous technique. The patient was 'obliged" by the physician to "remember," assisted by pressure upon the forehead, The new technical procedure led to an *unexpected* new observation. In the case of Elisabeth von R.,[8] Freud discovered that there were periods when his patient refused cooperation and would not produce the asked-for memories, The patient had a "resistance" to the emergence of these thoughts, a resistance which had to be overcome by the work of the treatment. These "resistances" arose in the interest of "defense" (a process of censorship) against ideas which would arouse painful affects. "....A psychical force, aversion on the part of the ego, had originally driven the pathogenic idea out of association and was now opposing its return to memory," Freud found, too, that insistence upon memory did not

---

7 Ibid, p. 154 and 268 ff.

8 *Freud's Psychoanalytic Procedure* 1904, *S.E.* 7, p. 250.

get him very far. It is at this point that he called into play the "pressure technique," with the explanation that the signal of hand pressure on the patient's forehead allowed for some relaxation of the conscious obstacle of the patient's "will" and allowed for the emergence of associative pathways However by 1904, he had abandoned the pressure technique and the laying on of hands.[9] Indeed, by 1904, he no longer required the patients to close their eyes, a procedure that had been adhered to during the production of *The Interpretation of Dreams.*[10] Freud said: "The session thus proceeds like a conversation between two people equally awake, but one of whom is spared every muscular exertion and every distracting sensory Impression which might divert his attention from his own mental activity, " By 1904, then, the general outline of procedure was that recognizable as characteristic of psychoanalysis,

It is important to retrace the rationale of the procedure in the theoretical concepts of hysteria and of the psychoneuroses in general, as they evolved in Freud 's early work and collaboration with Breuer. The initial view held by Breuer and Freud and presented in the introductory section of the *Studies* [11] was that some hysterical patients could not easily establish the point of origin of their illness because they had "no suspicion of the causal connection between the precipitating event and the pathological phenomenon." An amnesia had taken place which had to be lifted by hypnosis, The symptoms of hysteria were seen to resemble those of traumatic neuroses and were related to traumatic events. In other cases, Breuer and Freud saw the symptoms as symbolized representations of the traumatic events. The symptoms disappeared when the forgotten event and its accompanying painful affect

---

9 *Freud's Psychoanalytic Procedure* 1904, S.E. 7, p. 250

10 *Fragment of an Analysis of a Case of Hysteria,* 1905.

11 Ibid, p. 10.

were brought to light, The discharge of the strangulated affect ("abreaction") was thus the cornerstone of the cathartic technique.

This schematic representation did not describe the actual state of affairs in the conduct of the treatment. Many other complexities appeared: the phenomenon of "resistance" being one of the first noted. Perhaps of equal significance in raising new and perplexing questions was the phenomenon of the "transference"[12] — "the worst obstacle we can come across.".... "The patient's relation to the physician is disturbed" for a variety of reasons and serves as a resistance. It was characteristic of Freud's creative genius that this "worst obstacle" was to become for him the chief vehicle for therapeutic effort and the rationales for the later development of technique were to be intimately connected with growing knowledge about "transference" and "resistance." By 1904, and the appearance of his brief article on procedure (in Lowenfeld book on obsessional neurosis).

Freud had clearly arrived at the point of view that the amnesias of his patients were the result of "repression" and the forces which brought the repression about were to be detected in the resistance against the recovery of lost memories. The distortions brought about by resistance could be subjected to "interpretation," so that the mental contents which had been "unconscious" could be made conscious to the patient.

The general pattern of the Interpretive effort had been arrived at in *The Interpretation of Dreams*, itself the consequence of Freud's extensive self-analysis. Freud's empirical observations had demonstrated that hypnosis, by evading the resistances, had given an incomplete picture of the play of mental forces and yielded incomplete information and transitory therapeutic success. The therapeutic task was n to remove the amnesias," or, expressed otherwise: "all repressions must be undone." The unconscious had to be made

---

12 Ibid. p. 15.

accessible to consciousness via overcoming the resistances. The procedure was to be limited to patients with hysteria and with obsessional neuroses.

Freud's increasing awareness of the rôle of sexual factors in the etiology of the psychoneuroses and the need to substantiate his views of hysteria led to the publication of the Dora case.[13] This paper had serious importance for the subject of technique because in it Freud attempted to demonstrate "how dream interpretation is woven into the history of a treatment and how it can become the means for filling in amnesias and elucidating symptoms"[14]

With the warning that dreams did not play such an important rôle in all cases, he set "about to show how his technique had evolved. (The subject of dreams in analysis was to be returned to in 1911, in a technical paper.). Dreams were seen as a detour "by which repression can be evaded."[15]

In the Dora paper he states that a technical discussion would be out of place, but he manages to give hints of the actual therapeutic task in the process of the psychological exposition. For example, he discusses the matter of case presentation and the recording of data. He says that he does not take notes during the session, preferring to write them afterwards, since such activity detracts from the material. He notes that his technique has changed since the publication *Studies of Hysteria* (1895). He has evolved the method of free association: the patient chooses the subject and proceeds from the mental surface. (This is casually presented, seemingly without awareness of the revolutionary method.)

He says that an accurate history cannot be obtained at the outset of the treatment of a hysteria because the patient cannot give it. There are omissions, amnesias and falsifications of memory. The work of the analysis, with the lifting of repressions, will allow for the possibility of an accurate

---

13 *A Fragment of an Analysis of a Case of Hysteria* 1905, S.E. 7 pp. 7 ff.
14 Ibid. p. 10.
15 Ibid. p. 15.

history being reconstructed at the end of the treatment(a subject to which he returned in the paper on "Constructions in Analysis" (1937).

Technical hints are given throughout the Dora paper: for example,

a. *doubts* are the first stages of repression.

b. one must not be content with patients saying "no" to an interpretation.

c. cautious questioning of the patient is called for when matters are unclear.

d. in sexual discussions, things must be called their proper names, Freud says, "J'appelle un chat un chat," These hints have as their purpose the *clarification* of the material *and* of the process by which communications are made by both patient and physician.

A large portion of the paper Is occupied with the way in which dream interpretation throws light on the meaning of the illness. In this brief comment the content will be by-passed in favor of the technical implications. Freud describes some maneuvers in which he actively sought to stimulate the patient's interest and curiosity. ('These are fascinating glimpses of the analyst's *active* intervention devices which later had to be abandoned since they interfere with the spontaneous emergence of material.) After interpreting a portion of the first dream, he promised the patient that he would t*ell her more at the next session.* He begins the next session with an "experiment." (The material of the dream which had been left hanging dealt with an accident that might take place at night.) Freud asked his patient if she had noticed a match-stand on his table, and did she know why children were not supposed to play with fire. In this way he introduces and allows for a discussion of enuresis. In subsequent material the patient recalls a portion of this "first" dream which was forgotten; it appears after some interpretive work; this marks it, for Freud, as having been subjected to some specially severe repression. In this instance the fragment is that the patient "smelled smoke" on awakening. Freud's conclusion from the material is that this illusion represented a wish to have another kiss from a smoker—a "transference wish." The subject of transference, Freud notes, had been somewhat neglected in the conduct of the treatment and eventually the treatment foundered on this obstacle. (The patient's vengefulness was not sufficiently appreciated.) In his discussion of transference, he notes that improvement occurs after the patient leaves e the treatment. This postponement is caused by the physician's own person—the transference, This phenomenon Is a new edition of experiences from the past. Only after the transference is resolved is there conviction on the part of the patient of the nature of interpretations. Freud warns of a technical difficulty: instead of reproduction, in the associations, of the content of transference, these fantasies may be "acted out." From his viewpoint, he notes that he *always avoids acting a part*.

Thus, we see that in 1905 Freud had begun to deal with problems to which he and other analysts were to devote the next fifty years in the evolution of technique;

a. the problem of reconstruction

b. insight and conviction

c. the rôle of dreams in analysis

d. the activity and active interventions of the analyst later to be approached by Ferenczi

e. transference, transference interpretations, transference resistance and the acting-out of transference fantasies

f. the caution against acting a part—a caution to be Ignored by Alexander in his quest for the "corrective emotional experience."

g. the cathartic technique with its emphasis upon abreaction is played down in favor of actively engaging the patient's curiosity, that is, the stimulation of what was later to be termed the "therapeutic alliance."

The banner of "abreaction" was to be carried by Ferenczi and Rank as forerunners of Alexander.

(However, it is important to remember that the problems presented at this point in analytic development were not precisely the same problems to be seen later. These were fore-runners bearing only rudimentary resemblance to the later problems. For example, at this point there was an insufficient theory of anxiety, the concepts of defense and resistance were not developed in relation to anxiety, there was no theory of narcissism, no structural approach to the mental apparatus, no appreciation of the process of working through, and an inadequate view of the concept of trauma)

Several of these technical issues will be returned to in the course of this study. However, it is worthwhile to look at Freud's evolving technique as seen in "Notes Upon a Case of Obsessional Neurosis" (1909). This paper is a model for the meticulous attention to detail required for analytic observation. It remains the classic model for the demonstration that analytic theory must proceed from such observations and not be arrived at by speculation. Freud notes at the outset that the structure of obsessional neurosis is difficult to discern and describe analytically; this difficulty is added to by the many resistances in varying form. offered by the patient. This reiterates the view that the patient is prevented by repression from giving an accurate picture of the illness. In effect, it sets the stage for the intricate work of reconstruction.

In contrast to the Dora case, this report clearly shows Freud at work. In initial interview serves as an introduction to the patient and his illness. The analysis proper begins at the next session. An explicit and detailed statement of the fundamental rule is offered. For the reader, he repeats Adler's advice that the first communications from the patient may be of special importance. The associations are most carefully scanned with the view of making them tell some eventually coherent story. The vagueness of the obsessional ideas must be made concrete. The appearance of conscious resistance to the continuation of work prompts Freud to offer an explicit explanation of resistance to the patient and to demand of him an absolute adherence to the basic rule. When the patient's narrative is vague, Freud requires of the patient that he repeat the material; this repetition and the meticulous attention to detail is done in order to lay bare the seeming confusion.

Freud reports opening the fourth analytic session with the question: "And how do you intend to proceed today?" This question was put forward to emphasize that Freud had to suppress his own curiosity about the content of the third session, allowed full freedom of: choice to the patient; this is a considerable. departure from the match-stand experiment in his treatment of Dora.

Freud offered the patient instruction and theoretical interpretations concerning psychoanalysis and its workings, He saw this as preparatory work for later interventions, These didactic statements were not designed to bring conviction, but to facilitate the emergence of fresh material conviction is attained only when the patient has himself worked over the material; as long as he is unconvinced the material is not exhausted.

As may be seen, at this point in Freud's developing technique, educational devices to encourage curiosity and self exploration were given a high degree of priority.

The technical issues also formed part of two papers in 1910, "The Future Prospects of Psychoanalytic Therapy"[16] (2) and "Wild Psychoanalysis."[17] in the first paper Freud pints out that the treatment consists of two parts: that at which the physician tells the patient and that in which the patient works over what he hears. This is the intellectual help of the analysis. However, there is a more powerful device of the analysis: the transference. Its

---

16 *S.E.* 1910 11, p, 141.

17 *S.E.* 1910 11, p. 221.

counterpart—the countertransference—is brought into technical discussion. Countertransference is seen in this paper as a therapeutic obstacle to be overcome by self-analysis. Modifications of the technique established for conversion hysteria were seen to be necessary in anxiety hysteria with the need of the phobic patient to expose himself to the phobic situation after a preliminary period of analysis. (This question coupled with the issue of gratification of sado-masochistic impulses in the analysis of obsessional patients was returned to by Freud, in 1 919, in the paper, "Lines of Advance in Psychoanalytic Therapy," (1) where he stated the "rule of abstinence." This subject will be taken up later.)

The wild analysis paper is significant in that Freud demonstrates that the neurotic patient is not simply ignorant of some critical facts. It is not that the information behind the amnesia must be supplied. Rather, it is that the root of the problem is in the inner resistances, since they called the ignorance into being and they maintain it. In order to interpret the unconscious material to the patient, two factors are necessary: (a) that by preparatory work, the material is in a preconscious state, and (b) that the transference to the physician be of such a quality as to prevent the patient's taking fresh flight. (A further description of the process of interpretation was to be elaborated in the 1915 paper on the Unconscious

The 1911 paper, "The Handling of Dream Interpretation in Psychoanalysis,"[18] was the first paper specifically devoted to instruction in technique. It takes up the actual style of handling dreams in a therapeutic setting. (This is in contrast to much of the material in the "Interpretation of Dreams") Freud warns against too great an interest in dream analysis as separate from the general conduct of the work. The analyst must be aware of what is at work on the surface of the patient's mind and what resistances are active. The interpretation which can be obtained in hour is sufficient and

---

18 *S.E.* 12, pp. 91 ff.

dream Interpretation is not to continue necessarily into the next session; the surface is again to be dealt with in accordance with the general rules for analytic conduct. A detailed "practice" of dream analysis is thus essayed and the technical papers to follow in 1911–1914 come the closest to a "Practice of Psychoanalysis" ever written by Freud. (The promise of such a text given in the 1910 paper on "future prospects" never materialized.)

"The Dynamics of Transference" (1912)[19] addresses itself not only to technical issues but also to the theory of transference. The question is raised as to why patients in analysis develop such intense transference feelings and why these feelings serve as such a powerful resistance (where in other forms of treatment it is the necessary condition of success).

The answers provided are that the question is illusory the transference is not due to the analysis, but to the neurosis itself. Furthermore, transference In analysis appears as a resistance because a) libidinal regression (Initiated by frustration of gratification in reality) resists change (i.e., the attraction of reality is weakened), and b) in order to free it, the attraction of the unconscious must be overcome, i.e., repression must be lifted.[20]

The requirement for the lifting of repression cannot take place without the transference. The repressed material may be transferred to the person of the analyst *(instead of being conscious remembered)* and thus satisfies the resistance.

In this we see a cornerstone of the technique as it was to evolve further, in that the unfolding of the repressed analytic material was understood to take place in varying forms in memories, distortions of memory, or reproduced in transference, dream and symptom as substitutes for conscious memory.

---

19 1912 12, pp. 99 ff.

20 The clinician will recognize these issues as important determinants for the evolution of the concept of "working through," which was to be taken up by Freud 1n 1917.

Recommendations to Physicians Practicing Psychoanalysis" (1912)[21] continued Freud's attempt at a systematic statement of practice. It was in this work that he described one major aspect of the analyst's task; the maintenance of an "evenly-hovering" (evenly-suspended) attention, This attention was to be without conscious the material and without excessive therapeutic zeal. It is in this paper that Freud suggests that the analyst should be like a mirror. This did not mean that the analyst was to be a blank wall; rather, it meant that he was not to interfere with the natural unfolding of the material.

The beautifully detailed paper "On Beginning the Treatment"[22] will not be discussed because of limitations of time, but it provides further discussion of the vagaries of resistance, as does the déjà raconté[23] paper.

Now what has been the point of this very extensive inquiry into the early history of Freud's technical papers? It is simply this: as Freud's knowledge of psychoanalysis grew, he became *increasingly aware of the necessity of developing a technique which would allow for the most precise unfolding and analysis of resistance.*

A constant interplay between technical and theoretical considerations took place, and the technical papers of 1910–1914 were produced at a time when the ferment of Freud's thought was to lead to the work on "The Unconscious" (1912), "Instincts and their Vicissitudes" (1915) and "Mourning and Melancholia" (1917), and eventually then to the development of the structural theory in "The Ego and the Id"(1923), the vast revision of drive theory in "Beyond the Pleasure Principle" and of the theory of anxiety as the ego's response to danger in "Inhibitions, Symptoms and Anxiety" (1926). In other words, the development of his technique was

---

21 *S.E.* 12, pp. 111 ff.

22 1913 *S.E.* 17, pp. 123 ff.

23 1914 *S.E* 13, pp. 201 ff.

in constant interplay with the increasing development of his thoughts about the development and function of that psychic aggregate we now refer to as the ego. [24]

All of this was presaged in "Further Recommendations in the Technique of Psychoanalysis II" (1914): "Recollection, Repetition and Working Through"[25]. Here Freud notes that in the development of technique the physician's task became less one of interpretation of the unconscious mental contents and increasingly one of the discovery of resistances. When the resistances are analyzed and removed, the forgotten situations and affects are recovered. "The aim of these different techniques has, of course, remained the same, descriptively speaking, it is to fill in gaps in memory; dynamically speaking, it is to overcome resistances due to repression.

This paper addresses itself first to an examination of the function of memory and the process of forgetting. Freud notes that the forgetting of experiences "reduces itself to shutting them off." When the patient talks about these forgotten things, he seldom fails to add:" As a matter of fact, I've always known it; only I've never thought of it." Actually, all that is essential is preserved in the screen-memories which represent the forgotten years of childhood as adequately as the manifest content of a dream represents the dream-thoughts,

Freud also touches upon those factors which could be "remembered" but were never previously conscious, as well as those things remembered which took place so early in childhood as to be insufficiently comprehended but which are *reproduced* in dreams. (This was to be beautifully demonstrated in the paper on the Wolf-man.)

---

24 With the recognition that what was manifest 1n the analysis as resistance represented the *intrapsychic* phenomena of *defense,* this development was to be systematized by .Anna Freud in 1936 in "The Ego and the Mechanisms of Defense."

25 *S.E.* 12, pp. 147 ff.

A special aspect of forgetting was to be seen in the situation In which the patient remembers nothing of some forgotten event but *reproduces it in action*, This acting out of the forgotten past is an aspect of a compulsion to repeat which will be understood as the patient's way of remembering, The transference itself is to be understood as a bit of' repetition and that this repetition extends to other aspects of current life, This therefore will involve aspects of the patient's current work, love-life, and so one "the greater the resistance, the more extensively will acting out (repetition) replace remembering." Allowing this repetition to take place (as part of the 1914 technique) brings with It the danger of deterioration of the patient's condition during the treatment. It is a real slice of life and not a laboratory phenomenon as was hypnotic recovery of Lost memories. The illness cannot be underestimated by the patient as he had done before the treatment; he is now forced to pay attention to it. Because of the danger of poorly controlled repetitions, the patient must promise to make no important decisions affecting his life during the course of the treatment. This should not paralyze all action. The analysis of the transference allows for the transformation of the compulsion to repeat into a motive for remembering The symptoms of the neurosis take on a transference meaning, and the neurosis is replaced by a transference neurosis which can be cured by the therapeutic work.

Resistances are not analyzed by naming them once. They come up repeatedly and must be repeatedly "worked- through." The working-through of resistances is the part of the work that effects the greatest changes in the patient, and this factor distinguishes analytic treatment from suggestion. Freud ends: "From a theoretical point of view, one may correlate it with abreacting' of the quotas of affect strangulated by repression an abreaction without which hypnotic treatment remained ineffective."

In this paper we find the introduction of the concepts of the repetition-compulsion am of working-through which were to have such profound effect upon Freud's future technical ideas. These ideas would be inextricably linked with the development of the structural hypothesis. It would stimulate Ferenczi and Rank to develop broad technical innovations to facilitate repetition in the transference.

Transference was the subject of Freud's 1915 paper, "Further Recommendations in the Technique of Psychoanalysis, Observations on Transference-Love."

The situation focused upon by this paper is the frequent one of a female patient falling in love with her physician and demanding its return. This event is to be clearly understood as a resistance. Although previous evidences of positive transference had facilitated the treatment, at a point where some painful aspect of the past was to be revealed the picture changes. The demand for returned love becomes obdurate and evidence of a resistance at work. The "resistance acts as agent provocateur intensifying the love of the patient and exaggerating her readiness for the sexual surrender, in order thereby to vindicate the action of her repression more emphatically by pointing to the dangers of such licentiousness."

The "analytic technique requires the physician to deny the patient who is longing for love the satisfaction she craves. *The treatment must be carried through in a state of abstinence*" (italics mine). This view has far wider transference implications than merely the present example—it is to be the cornerstone of technical dealings with all transference manifestations. The analyst must take a course for which there is "no prototype in real life." "He must guard against ignoring the transference love, scaring it away or making the patient disgusted with it; and just as resolutely must he withhold any response to it. What must be interpreted Is the resistance under the guise of love. Secondly one must demonstrate the repetitions from the past. However, the genuineness of the feeling is not to be disputed; in life, falling in love is equally determined by many repetitions and unreal estimates of the current situation

The emphasis on abstinence is the important center of the paper.

"From the History of An Infantile Neurosis" (1918)[26] was written in 1914–15 as part of a polemic (with "On the History of the Psychoanalytic Movement") against the views of Jung and Adler. Jung had discarded his earlier psychoanalytic views and rejected the rôle of infantile sexuality in the genesis of neurosis. He had turned away from concern with the early history of the individual and toward an increasingly mystical concern with the pre-history of the race. Adler, on the other hand, rejected Freud's views in favor of a simplistic schema in which a search for power became the central issue of neurosis.

The paper addresses itself to the elucidation of an adult patient's infantile neurosis.[27] This neurosis was analyzed fifteen years after the termination of a childhood phobia; the analysis was occasioned by an adult "neurosis" of grave proportions. The case material throws light upon the distortions caused by retrospection. However, the design of the presentation was to demonstrate that the infantile neurosis was not simply a retrospective distortion, regressively arrived at, so that the patient might escape from the present. In brief, it was to demonstrate *conclusively* the rôle of infantile sexuality in the neuroses. That the case was extremely difficult led to its striking content. Freud comments that we learn from the difficult cases and in these cases it is necessary to renounce short sighted therapeutic ambition.

There is one important technical innovation in this paper, a heroic measure was taken to overcome the patient's resistance of apathy. A date was set for the termination of the analysis, no matter how far it had advanced. This led to a giving way of resistance and the resolution of some aspects of the illness.[28] This innovation was to have the most far-reaching and unforeseen consequences for the history of psychoanalytic technique. It was

---

26 *C.P.* 3, p. 473 ff.

27 Later shown by Ruth Mack Brunswick to be a fore-runner of a paranoid schizophrenia.

28 Ibid. p. 478.

to be a central concern with both Ferenczi and Rank: an important aspect their jointly written 1923 work, one aspect of Ferenczi's "activity," and to be reduced to absurdity in Rank's birth trauma therapy.

The case report does not concern itself with the patient's current illness. It concentrates upon the infantile precursors, and, in particular, upon a remembered dream of childhood. Its content is too well known to analysts to bear repetition. Only the technique be looked at. The case was unfavorable from many aspects.[29] The patient came from another culture (he was Russian) and his style of' thinking was foreign to Freud, A "completely unbridled instinctual life" necessitated "a long process of preparatory education. Unfortunately, we do not know how this preparatory work was undertaken.

The story of his childhood was told by the patient from two sources; his memory and his recollection of family stories told to him about himself. Of the latter, Freud says that such stories are employable as authentic material.[30]

However, he advises against making new inquiries of relatives about the patient's history. Their stories may be distorted, confidence in the analysis is shaken and a court of appeal is set up over it.

In attempting to discern the point of origin of one of the childhood symptoms, Freud describes offering a construction of a castration threat by governess.[31] He says such constructions never do damage if they are mistaken but they are not put forward unless they will lead to some nearer approximation of the truth.

The Wolf-dream (when patient was 4) was remembered· as having a lasting sense of reality; this was connected to the fact that the latent content referred to some real event. This real event was the reconstructed

---

29 p. 585.

30 p. 481, footnote 2.

31 p. 486.

primal scene, observed by the patient at one-and-a-half years of age. This reconstructed scene, the observation of the parental coitus a tergo, is the center of the paper's viewpoint. Freud notes here that objectors to the rôle played by childhood sexuality in the etiology of the neuroses, would prefer to see these events in the light previously described. That is, that they are the regressive expression (via imagination) of problems avoided in the present. However, no alteration in technique would be admissible even if this were the case. The fantasies would still have to be explored and their relation to reality would still have to be established. The primal scene material had to be constructed—it was not recollected. However, Freud cautions, dreaming is a form of remembering.

A regressive shrinking away from current conflict is one part of the process of neurosis, the other part is the forward movement from the impressions of childhood. (1) These factors lead to the development of symptoms. The childhood experiences determine "at which point the individual shall fail to master the real problems of life." These infantile experiences and the infantile neurosis prove that neurosis can proceed only from the inability to master the instinctual push and not only from an evasion of the problems of life. Every neurosis in adult life is based upon an infantile neurosis which, however, might not have been severe enough to attract attention.[32] The technical requirement of adequate appraisal of the infantile neurosis is here underscored.

At the Budapest Congress in 1918, Freud gave a rare technical paper, "Turnings in the Ways of Psychoanalytic Therapy." Freud was assessing new directions in which the therapy might develop. His specific attention was toward Ferenczi's ideas of "activity." By "activity," Freud meant those means of stimulating the emergence of new material so that resistances might be uncovered and the repressed made conscious. That is, "activity"

---

32 p. 579.

was to facilitate the well-known analytic aim and not replace it. Above all, the work was to be carried out in a state of abstinence. Activity was not to be a mask for transference gratification. The patient's sufferings must not *prematurely* come to an end; the analyst must oppose *premature* substitutive gratifications,

Another form of activity is necessary in phobic patients who must be induced to confront the phobic situation so that new material will be available. With certain obsessive patients, passive waiting is to be avoided. Here Freud was obviously referring to his experience with the Wolf-man (see that discussion) and the need for setting a date for termination.

In the end of the paper, Freud was looking to the possibility that great numbers of poorer patients might be treated in clinics; in that event where the need for increased service to the community dominated the task, "the pure gold of analysis" might have to be alloyed to the "copper of direct suggestion." He here introduced the concept of psychoanalytically-oriented psychotherapy.

At this point it will be necessary to turn away from Freud's work to a monograph written by Sandor Ferenczi and Otto Rank, "Entwicklungsziele der Psychoanalyse" 1923 (translated as "The Development of Psychoanalysis," 1925), This work, of enormous impact and influence in its day, is now hardly read. However, its significance as the forerunner of a vast variety of technical variations psychoanalytic schisms make its careful study imperative to the historian. Ferenczi and Rank were interested in emphasizing the rôle of abreaction in psychoanalytic therapy. To this end they see the essential aspects of technique as being related to the *experiencing* in the analytic situation (a term they coined) of the infantile wishes and traumata, The crux of their technical argument is that the analyst should not impart the theoretical knowledge which occurs to him in connection with the patient's associations; he should only impart what the patient requires for understanding *the analytic experience.*

They arrive at this point of view through the following pathways: They use Freud's working through paper of 1911 as a point of departure. In that work they emphasize that Freud treated repetition as a resistance (missing the point that Freud was demonstrating that certain repetitions were resistances to remembering but other repetitions were attempts at mastery). Ferenczi and Rank viewed repetition as *essential* and as a form of communication to be interpreted to the patient. To them, the chief rôle in technique belongs to repetition and *not* to remembering. *Via interpretation,* this repetition gives way to remembering.

The chapter on "The Analytic Situation" was apparently written entirely by Rank. He saw this situation consisting of an unwinding of the libidinal development. This artificial process is inaugurated by the transference and Its course determined by the transference. The analytic task is to watch this unwinding of the libido, and where he notices a disturbance in the process in the form of a resistance, he intervenes. The attitude of the analyst is to remain "passive" in the face of the libidinal repetitions, and "active" in its interpretation where resistance arises. It is necessary to make conscious those trends of the libido that were never conscious but were repressed at once. The patient is thus able really to "experience" these infantile wishes for the first time. The chief resistance to this process is infantile anxiety and unconscious guilt. Analysis of this guilt is then expected to lead to the emergence of libidinal tendencies and consequent new solutions in life (through repudiation, new ego-ideals, sublimation, or direct expression). The creation of the analytic situation allows the expression and satisfaction of some previously libidinal wishes (if only in fantasy). Some of these wishes may be repeated in life to remove them from the analysis—that is the problem of acting out. This must be prevented by interpretation, or, in extreme cases, by the active intervention of forbidding the behavior. This accorded with Ferenczi's view that libidinal privation is essential to attaining reproduction in the analysis. The process for the resolution of transference is seen as requiring a "certain tine" to run its course; to this end they set a time limit on the last portion of the analysis, that is to say, they took Freud's attempted solution of the Wolf-man's resistance of apathy and made a general rule for all patients. (This issue of a "certain time" and setting a time limit for the treatment was later to be reduced to total absurdity by Rank in the birth-trauma technique.)

The analytic task was to uncover the infantile neurosis back of the clinical neurosis, even if the preliminary stages had never been manifest. (This emphasis on the reproduction of the Infantile neurosis through regression was later to lead Ferenczi in the path of actually treating the patients as if they were children. One can also recognize in this general schema Alexander's technique of parental rôle-playing.) At the time of this paper, however, Ferenczi was clearly of the opinion that the patient must learn in the painful transference situation that it was not possible to gratify the infantile longings.

In dealing with issues of interpretation, they take the view that interventions should only be made when resistances require it for the libidinal unwinding." They should be reserved for big situations and not for overzealous Interpretation of detail. They emphasize, by implication, that interpretations should be in the context of the transference. (This idea was later taken up by James Strachey in his views of the process of interpretation.[33] Strachey, who accepted Melanie Klein's views of superego development and function, saw transference interpretations as the only effective interpretations, since they dealt with the immediate and tangible e mis allows for introjection of a "good n image of the analyst to replace "bad" images in the superego).

---

33 The Nature of the Therapeutic Action of Psychoanalysis; Int. J. Psa. *XV*, 1934; pp. 127-159.

The emphasis in Ferenczi and Rank's work was the value of "experience" in the transference of the original pathogenic constellations and the therapeutic factor was abreaction. Affective factors of experience were to be substituted for intellectual processes in this light they saw as a future development the readmission of hypnosis or direct suggestion into the technique and had the hope of devising means for shortening and simplifying the treatment.

By their emphasis on abreaction they had failed to see the increasing need for working through as a necessary factor in the therapeutic process.

The paper was a case of special pleading for the "emotional experience" as against intellectual reconstruction, as if these were antithetical tasks. Though they take some pains to point out that "experience" must precede remembering, so that reconstructions may be viewed with conviction, this part of their message is lost in the text. The work was an example of psychoanalytic reductionism—an attempt at grossly oversimplifying a complex field of work.

This reductionism was the hallmark of Wilhelm Reich's character analysis, where character was viewed as an armor, a resistance which must be stripped from the patient layer by layer. This work which appeared in its original form in 1928, was expanded by Reich into a system of therapy with a highly reductionist viewpoint. As is well known, it had a wide effect upon analytic technique and analysts for a while, One of its frequent results was its relentless pressure upon the patients to fall back upon regression as a defense. Its results were unhappy, to say the least. Nevertheless, the idea of the careful analysis of character traits within the context of the remainder of analytic work remains with us as a cornerstone of our technique. With this work the need to inspect and analyze the ego's habitual modes of dealing with reality and the other psychic agencies was given further impetus.

Coming on the heels of The Ego and the Id and of Inhibitions. Symptoms, and Anxiety, it paved the way for those contributions of technique implicit in Anna Freud's The Ego and the Mechanisms of Defense.

Anna Freud's monograph The Ego and the Mechanism of Defense (1936), is not dedicated to the issue of technique, but its impact upon technique has been very marked. It spelled out in some detail that the pre-structural issue of psychoanalytic "resistance" would have to be viewed within the structural concept of the ego defenses.

This work saw all the psychic agencies viewed through the ego and presented by the ego, subjected to the ego's defensive distortions. It continued Freud's view that the—resistances—defenses would have to be analyzed in order that the repressed content might emerge, and it emphasized the unconscious quality of the defensive process. The ego in conflict was Miss Freud's primary concern. In contrast to this work and complementing it, was Heinz Hartmann's work on adaptation. Out of the need for the development of a concept of mental health, Hartmann had examined the non- conflictual aspects of the ego as well as that involved in conflict. The issue of autonomous ego functioning was to become a central one in the developing psychoanalytic ego psychology. This was seen as a necessity by some, in order to establish psychoanalysis as a general psychology. Hartmann's concern with the problems of adaptation turned a new view upon the issues of the ego's dealings with reality. This view avoided Adler's earlier reductionism and over-simplification. It saw the problem in developmental terms and thus has served as a ground-plan for psychoanalytically inspired researches into direct observation of child development. Its implications for technique were to be arrived at only when more complex aspects of structure formation in development had been studied, and this in collaboration with Kris and Loewenstein.

However, while these important papers in the thirties were under discussion, a great series of psychoanalytic schisms and battles were taking place, many of them around the question of technique. None of the issues were entirely new, and most had been presaged in Jung, Adler, Rank and Ferenczi. The technical problems involved dealt with simplifying the treatment, shortening the treatment, the rôle of present reality, the attempt to avoid or deny the rôle of the infantile neurosis and infantile sexuality, giving a special rôle to the issue of adaptation, attempting to manipulate transference by rôleplaying, and seeing the treatment as determined by corrective emotional experiences. With these technical variations are associated the names of Sullivan, Horney, Rado and Alexander. The English School, under Melanie Klein, entered into a different backwater by crediting early infantile states with a high degree of specialized ego functioning and thus developing a technical viewpoint in which the Anlage for future illness were already present in the very young infant. Time prevents us from considering these viewpoints in detail. Suffice it to say each of these viewpoints derived from one facet of psychoanalytic technique, or was a contravention of one facet. By attempting this reductionism, these views denied the complexity of the task, i.e., the minute examination of the interactions of the ego with the drives, superego, reality and the repetition compulsion, This was the complex polyphonic view offered by Waelder in his "Principle of Multiple Function" 1936).

At the end of his career, Freud turned his attention once more to some technical issues, "Analysis Terminable and Interminable" (1937) surveyed Freud 's entire analytic experience, using as its point of departure the lengthiness of psychoanalytic therapy, it proceeds from that point to a wide-ranging discussion of the limitations of that therapy,

Freud reviews his attempt to combat the Wolf-man's apathetic resistance by setting a date for the termination of the treatment. He notes its limited usefulness and the need for perfect timing in its employment. However, the concern for accelerating analytic progress is only the opening for a discussion of the question of whether there is a natural end to an analysis. By end of the analysis is meant whether the change in the patient has been so great that further work would be superfluous. Some cases are able to be conducted in this fashion; the results occurred in cases in which "no noticeable modification had taken place in the patient's ego and the causation of his illness was pre-eminently traumatic." He contrasts this to interminable cases in which the problems are a profound "constitutional strength of instinct and an unfavorable modification of the ego in the defensive conflict." His attention Is then turned to the essential point of view of this work: an inquiry into the obstacles to cure.

The treatment of more difficult cases and the greater therapeutic challenge makes the question of shortening treatment superfluous.

The three major factors determining the results of analysis are traumatic origins, strength of instinct and ego modification. The latter two are extensively discussed. Freud says that in previous works he had given more attention to the dynamic and topographical aspects and lese to the economic aspects of neurosis. In considering the quantitative relationships of drives to ego forces, he makes clear that the problem is one of balance. The drives cannot be abolished, they must be "tamed," Early attempts at repression created ineffective defenses against drive irruption, The work of analysis corrects the original process of repression by the creation of stronger and more reliable defensive balance. We offer greatest therapeutic help by our attention to the patient's ego and its defensive constellations.

Patients cannot be protected against future conflict, and it is not really possible to activate conflicts not actually manifest, Merely informing the patient of potential future pitfalls does little good.

The factor of ego-modification influences the capacity for a therapeutic alliance. Disturbances in the ego prevent the necessary cooperation. In the attempt of the developing child to simultaneously master the instincts and to deal with the environment, there is a blurring and shifting of what is external and what is internal. To avoid anxiety, varying defensive mechanisms are used by the ego. These mechanisms take their toll in the form of distortions of the ego and will be reflected in analysis in the form of resistances. The ego treats recovery as a new danger to be met with the old weapons. The extent and fixity of these ego-modifications 1 limit the efficacy of analysis.

This leads to the one really new idea of the work: i.e., each selects only *certain* defense mechanisms. This suggested to Freud that each individual ego is endowed from the beginning with its own peculiar dispositions and tendencies. However, there are other resistances, coming from other sources than the defenses. There are those patients who display "an adhesiveness of the libido." Others seem to display an exhaustion of the capacity for change the resistance of the id." In still others, guilt and the need for punishment cause the patient to cling to suffering; part of it is to be understood in the nature of the superego, part of it in a less well-understood primary masochism. The spontaneous tendency to conflict is related to an element of free aggressiveness.

A further source of difficulty in analytic work comes from the personality of the analyst and Freud recommends periodic re-analysis for practitioners.

Though analysis may seem to be interminable, in practice it is not. The practical task of analysis "is to secure the best possible psychological conditions for the functioning of the ego."

The paper ends by a discussion of the psychological bedrock which offers extraordinary difficulties: penis envy in women, and in men "the struggle against their passive attitude towards other men." That is to say, the vicissitudes of the castration complex lead us to an analytical end-point.

This paper was the logical conclusion to the body of Freud's work, it clearly states that the task of analysis is to allow for the better functioning of the ego. The dynamic struggle between drives and ego is viewed in more precise terms by the emphasis upon quantitative drive factors on the one hand, and defensive constellations and ego distortions on the other. This paper has been viewed by some as a pessimistic statement of the deficiencies of analytic therapy. Careful reading demonstrates that it is precisely the opposite. a signpost for future analytic work. By indicating situations where analysis is difficult, it pointed toward the need for research into the functioning and development of the ego and the biological development of the drives.

An unfinished fragment written in 1938 but not published until two years later concentrates upon the issue of defense. In "Splitting of the Ego in the Defensive Process."[34] Freud returns to a subject previously dealt with in the paper on "Fetishism" (1927).[35] Evidently Freud felt that the views offered in the work on fetishism had a broader application in understanding the process of defense. me essence of the undeveloped idea is this: certain children respond to powerful instinctual demands which come into conflict with reality by two contrary reactions On one hand, the gratification is not relinquished, on the other hand the dangers of reality are given obeisance. The cost of this ingenuity Is an ever-widening split in the ego, a disturbance in the ego's synthetic function.

Freud's 1937 paper on "Constructions in Analysis"[36] returns his attention to the material so beautifully described in the Wolf-man. It is the work of analysis, among other tasks, to give a trustworthy picture of the "patient's forgotten years," to offer the patient a reliable reconstruction of the past, The work of that reconstruction demands confirmatory evidence from the patient; however, it is the *indirect* confirmatory evidence that we seek. That is, we await such things as the patient's saying "I've never thought of that," or giving associations of analogous material. The patient's attitude toward the construction is certainly not ignored. it is analyzed as is all the rest of the material. Freud describes then a special circumstance in which certain patients respond to a construction by vivid recollection *not of the event* but of' some minor detail surrounding the event. Resistance has displaced the

---

34 *C.P.* Vol. 5, p. 372.

35 Ibid. p. 198.

36 Ibid. p. J58.

upward drive of the repressed from the event to a detail, The vividness of these experiences allows Freud to speculate upon the nature of hallucinations and delusions. These phenomena, he states, are so impervious to reason because they contain an element of historic infantile truth which is inserted in the place of the rejected reality. This context then is the same as that of the ego-splitting paper in its awareness of the defensive process. It also tends to throw some light upon the ending of "Analysis Terminable and Interminable;" i.e., it suggests that it is the fragment of historic Infantile truth that makes for the extraordinary tenacity of attitudes stemming from the castration complex.

The paper on "Constructions" once again presents Freud's view of the necessity of accurate re-construction and memory as the matrix upon which interpretations must be made, as well as the outcome of such interpretations. It refutes the Rank-Ferenczi one-sided emphasis on "affective experience."

The issues presented by Freud in his final papers still remain before us. Probably the most striking developments in modern technique have been in recognizing the central röle of the process of working through—i.e., the exercise of the principle of multiple function in technical action. It is the work of analysis to see the tasks set before the ego and the task it sets upon itself (passive and active ego problems) in repeated form. These must be repeatedly worked over via interpretation. This entire process becomes specially important in the light of renewed interest in actual infantile traumatic experience.'

Heinz Hartmann, in his 1951 contribution on the implications of ego psychology for technique, suggests that current technique has lagged behind our knowledge. He expressed the view that discrete ego functions must be studied with the same exactitude as we had studied the process of defense. He particularly emphasized the necessity of studying speech and the use of language, since these functions are critical in the analytic process. (This general view had been expressed by Hartmann earlier in his work; in objecting to the use of such terms as "precocious development of the ego" in obsessional neurosis, he had insisted upon the necessity of specifying "which functions" of the ego were precociously developed.) This hint from Hartmann stimulated me to attempt such study in a number of analyses.

However, the problem in studying functions with a high degree of autonomy is inherent in the degree of autonomy. Psychoanalysis is, after all, in Kris's terms, the "study of human behavior viewed as conflict." We cannot analyze what is not in conflict. Freud had pointed to this difficulty in "Analysis Terminable and Interminable," and there had questioned the feasibility or wisdom of creating new conflict. experience has demonstrated difficult it is to create new conflict—one has only to see the problem of attempting to have patients examine their character traits. To create distance from ego syntonic traits and functions is a formidable task, even when these traits developed out of conflict. Where functions were little involved in conflict at their inception, the task is almost impossible,

It may be instructive, then, to present two small clinical vignettes in which speech and language functions, having arisen in conflict, could be analyzed. As usual with our special means of observation, we may be able to extrapolate from the pathological to the normal. In this material it will become clear that the obstacle to examining autonomous ego functions is the ego's narcissistic investment. The very autonomy of these functions serves as one basis of the ego's self-love.   ,

Narcissistic wounds and mortifications may lead to increased defensive protection at one level, but also to analyzability of the involved functions at another level. The patient will analyze the impaired function if there is the unconscious expectation that the narcissistic wound will be repaired. (In this regard it would be well to remember Nunberg's view of the will to recovery; the patient enters into the analytic work with the Will to recovery where his unconscious expectations are that the analysis will make his infantile wishes come true.)

Grammatical errors may exist as parapraxes, as character traits, or as educational defects,

Grammar, the rules of language, bears closely upon the function of the superego and its connection to the rules of life. Isakower has pointed to this connection. When one raises a question with a patient who makes a grammatical error, the patient usually responds with annoyance and anger. In the midst of narcissistic rage, the patient accuses the analyst of pedantry, of interrupting the train of thought for nonsensical reasons, etc.

A young man In analysis for a complex neurosis repeatedly was confused about whether to say "I" or "me" in any given sentence, Though the issue of whether to use the nominative or objective case is common in people of poor education, the patient was very well educated. I presented this problem to him, and he Immediately proceeded to the work of analyzing this along with a tendency to malapropisms, As he associated to the question of "I" or "me," He became aware that the confusion was also "You" or "I." That is to say, the confusion was in the sphere of subject vs. object. Previous analytic work had concerned itself with the extent of his identification with his poorly educated, chronically depressed mother, His mother's withdrawal from him in a depressive psychosis when he was had stimulated this identification. Her speech was marred by frequent malapropisms, His father, well-spoken and educated, had been rejected by the patient as a suitable ideal, The father was an ineffective passive person, who fled in the face of difficulties. The R I-me" "You-I W confusion reflected not only the content of the identification with the mother, but an aspect of the blurring of boundaries which was a formal aspect of this identification. The patient eagerly cooperated with the work because it enhanced his phallic narcissistic image of himself, so that he felt less like his sick mother and more like the idealized transference figure of the analyst.

The second case demonstrates the way in which the *language* spoken may determine one's attitude while speaking that language

A young man, raised in a multilingual household in a European country, was always viewed as being stupid by his family and teachers His persistent wish in childhood was that he be the "next to last" on the class marking roll, rather than the dullest boy in class. An experience during the War galvanized his life. Caught with his family at the Battle of Dunkerque, they observed that all troops except the English had thrown away their arms and fled. The English remained to fight a rear-guard action in order to withdraw to England to fight again. As he described a small group of English soldiers leaving for the beach singing Tipperary, he burst into tears. Some years later he learned English and never having had formal high school education he acquired a Bachelor's degree at one of our major universi ties in one year. In English, the language of rectitude and honor, he showed a genius which has been carried out in his career. It is interesting to note that cruelty and business dishonor were part of his family's tradition. The patient was unconscious of the connection between his use of English and his capacity to learn. He, too, was eager to analyze these language issues because they had enhanced his narcissistic self-representation.

However, these successful vignettes highlight the difficulty in ordinarily analyzing the ego functions related to speech and language by pointing to the issue of the narcissistic investment.

To Freud's view of the barriers to analytic work mentioned in Analysis Terminable and Interminable we must thus add the resistance offered by the ego's narcissism to the investigation of those autonomous functions which were won by such labor in the course of development. This presents us with the next great technical challenge: the issue of the investigation of factors outside of conflicts. There are as yet no answers.

REFERENCES

Breuer, J. & Freud, S. (1893). Studies in Hysteria. *Standard Edition* 2:1-305.

Ferenczi, S. & Rank, O. (1924). *The Development of Psycho-Analysis*. Eastford, CT: Martino Fine Books, 2012.

Freud, A. (1936). *The Ego and the Mechanisms of Defence.* Oxfordshire: Routledge, 1992.

Freud, S. (1900) .The Interpretation of Dreams. *Standard Edition* 4:ix–627.

——— (1909). Notes Upon a Case of Obsessional Neurosis. *Standard Edition* 10:151–318.

——— (1910). 'Wild' Psycho-Analysis. *Standard Edition* 11:219–228.

VII.

——— (1910). The Future Prospects of Psycho-Analytic Therapy. *Standard Edition* 11:139–152.

——— 1919). Lines of Advance in Psycho-Analytic Therapy. *Standard Edition* 17:157–168.

——— (1911) .The Handling of Dream-Interpretation in Psycho-Analysis. *Standard Edition* 12:89–96.

——— (1912). The Dynamics of Transference. *Standard Edition* 12:97–108.

——— (1912). Recommendations to Physicians Practising Psycho-Analysis. *Standard Edition* 12:109–120.

——— (1912). A Note on the Unconscious in Psycho-Analysis. *Standard Edition* 12:255–266.

——— (1913). On Beginning the Treatment (Further Recommendations on the Technique of Psycho-Analysis I). *Standard Edition* 12:121–144.

——— (1914). Fausse Reconnaissance ('Déjà Raconteé') in Psycho-Analytic Treatment. *Standard Edition* 13:199–207.

——— (1915). Instincts and their Vicissitudes. *Standard Edition* 14:109–140.

————— (1917). Introductory Lectures on Psycho-Analysis. *Standard Edition*16:241–463.

————— (1917). Mourning and Melancholia. *Standard Edition* 14:237–258.

————— (1918) From the History of an Infantile Neurosis. *Standard Edition* 17:1–124.

—————. (1920). Beyond the Pleasure Principle. *Standard Edition 18*:1–64.

————— (1926). Inhibitions, Symptoms and Anxiety. *Standard Edition* 20:75–176.

————— (1914). Remembering, Repeating and Working-Through (Further Recommendations on the Technique of Psycho-Analysis II). *Standard Edition* 12:145–156.

————— (1915). Observations on Transference-Love (Further Recommendations on the Technique of Psycho-Analysis III). *Standard Edition* 12:157–171.

————— (1918). From the History of an Infantile Neurosis. *Standard Edition* 127:1–124.

————— (1923). The Ego and the Id. *Standard Edition* 19:1–66.

————— (1937). Constructions in Analysis. *Standard Edition* 23:255–270.

————— (1937). Analysis Terminable and Interminable. *Standard Edition* 23:209–254.

————— (1938). Splitting of the Ego in the Process of Defence. *Standard Edition* 23:271–278.

Hartmann, H. (1951). Technical Implications of Ego Psychology. *Psychoanalytic Quarterly* 20:31–43.

Kris, E. (1956). The Personal Myth—A Problem in Psychoanalytic Technique. *Journal of the American Psychoanalytic Association* 4:653–681.

Kuhn, T.S. (1962). *The Structure of Scientific Revolutions:* 50th Anniversary Edition. Chicago: University of Chicago Press, 2012.

Strachey , J. (1904). Freud's Psycho-Analytic Procedure (1904 [1903]). *Standard Edition.*

——— (1934). The Nature of the Therapeutic Action of Psychoanalysis. *International Journal of Psychoanalysis* XV, pp. 127–159.

CHAPTER 18

Discussions for the Panel: The Relevance of Frequency of Sessions to the Creation of an Analytic Experience

Dr. Arnold Rothstein Chairman 1996 American Psychoanalytic Association Los Angeles

ON THE RELEVANCE OF FREQUENCY

General Comments

For the purposes of discussion of these four fascinating cases, I propose that we distinguish between *analytic atmosphere, analytic experience*, and *analytic process*. Let me try to describe the differences among them. By *psychoanalytic atmosphere*, I mean the following: a person (every degree our equal) contacts us because of some suffering. The initial contact usually begins when the patient calls us on the telephone. The contact has started before the phone was lifted; in the patient's thoughts and imagination. Is your response welcoming, helpful? The patient wants to ask some questions. What answers does he/she get? The appointment is made, and the interview begun. Do you let the patient tell the story his/her way, or do you set the agenda by asking questions? Is the atmosphere of free interchange established from the onset? The questionnaire-style or DSM-IV interview (or its predecessors), however helpful diagnostically in some circumstances, tells the patient that the agenda is *yours*. The psychoanalytic atmosphere is established by your not interfering with the patient's agenda, by your helpful listening, your recognition of affects expressed or hidden and your attention to the body and facial languages which are important parts of the communication. What matters in the *atmosphere* is a human connection; the valence of that connection from the patient may be positive or negative, shallow or strong. You will have your reactions; what matters is that you want to be helpful and offer that help, and that the patient wants your help. *Atmosphere* is, for the most part, set by you.

By analytic *experience* I understand a special form of conversation (as described by Siegfried Bernfeld) in which there is a differential grade in the röles of the participants. We generally listen more than we speak. We try not to intrude.

We may or may not have asked the patient to use the couch in a recumbent position and have asked the patient to speak freely. However, no one is *capable* of full free association. The request is made *not* for compliance but to uncover the inevitable conflicts to which the request gives rise. The ease or difficulty with candor is the introduction to resistance. We have set the conditions for a technical regression that will serve the purposes of the analysis and facilitate some freeing-up of idea and affect. We do not want merely to be told an interesting story about the patient's life; neurosis and character are *not* archeological fragments dug out of the past. We want to set the conditions for the *re-living with us* of pathogenic conflicts; and, the *here and now experiences* are to be interpreted by *both* participants. That is to say, *both participants* enter the analytic *experience;* the patient attempting to freely associate with all the attendant affects, the analyst attempting the counterpart in what we have termed the "freely-hovering attention." This psychoanalytic *experience* may take place in the first session. At the far end of a spectrum it doesn't take place at all. The *frequency of sessions* per week will determine the intensity of the psychoanalytic experience; that is what this panel is about. And that is what Dr. Rothstein has charged us to explore.

There is a further and perhaps more important aspect of discourse: that is, *psychoanalytic process*. Here I refer to that aspect of analytic work in which aspects of "transference" and "resistance/defense" either undergo some change over time *or* do not change over time. Aspects of this *process* involve *both* analyst and analysand. A series of process changes are usually accompanied by insight, and some symptomatic improvement and a "stagnant process" is usually accompanied by endless repetitions of stereotyped behavior (also by both participants).

Now many colleagues differ upon what they consider "psychoanalysis," placing different emphases upon different aspects of the work. Some seem more interested in the here-and-now phenomena, some more on genetic data, on experiences outside the analytic hour as well as inside, and so forth. Some focus on the "new" experience of the "analytic" experience. Here we must be cautious in our evaluations. Character (understood as having a repetitive *structure*) represents a barrier to "new" experience (even new experience in the transference). The analysis of the barrier-resistance function of character is difficult in both participants, this aspect of exploration and analysis always treading on both sets of narcissistic toes.

Whether the psychoanalytic *experience* leads to a psychoanalytic *process* is not always predictable. I would now like to introduce another concept: psychoanalytic *intensity,* that is, the ideational and affective *charge* with which the psychoanalytic work is approached. This is also relevant to frequency: some patients and some analysts can exhibit high or low levels of intensity whether they meet "x" or "y" numbers of sessions per week. (I have come to prefer seeing patients four or five times a week. I have seen one patient three times, and several patients six times.) My own experience and the experience of my analysands and my students has led me to correlate more frequent meetings with facilitated technical regressions, heightened *intensity of experience* and heightened tendencies toward process changes accompanied by insight. This is especially true in the understanding of aggression and sadism. (Here I refer you to Ernst Kris on the dark-side of the good hour, Martin Stein on the issues of unobjectionable transference and the necessity of the analysis of negative transference and Paul Gray and the analysis of aggression through the interpretation of resistance.)

REFERENCES

Bernfeld, S. (1985). The Facts of Observation in Psychoanalysis. *International Review of Psychoanalysis* 12:342–351.

Kris, E. (1956). On Some Vicissitudes of Insight in Psycho-Analysis. *International Journal of Psychoanalysis* 37:445–455.

Stein, M. H. (1981) .The Unobjectionable Part of the Transference. *Journal of the American Psychoanalytic Association* 29:869–892..

Gray, P. (2000) .On the Receiving End: Facilitating the Analysis of Conflicted Drive Derivatives of Aggression. *Journal of the American Psychoanalytic Association* 48:219–236.

www.ingramcontent.com/pod-product-compliance
Lightning Source LLC
Chambersburg PA
CBHW062115020426
42335CB00013B/968